Sex Addiction

Case Studies and Management

Sex Addiction
Case Studies and Management

Ralph H. Earle, Ph.D.
and Marcus R. Earle, Ph.D.

with Kevin Osborn

BRUNNER/MAZEL *Publishers* • NEW YORK

Library of Congress Cataloging-in-Publication Data

Earle, Ralph (Ralph H.)
    Sex addiction: case studies and management / Ralph H. Earle and
Marcus R. Earle.
        p.   cm.
    Includes bibliographical references and indexes.
    ISBN 0-87630-785-3
    1. Sex addiction–Treatment.   2. Sex addiction–Treatment–Case
studies.   I. Earle, Marcus R.   II. Title.
RC560.S43E23   1995
616.85'83–dc20
                                                                95-30129
                                                                CIP

Published by
BRUNNER/MAZEL, Inc.
19 Union Square West
New York, New York 10003
Manufactured in the United States of America

10   9   8   7   6   5   4   3   2   1

Contents

v

Preface

A New Look at Sex Addiction

In the six years since the publication of *Lonely All the Time: Recognizing, Understanding, and Overcoming Sex Addiction for Addicts and Co-Dependents* (Earle & Crow, 1989), we have learned a great deal more about sex addiction. We have integrated new approaches to sex addiction, broadened the scope of our treatment, incorporated new treatment modalities, and added new staff members whose specialties augment the treatment of sex addicts and their families. Although we have made significant advances, we remain aware that the treatment of sex addiction is an evolutionary process. As we review the text one final time prior to publication, we are reminded how rapidly changes are occurring in our treatment program at Psychological Counseling Services. Ongoing research in the field, the practice of our own staff, and most of all, the experience of our patients continue to spark changes—some dramatic, some more subtle—in our overall treatment program for sex addiction.

One program we recently developed is called intensive therapy, which seems especially helpful in treating patients who are "stuck" in the process of recovery or who are facing a current crisis that necessitates more intensive therapeutic involvement. This two- to five-week program allows colleagues throughout the United States and Canada to refer clients to us for short-term, intensive treatment customized to the needs of the individual patient. Our intensive program does not replace, but rather complements, the treatment program provided by the referring therapist, who continues to be the patient's primary therapist. Indeed, we enjoy working with and learning from referring therapists, whose input helps us in the design of effective, brief treatment.

We owe a deep dept of gratitude for the contributions of Barbara Bagan, Ph.D., creative-art therapies and family issues; Donald W. Hall, Ph.D., spirituality; William Harnell, Ph.D., relapse prevention and assessment; Elaine Katzman, Ph.D., R.N., healthy sexuality; Marilyn Murray, M.A., Scindo-Syndrome model; Carol Ross, B.A., false memory syndrome; Roxanne Witte, Ph.D., mother/daughter issues; Paul Simpson, Ed.D., sexual addiction cycle; Brad Olson, M. Ed., cycle of anger; and Marcie Edmonds, M.S., M.C., research support. The team approach taken by the PCS staff in writing this book proves that the whole is larger than the sum of its parts. A very special thanks to Kevin Osborn, who is an incredible writer and helped to bring things together. Thanks to Mark Tracten of Brunner/Mazel for his continuing support. Two other people have been very significant in the completion of this text: Marsha Sherer, who both typed and critiqued the text; and Natalie Gilman of Brunner/Mazel, who through her editorial staff provided very helpful corrections. We wish to thank our wives, Glenda and Robin, for their patient support during the extensive time needed to work on this book. Most of all, thanks to the patients whose stories continue to educate us and whose contributions to this book have been invaluable.

We have written this book for the benefit of both patients as well as colleagues. For our colleagues, we believe that we have provided new and useful information and innovative, integrative treatment approaches to sex addiction. For patients, we hope this will promote an openness to treatment and to a variety of treatment modalities that will help advance recovery. One step at a time.

Ralph H. Earle, Ph.D.
Marcus R. Earle, Ph.D.

Sex Addiction

Case Studies and Management

The Assessment of Sex Addiction and an Overview of Treatment Modalities

Patrick Carnes first called attention to the growing problem of sex addiction (Carnes, 1983) over 10 years ago, yet relatively few sex addicts today receive the treatment they need. Failure to treat sex addiction is most acute among treatment programs for sex offenders. Certainly, not all sex offenders demonstrate sex addiction, just as not all sex addicts commit criminal sexual offenses. However, given the high rate of recidivism among sex offenders, one can only speculate as to why the treatment programs for this population do not include addiction models with other therapeutic modalities. According to very recent statistics from The Safer Society Press, 44.3 percent of sex offender treatment personnel do include the addictive cycle.

INCORPORATING THE ADDICTION MODEL INTO SEX OFFENDER TREATMENT PROGRAMS

When sex offenders repeat their offenses, they cause severe damage to their victims. For this reason, sex offender treatment programs have focused on preventing relapse at all costs (Laws, 1989). Though the very notion of "relapse prevention" grew out of addiction models, many clinicians still shy away from the concept of sex addiction or sexual compulsion. This resistance stems in part from controversy in recent

years regarding the use of the term sex addiction. To our way of thinking, however, the terminology chosen is not nearly as important as the
goal of eliciting genuine changes in behavior. In our practice, we customize treatment to suit the recovery needs of each individual patient.
In our efforts to empower our patients, we give them choices regarding terminology, encouraging patients to understand the nature of their
problem in the terms that will help advance their own recovery. For
most patients who engage in compulsive sexual behaviors, the term
sex addict seems best suited to this goal. Many clinicians, however,
resist using this term, especially in reference to sex offenders, because
it seems to imply that the offender has no control. Indeed, 12-step programs, a mainstay of almost all addiction treatment programs, emphasize "giving up control." To clinicians doing their best to instill a sense
of control in their clients, and strongly emphasizing the need for individual responsibility and accountability, this concept may at first seem
irresponsible and even abhorrent: Could anyone prescribe a worse
strategy to an addict—especially one whose addiction traumatizes
others?

When viewed as a therapeutic strategy, however, giving up control
has a powerful impact. Addicts who embrace this concept do not go
downhill even faster as might be expected; they begin, instead, the
uphill climb of recovery. Bateson (1971) examines this apparent paradox of control in "The Cybernetics of Self: A Fear of Alcoholism." He
describes surrender or giving up control as an epistemological shift to
a higher level of control: a "meta-control." By purposefully surrendering, the addict can escape the double bind of control versus noncontrol.

In personality terms, the alcoholic's self is constructed in a bipolar
manner consisting of good versus bad introjects that continually oscil-
late. Quite often the sex addict presents as a socially responsible individual of high moral standards to compensate for an unintegrated and
dissociated dark side or shadow (Jung, 1951). Horowitz (1976) describes
a similar numbing/intrusion dynamic in examining posttraumatic stress,
a dynamic Marilyn Murray (1985) attributes to the struggle between
the "Controlling Child" and the "Sobbing Hurting Child." A cycle of
control/release has also been observed in shame-bound families (Fossun
& Mason, 1986).

As the two poles of a personality mutually implicate each other,
therapies based on a correctional model—that is, those traditionally

employed by most sex offender treatment programs–that attempt to reinforce the good side or extinguish the bad side will frequently prove ineffective. Although the sex addict/offender may appear to make some initial progress in programs that use such an approach, this very often represents nothing more than an accommodation by "the controlling self." For treatment of any addiction to succeed, the dynamic of control versus noncontrol–circular, symmetrical, escalating, and central to the addictive process–must be dealt with. Often addicts make valiant attempts to control themselves, which is remaining sober for months or even years at a time, which is a process known as white knuckling. However, the self-control is an illusion, one that rarely keeps an addict sober forever. Therapy must break through this illusion for the addict to have any hope of lasting recovery. Although many different therapies, from insight-oriented to behavioral, can break an addict's denial, the treatment effects will be compromised unless the treatment program acknowledges the addictive cycle of overcontrol/undercontrol.

EVALUATION AND ASSESSMENT

Sex addicts, whether offenders or not, require a comprehensive assessment for proper treatment. Typically, assessment should include a complete clinical history and psychosocial history, a thorough sexual history, objective and (rarely) projective personality testing, sexual behavior inventories, a family interview if possible, and–especially in the case of adult offenders–a clinical polygraph examination and frequently a penile plethysmograph. A physical examination, preferably by a urologist or gynecologist, is frequently advised as the process of sex addiction can lead to internal or external damage to the genitalia. The clinician should also look for signs of neuropsychological disturbance, especially in cases involving known or suspected trauma or a substantial history of drug or alcohol addiction. We recommend a comprehensive personality inventory, such as the Minnesota Multiphasic Personality Inventory-2 (MMPI-2), since anxiety and depression, as well and as narcissistic, borderline sociopathic personality disorders are often comorbid with sex addiction. The Millon Clinical Multiaxial Inventory-3 can help differentiate personality dysfunction. Although no one personality is characteristic of sex addiction and personality tests cannot accurately predict recidivism, they are essential in treatment planning and in making diagnostic decisions.

The therapist can obtain information critical to treatment through a clinical sex history. The sex history must explore thoroughly such basic issues as gender identity, conflict, gender role, and sexual preference. Too often, clinicians ignore or only touch on these issues, and consequently miss important information. A complete chronology of the addict's childhood and adolescent sexual behavior, including both normal and deviant sexual activities, is essential. Close attention to masturbation patterns can provide early clues to the development of sexually compulsive behavior. Since even the most cooperative clients may provide vague and superficial answers in giving their sexual history, the therapist needs to question the client specifically in order to obtain detailed information. Questions that draw on assumed knowledge ("How often did you masturbate?") will prove more effective than general questions ("Have you ever masturbated?").

Sexual behavior inventories, such as the Multiphasic Sex Inventory (MSI) (Nichols & Molinder, 1984) or the Clarke Sexual History Questionnaire (Paitich, et al., 1977), can also elicit information helpful in planning treatment for the sex addict. In administering such tests to sex addicts, however, the therapist should take note of certain precautions. The originators of sexual behavior inventories did not base their tests on a sex addiction model and did not intend them to measure sex addiction. Because the MSI, for instance, has as one of its primary aims the measurement of behaviors associated with child molestation and rape, we use it primarily for testing sex addicts who have committed sexual offenses. When administering the MSI to a sex addict, particularly a nonoffender, therapists should exercise caution in interpretation in order to avoid reaching false conclusions.

Like most sexual behavior inventories, the MSI embraces a theoretical model of normal sexuality that might otherwise be called chauvinistic or sexist. The test items appear to differentiate aggressive or pedophilic behaviors from consenting, heterosexual adult behaviors, but they do not clearly differentiate levels of intimacy within adult sexual behaviors. In fact, items on the inventory strongly reflect the designers' evaluation of nonintimate sexuality as normal. Examinees score in the proper direction, for instance, if they indicate a desire to go to topless bars or that they would become aroused by a woman simply because she was not wearing panties. Although it may in fact be considered "normal" for men in our society to find these situations (as opposed to scenarios involving children, for example) arousing, such arousal still indicates an objectified, dehumanized attitude toward women. For a pedophilic sex offender who is not a sex addict, appropriate treatment goals might include the transfer of arousal from children to adults. For a sex addict, however, such a strategy would make little sense, since most heterosexual sex addicts already sexualize adults of the opposite sex. Thus the MSI does not accurately indicate progress in the sex addict's treatment, because progress for the sex addict involves *not* sexualizing or objectifying others, whether adults or children.

The test fails to differentiate objectified sex from intimate sex, resulting in conflict and confusion among sex addicts taking the MSI. Those who "work their program"—that is, follow a 12-step program, abide by their sobriety contract, and participate in therapy—know that perceiving another person as a sex object should serve as a red flag, alerting them to the hold their addiction exerts. As the MSI forces the examinee to choose between items, sex addicts who take the test experience a double bind: If they admit that they find women who do not wear panties attractive, they are not working their program; if they answer No, they judge themselves as being in denial. Another confusing aspect of the MSI concerns its use of questions, particularly on the obsessions scale, framed in both the past and the present tense. Examinees report not knowing whether the question refers to their past behavior (their deviant lifestyle) or the present behavior (their recovery program). Because many sex addicts fail to report their confusion to the examiner, test results may not reflect an accurate picture of the client. For this reason, the examiner must thoroughly explain the test to each examinee beforehand and offer the opportunity for the test taker to discuss any concerns about the inventory afterward. Otherwise, the meaning of test scores will lack clarity and thereby confound rather than facilitate treatment planning. Similarly, using the MSI to measure pre-post-outcome without attending to these precautions can easily lead to false conclusions.

In addition to a complete clinical and sexual history and personality assessment, treatment programs for sex addicts who are also sex offenders should include a polygraph examination and (for most adult male sex offenders as well as nonoffenders who raise a therapeutic concern that they might offend) a penile plethysmography. Despite the considerable controversy regarding the reliability, validity, and ethics of using the procedure (Lalumiere & Quinsey, 1991; McConaghy, 1988), we believe it serves a useful function if the therapist understands the limitations and administers it in a humanistic fashion. Sex addicts, especially those who commit criminal offenses, are notoriously unreliable as self-reporters. Therefore, a clinical polygraph can sometimes cut quickly through a patient's denial. As with all clinical procedures, polygraphs must be tailored to the particular characteristics and history of the individual patient. Standardized polygraphs that use the same or similar questions for everyone have less value, often yielding misleading results. We advise the use of an independent, licensed polygrapher who has expertise in administering the test to sex offenders. The therapist and the polygrapher can work together to ensure maximum validity by constructing test questions that specifically address issues and concerns relevant to the individual addict.

In preparing for a polygraph assessment, therapists, parole officers, and interested officers of the court should submit questions to the polygrapher. We typically use the initial polygraph to ask the patient questions related to the self-reported sexual history already obtained by the primary therapist. The sexual history obtained by the polygrapher then allows the therapist to evaluate the accuracy and completeness of the self-assessment. Although questions must be specifically tailored to the individual patient, questions might include:

- Is it true that since the age of 18 you have not had any sexual contact with another male?
- Is it true that you have not used any form of pornography since 1985?
- Have you ever used physical force or physical abuse to obtain sex?

Subsequent polygraphs can then help determine a patient's treatment compliance. Issues typically addressed include such questions as:
- Have you had any sexual fantasies involving your victim since your last polygraph?

- Have you violated the terms of your therapeutic contract?
- Have you reoffended or attempted to reoffend sexually?

Penile plethysmography can also provide essential information to the clinician regarding the addict's arousal patterns. Unfortunately, the normative basis for penile plethysmography is limited at best. No one has yet determined empirically what "normal arousal patterns" are, nor has cross-cultural or crossethnic group research been done on penile plethysmography. The various ratios or indexes devised to compare deviant and nondeviant arousal (Abel et al., 1978) rely on very limited research and draw overly simplistic conclusions. Despite its limitations, we regard penile plethysmography as a useful tool in developing hypotheses for treatment planning and in obtaining admissions from the sex addict. We also believe, however, that some courts and some treatment programs put entirely too much faith in it. To interpret penile plethysmography in terms of "factual data," to view it as an indicator of guilt or innocence, extends the parameters of the procedure far beyond the limitations at this time.

Sex addicts have very idiosyncratic arousal patterns and often demonstrate arousal in many categories of stimuli. Often, however, this represents a secondary escalation of the addict's compulsivity rather than the patient's primary orientation. As almost everything has a sexual connotation to a sex addict, plethysmography may not prove very helpful in determining the addict's "real" sexual preferences. In addition, the stimuli content utilized in plethysmography may trigger dissociated sexual cues based on a model of state-dependent learning of the addict's own past trauma or victimization (Overton, 1973). At this stage of research, the significance of a client's arousal pattern cannot be determined with any degree of certainty.

CASE 1-1

David, married with three stepdaughters, turned himself in for repeatedly molesting Jenny, his 18-year-old stepdaughter, over the course of the previous eight years. Having received some treatment from other sources through referral from the probation department, he first came to us for therapy three months after his

arrest. David had already taken the MMPI-2. The most significant result seemed to be the 85 he scored on the depression scale.
Within the first week of treatment with us, we administered both
the MSI and a penile plethysmograph. Before taking the plethysmograph, David reported that he had consumed no alcohol or
drugs over the last 24 hours, had no sexually transmitted diseases,
and had not ejaculated in 48 hours. Although we no longer employ visual stimuli in administering plethysmography, relying instead on audiotapes to create fantasy scenarios, the test at that
time consisted of 26 slides of nude men, women, boys, girls, and
infants. David showed no physical response to any of the subjects. Questioned about his lack of arousal, David explained that
he was having a hard time relaxing, that none of the subjects
seemed very attractive to him, and that his job as a nurse may
have desensitized him to nudity. In fact, the lack of physiological
arousal could have been attributed to one or more of the following factors: the explanations David offered, inhibited desire, in-
tentional suppression, or extremely slow arousal patterns. However, due to the total absence of response we had to regard the
plethysmograph results as inconclusive.

Plethysmographs were repeated at regular intervals throughout David's therapy program. He showed absolutely no physiological arousal on any of them. After a year, he offered another
potential reason for his lack of arousal: within the context of
his recovery program, staring was considered an inappropriate
behavior. Thus the entire test—which involved staring at slides—
presented a conflict for him. This case illustrates just some of the
difficulties that penile plethysmography can present when used
as a tool in the assessment of sex addicts.

TREATMENT OVERVIEW

Just as the assessment of sex addicts is a complex undertaking, so
too is their treatment. Taking into account the multiple levels of systems involving the sex addict, his or her family, and in the case of sex
offenders, the victim(s), as well as lawyers, courts, and various agencies, we employ a treatment team consisting of different specialists and

multiple theoretical viewpoints. We consider a multimodality approach to be more effective than a single provider or a program oriented around one common theme or modality.

We believe it critical, for example, to involve the family of the sex addict in treatment whenever possible. Many treatment programs, especially those for sex offenders, focus exclusively on the individual sex addict to the detriment of other family members and the family system as a whole. Although we agree that the elimination of sexually compulsive behavior, particularly behavior that victimizes others, should be the primary goal of treatment, we think it unfortunate that so many programs put the addict's family in second place. Such an approach actually reinforces codependent tendencies by sending other family members the message that they have no importance of their own, apart from their relation to the addict. It also indirectly feeds the narcissism of the sex addict, who has probably already learned that (s)he can gain a lot of attention through "bad" behavior. In the case of sex offenders who are addicts, legal proceedings already concentrate solely on the offender. If the treatment program mirrors this focus, neglecting the sex addict's spouse and children, it in effect revictimizes them. Apart from such considerations, it is also in the best interest of the sex addict to involve the family in recovery. From a systems perspective, pathological family interaction can maintain deviant behavior. The absence of intensive family therapy therefore only increases the likelihood of relapse.

Long-term sobriety depends also on dealing with the addict's family-of-origin issues. The current behavior pattern of sex offenders tends to repeat their own childhood victimization (Schwartz, 1992). We believe this also to be true of sex addicts who do not commit criminal offenses. In dealing with the addict's own victimization, the therapist can choose from a number of helpful therapeutic modalities. With some modifications, treatment models used with incest victims (Courtois, 1988; Gil, 1988) can be effective in treating the addict's victimization whether incestuous or not. A family genogram, a procedure called the trauma egg, family-of-origin sessions, and other modalities further described in Chapter 2 can help the sex addict gather information, unearth issues, and begin to express affect associated with childhood trauma. As addicts begin to connect with the pain in their past, more intensive modalities such as "restoration" therapy (Murray, 1985) and psychodrama can prove useful. Art therapy (Prochelo, 1991; 1993) offers a valuable therapeutic tool as preverbal victimization can sometimes only be accessed through iconic modalities.

Since most sex addicts have deficits in the areas of social skills, interpersonal communication, stress control, anger management, and victim empathy, cognitive behavioral intervention and educational therapy offered in the context of individual and/or group therapy play a critical role in long-term recovery. The addict must also thoroughly identify and understand the deviant cycle (the antecedent to acting out), a concept that fits nicely with a systemic/circular understanding of the addictive process. The deviant cycle consists of four phases: a buildup phase; the period when the sex addict acts out; subsequent justification of the acting out; and the intermediate phase when the addict pretends to be normal (Bays & Freeman-Longo, 1989). Although the deviant cycle is typically used as a framework for focusing on present and deviant behaviors, it can also be expanded beyond its orientation in the present to encompass repetitive cycles of past family-of-origin issues. Anger, for example, may follow a similar cycle. Children in dysfunctional families, who seldom learn how to express anger appropriately, may allow their anger to build up until it explodes. After acting out in ways destructive to self or others, these children (or adult children) will typically attempt to justify their angry outburst and then pretend to have no anger whatsoever. Recovering sex addicts who become aware of the cyclical nature of their sexual behavior often find it easy to recognize other cyclical patterns in their behavior, cognitions, or emotions. Understanding the deviant cycle can thus lead to treatment of multiple aspects of the patient's disorder under a unitary framework.

Any effective treatment for sex addiction must address the issue of deviant arousal patterns. However, the therapist needs to bear in mind certain precautions. The early stages of treatment for sex addiction involve sobriety from all sexual behavior, especially masturbation. In early sobriety, the sex addict usually cannot distinguish between appropriate and inappropriate masturbation. Trying to teach this distinction in the early stages of treatment will only reinforce the addict's urge to masturbate. For this reason, we strongly discourage the use of masturbation as part of arousal training until later stages of therapy.

Arousal training for the sex addict must aim not only toward decreasing deviant arousal, but also toward the more far-reaching goal of developing healthy sexuality. For the sex addict, healthy sexuality must center on the development of an intimate sexual relationship with one appropriate partner (Katzman, 1993). This complex goal cannot be achieved through arousal training alone, but must be integrated throughout the entire treatment program. Indeed, inappropriate arousal training can undermine the long-term goal of developing healthy sexuality. Returning to the example cited above in discussing the MSI, arousal training conducted with the aim of transferring an addict's arousal from children to women's breasts will only further the addictive process.

Aversive conditioning as part of arousal training for sex addicts can also result in the strengthening of the addictive cycle. Aversive conditioning can further victimize the sex addict, and while it may at first appear successful, it can in the long run increase the addict's overwhelming sense of shame and powerlessness, again initiating the deviant cycle. For this reason, we avoid using aversive conditioning unless absolutely required—and then only with the complete cooperation of the client. We caution against placing the sex addict in the double bind of having to choose between submitting to aversive conditioning and expulsion from the treatment program. The therapist should first attempt to work with deviant arousal through cognitive techniques aimed at controlling the obsessions behind arousal.

In more severe cases of sex addiction, promising research into the neurobiological substrate of obsessive-compulsive behavior may offer the clinician more treatment modalities in the future. Stein et al. (1992) suggest that compulsivity and impulsivity may lie on a phenomenological and neurobiological continuum, with sex addiction falling at the compulsive end of the spectrum and paraphilias at the impulsive end. They also report that serotonergic reuptake inhibitors such as fluoxetine and fluvoxamine have shown some promise in controlling sexual obsessions.

Electroencephalographic research has shown great promise in expanding our understanding of the neurobiology of obsessional behavior. Research into abnormal brain-wave functioning in alcoholics began in the 1940s (Funderburk, 1949). Recently, investigators found that using electroencephalographic feedback to increase an alcoholic's alpha-theta brain-wave functioning substantially reduces relapse rates and produces positive fundamental changes in personality variables (Peniston & Kulkosky, 1989, 1990). Ongoing research applies alpha-theta brain-wave training not only in the treatment of alcoholism, but of many other addictions as well. Some clinicians have already begun using this technique with sex addicts, and have reported favorable results.

Finally, in our view, treatment of the sex addict cannot be considered complete unless it addresses the question of spirituality. The addict's attitude toward religion can provide important diagnostic clues. Does the sex addict regard his or her life as meaningless? Does the patient see God's grace as an easy path to forgiveness? Does the addict adhere to rigid and absolutist concepts of religion? By examining the patient's religious views in the context of his or her personality dysfunctions, the clinician can differentiate between valid expressions of spirituality and defensive religiosity.

In the context of recovery, spirituality involves dealing with one's deepest levels of pain and suffering and also the pain inflicted upon others. This, far more than any cognitive material, provides the basis for authentic victim empathy.

True spiritual development takes time and demands concurrent psychological development. A Jungian framework can promote the integration of psychological and spiritual development (Jung, 1951). "God is in the details," as the saying goes; and it is in the sex addict's small insights and changes in behavior that significant moral and spiritual growth can be detected.

2

Looking at Families of Origin
The Etiology of Sex Addiction

Sex addicts are made, not born. As detailed in *Lonely All the Time* (Earle & Crow, 1989), the etiological factors that contribute to the development of sex addictions are many. Traumatic childhood events—years of sexual, physical, or emotional abuse and victimization, divorce, the death of a parent or sibling—often play a part. Prohibitive messages about sex—that sexual desires and sexual acts are sinful, dirty, illicit, and/or demeaning—can provide fertile ground for the development of sexual compulsions. Poor modeling also provides critical component in the etiology of sex addiction. Most sex addicts come from homes in which parents lacked communication skills, offered little affection or support to each other or their children, consistently betrayed their children's trust, and were frequently absent altogether. Rigid and arbitrary family rules, constant, often abusive criticism, and harsh punishment for breaking the rules or failing to live up to strict standards can also contribute to the development of sex addiction.

CASE 2-1

Maria, 33 years old, married, with two children, came to us seeking help to stop her pattern of compulsive extramarital affairs, a pattern that had persisted for nearly 12 years. She acknowledged that 95 percent of her day was spent fantasizing about men and planning her next seduction. The amount of time spent in fantasy made it hard for her to get any work done, and she resented her husband's or children's intrusion into her fantasy world.

In the initial exploration of her family, Maria revealed that her father had ruled the home with an iron hand. An alcoholic, he tyrannized the family, often beating his wife and Maria's two sisters and once threatening her older sister with a knife. Maria said of her mother that she "acts as if she can't control anything" and "plays the part of the martyr," submitting to her husband's rage without question or objection. To escape her father's violence, Maria said she took the part of the "good little girl." Maria saw this strategy as a success, claiming that she "wasn't affected by the physical violence."

Her father, a Catholic, laid down strict rules for his wife and three daughters. His wife (and daughters) were expected to serve him, providing for his every need. Although he was an alcoholic and chain smoker, he forbade his children to drink or smoke. Sex was also forbidden. Talk about sexual matters was not permitted, and the girls were not allowed even to date until they were 19 years old.

All the sex addicts we have treated experienced some type of painful childhood. Their backgrounds left countless invisible wounds, scars that would become manifest in compulsive sexual behavior. The unresolved childhood issues that plague sex addicts include:

- *Low self-esteem:* Sex addicts carry into their adult lives a profound sense that they are unwanted, unloved, and unworthy. "He made me feel useless," Maria remembers, "and that I was a terrible person and that I was worth nothing." If their parents demonstrated any affection at all for them, it was only under prescribed conditions: that they obey the unwritten rules, that they excel, that they not mar the family facade. Maria tried to do everything possible to please her father, yet still felt that whatever she did was not "good enough."
- *Abandonment fears:* The actual loss of a parent through death or divorce, or the threatened loss of a parent through the imposition of conditional love, produces a powerful fear of abandonment. Sex addicts believe that anyone they allow themselves to get close to will abandon or reject them. Al-

though Maria's father never left the home, she felt rejected by him.

- *Blurred boundaries:* Discouraged from any attempts at individuation, sex addicts remain tied to their families of origin long after leaving the home. Salvadore Minuchin (1974) describes how children can become enmeshed with or disengaged from their parents. An enmeshed child and parent become overinvolved in each other's lives, while a disengaged dyad is disconnected in their interactions. These operating extremes, as Minuchin identifies, lead to problems in adult life:

> A highly enmeshed subsystem of mother and children, for example, can exclude father, who becomes disengaged in the extreme. The resulting undermining of the children's independence might be an important factor in the development of symptoms. (p. 55)

Maria was deeply enmeshed in her mother's life, while apparently disengaged in her relationship with her father. Maria had started her own family 12 years earlier, yet when she first came to us, she was still caught up in trying to take care of her mother: taking charge of renovating her parents' house for her mother because "my father wouldn't do it." Children of compulsive parents conclude, or are directly told by their parents, that their parents' problem is their problem. They believe that they can magically control their parents' feelings and behavior, as Maria tried to do by becoming the perfect daughter. Sex addicts have little foundation for and almost no encouragement to develop an identity apart from their role in the dysfunctional family drama.

- *Mood disorders:* Sex addicts learn in childhood that feelings are dangerous. Those who were traumatized separated from feelings they found unbearable. Those who were punished for expressing feelings of anger or sadness, for example, also learned how to mask their feelings, often even from themselves. Maria, for example, began to acknowledge in therapy that she buries her feelings and "acts as if nothing at all is bothering me." To defend against dangerous emotions, the children who would later become sex addicts cut themselves off from their feelings, numbing themselves to the presence of emotions.

- *Dehumanizing sexual attitudes*: Sex addicts have little or no sense of sex as a "natural function," as Dr. William Masters recognized it. The kind of sexual repression that existed in Maria's childhood home is common among sex addicts. The result is that many sex addicts harbor the conviction that any sexual acts or desires are wrong, a confirmation of their sense of essential unworthiness. Paradoxically, many sex addicts see sex as the only thing they are good at, the only basis for self-worth. Sexually compulsive behavior offers the illusion of intimacy, a false sense of the connection that they desperately want. Yet because they cannot achieve real intimacy, sex becomes dehumanized and objectified. Sex serves as a vehicle not for mutual intimacy, but for a temporary escape from loneliness and pain.

- *Undeveloped social skills*: Sex addicts seldom have learned how to communicate honestly and deeply with others. Maria's two strongest models—her father's explosive temper and her mother's painful silence—taught her that communication was dangerous. Poor modeling in the home and the response of rejection or punishment for any honest expression of thoughts or feelings leave sex addicts incapable of achieving intimacy: unwilling and unable to open up or become vulnerable with others.

- *Secretiveness and superficiality*: Often, sex addicts grow up in homes where appearances matter more than anything, thus they become experts at the art of maintaining a good facade. Because they feel inherently "bad," sex addicts try to preserve their good image at all costs. Many sex addicts become adept at hiding their lack of social skills behind a veneer of charm, but do not know how to move beyond superficial communication; indeed they cannot go deeper without destroying the facade and revealing the secrets they have struggled a lifetime to keep.

- *Distrust*: The fear of abandonment leads sex addicts to conclude that they cannot depend on others. Their feelings of unworthiness also foster the belief that they cannot trust themselves. Unable to trust themselves or others, sex addicts see only one hope: escape from the pain, emptiness, and despair.

- *Escape strategies:* As children, sex addicts almost invariably observed just one technique to deal with unpleasant realities (pain, anger, stress): escape through compulsive behaviors. Maria took note of her father's alcoholism and compulsive gambling as well as of her mother's escape into excessive religiosity. Family histories of sex addicts are riddled with alcoholism, eating disorders, oppressive religious belief systems, compulsive gambling, and, of course, compulsive sexual behavior.

- *Isolation and profound loneliness:* Unable to trust others, sex addicts attempt to defend against their own abandonment fears by isolating themselves. By not getting close to anyone else, they protect themselves from the threat of pain that has characterized their close relationships. Yet their isolation, their distrust, and their secretiveness leave sex addicts in lonely despair. Lacking the social skills needed to escape this loneliness, they find temporary refuge in the illusion of intimacy offered by their sexual compulsions.

FAMILY HISTORY

Since sex addicts' families of origin play such a critical role in paving the way for the compulsive behavior, therapists and their sex-addicted patients need to examine and reexamine the family history. We begin looking at the family of origin in the first session. We take a family history and help prepare both a genogram and a trauma egg at the very first stage of treatment. In addition, we have found a number of other tools and techniques (detailed in the text that follows) particularly useful in evaluating, understanding, and establishing boundaries with our patients' families of origin.

Throughout this process of family examination, we emphasize the use of these techniques as a valuable source of self-understanding. We do not look at the family in order to affix blame or to justify self-pity, though understandably, most patients will react with blame or self-pity. The therapist's job in such situations is to help the patients see that remaining stuck in these emotions can trigger relapse into compulsive sexual behaviors. With the therapist's help, they need to work through the anger and sadness they feel toward their families of origin, not use it as an excuse for further acting out. Throughout our therapy program for sex addicts, we stress the addict's responsibility for his or her behavior. Understanding the underlying causes of their compulsive behavior does not relieve sex addicts of responsibility for their actions, or for changing their patterns of behavior.

Used to promote healing rather than backsliding, a thorough understanding of family history can empower sexually addicted patients. Identifying and examining multigenerational cycles of abuse, far from leaving patients helpless, despairing, and resigned to their fates, can motivate sex addicts to do everything possible to interrupt the cycle. Having recognized family patterns, recovering sex addicts want to prevent their children and grandchildren from going through the same pain and abuse that they—and their parents and grandparents—endured.

Genogram

Because we attach such importance to the influence of family history, we ask every new patient diagnosed or potentially diagnosed as a sex addict to prepare a genogram detailing the characteristics and patterns in his or her family of origin. We believe in a multigenerational transmission process for compulsive behaviors; that is, emotional problems and resulting adaptive compulsive behaviors can be traced to the relationship between a patient's parents, and between their parents, continuing back for several generations. Only by understanding one's family of origin is it possible for sex addicts to become differentiated and autonomous (Bowen, 1978). The genogram should therefore span at least three generations, including grandparents, parents, aunts, uncles, siblings, self, and children.

In helping to prepare the genogram, we encourage our sexually compulsive (and codependent) patients to pay particular attention to:

- The presence of addictions or compulsive behavior, especially sex addiction, in any family members;
- Divorce of parents or grandparents (as divorce was rare in earlier generations except in cases of extreme dysfunction,

it often provides an important clue to deeper problems);
- Personal characteristics of family members;
- How family members communicated and expressed emotion;
- Religious and ethnic background (excessively strict or overly permissive) and its influence on parenting styles;
- The patients' evaluation of the quality and dynamics of their parents' and other family members' marriages;
- Styles of parenting, not only that of the patients' parents, but also those of grandparents, siblings, and the patients themselves;
- The nature of conflicts among siblings;
- The accepted roles of men and women within the family;
- Messages received from other family members regarding sex and sexuality;
- Family secrets;
- Any suspected or known instances of incest, abuse (sexual, physical, verbal, emotional), or neglect;
- Family rules, both spoken and unspoken.

CASE 2-1 (*continued*)

Every family has a story; the genogram provides a vehicle for telling this story, often for the first time. Maria's genogram (see Figure 2.1) revealed her multigenerational patterns of marital stress, not unlike that which she was currently experiencing in her own marriage to Carter. All of her grandparents were divorced. Her mother's parents had divorced when her mother was 12 years old; her father's when he was 18. Maria has had no contact with her paternal grandfather, whom she believes lives in Mexico. She has also never met her maternal grandmother, and in fact does not even know her name. She recognized compulsive behavior in her father (alcoholism, gambling, smoking, womanizing), and in both of her sisters (alcoholism, obsessive-compulsive tendencies). She characterized her mother as a "people-pleasing codependent." Her parents were Catholic (her mother having converted from the Baptist faith) and had strict rules about their daughters' sexuality. Except for laying down the law (no dating,

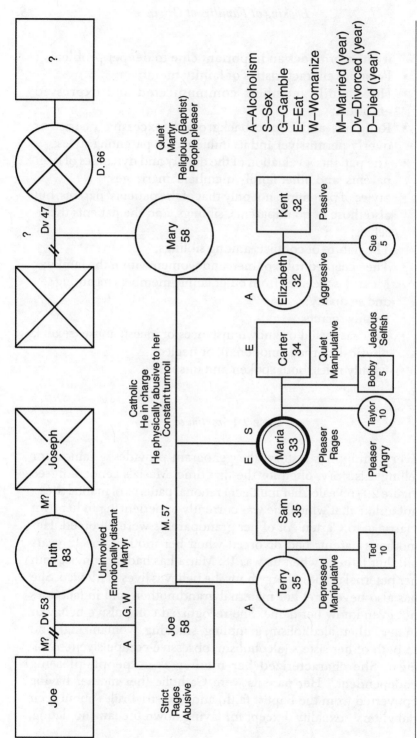

Figure 2.1. Maria's genogram.

and by implication no sex, until they were adults), sex was never spoken about in the home.

The genogram, an important tool for any therapist who takes a family systems approach, offers sex addicts—and any patients—a graphic representation of family members, family rules, and family dynamics. Preparing a genogram encourages patients to look at their families in a new way. It introduces sex addicts to the family systems perspective, rather than focusing exclusively on their individual histories, experiences, and perceptions. In concentrating attention on the family, its structure, and primary relationships, the process of preparing a genogram provides sex addicts with an historical context for their own compulsive behavior. In most cases, the genogram allows sex addicts to clearly see that their family has a history of not dealing with reality. It establishes a cognitive connection between current behavior and the problems of the patient's family of origin, clarifying the impact of the past on what the patient considers normal and on what (s)he has done.

Often, this sobering process begins to break down unconscious defense mechanisms designed and implemented to protect the patient's self-image and that of the family. Patients begin to realize, often for the first time since childhood (when those defenses were first activated), that their "perfect" childhoods were far from perfect. Yet even in cases when the genogram draws only on knowledge the addict already had, because it collects information about all the parts of the family, it provides a more complete portrait for the patient. The best tool we know to explore family patterns and unearth family secrets, the genogram pulls together all the pieces of the puzzle that make up the sex addict's family history.

Telephone Calls

We often encourage our patients, in completing a genogram, to conduct further research and investigation into their family history. Rather than rely exclusively on their own memory, which may not be entirely reliable, sex addicts often find it helpful to consult with other (non-abusive) family members. Siblings, for example, can often provide additional perspectives that allow the patient to paint a more comprehensive and accurate picture. By checking out their impressions with other family members, by sharing and comparing memories, sex addicts can gather more information to help augment, validate, or invalidate their own recollections.

CASE 2-1 (continued)

After several months in therapy, Maria called both of her sisters to talk about the family's past. Her younger sister, Elizabeth, stonewalled. She denied that the family had any problems and ultimately hung up on Maria. Her older sister, Terry, however, opened up in response to her call. In addition to confirming Maria's impressions of her parents and home life, Terry added another piece of information. Terry recalled that her father would occasionally bring other men into the home for dinner or drinks. Prompted by Terry, Maria remembered these occasions, which began when they were very young and continued throughout their adolescence. When their father's friends visited, the girls overheard a lot of sexual talk—mostly jokes and innuendoes. The men also regularly flirted with the young girls, who both remember sometimes flirting back.

Especially after the patient has benefited from some therapy, phone calls can be valuable in opening up family conversations. In most cases, such phone calls represent the first time family members have ever candidly discussed their experiences in and feelings about their home life. In addition to tapping into additional sources of information about the family, these phone calls put into practice the sex addict's developing communication skills, and in the precise setting where they have been most sorely lacking. When a phone call to another family member is met with a positive response, it can break open the family system of secrets. Adult siblings like Maria and Terry will find that they can talk about both the pain caused by the family and the good memories they share. Although it may represent only a small step forward, such a phone call can thus mark the first change toward healthier, more open family dynamics.

Trauma Egg or Lifeline

Another tool we employ with all of our patients to explore their pasts is a lifeline or trauma egg. A lifeline offers a linear representation of the significant events in a sex addict's life, beginning with the earliest memories of childhood. A trauma egg is nonlinear, offering a graphic representation of childhood (and adult) trauma.

Within the first four or five sessions, we ask all patients to draw an egg on a large piece of paper. Offering patients a wide variety of colored markers, we ask them to choose among the colors and to write inside the egg a capsule description of the earliest traumatic event—or long-term traumatic circumstances—they can remember. We then encourage the patient to fill up the egg with all the traumatic events or circumstances in their lives. Around the outside of the egg, we tell the patient to list any positive influences, including any events or relationships that helped nurture them.

CASE 2-2

Sam, a minister, was suffering from what he called a secret life of chronic masturbation to pornography when he came to us for help. A self-described TV addict and compulsive overeater, Sam had begun to frequent adult bookstores and had grown increasingly fearful of getting caught. In the course of a two-week intensive therapy program, we asked Sam to draw a trauma egg (see Figure 2.2). This exercise helped Sam to understand his isolation, his overwhelming sense of shame, and his use of masturbation for self-medication as long-standing patterns, rather than recent developments. At age 10, two separate events had established a powerful foundation for his shame. His father had publicly ridiculed Sam for holding his penis in the outfield during a Little League game. Shortly thereafter, the nuns who taught at his parochial school punished Sam for chasing girls into the bathroom by forcing him to play with the girls for a week. These early incidents fueled Sam's feelings of inadequacy. At age 15, Sam stayed in an adjacent room as his brother and other boys from his neighborhood raped the girl who lived next door to him. Sam, who felt

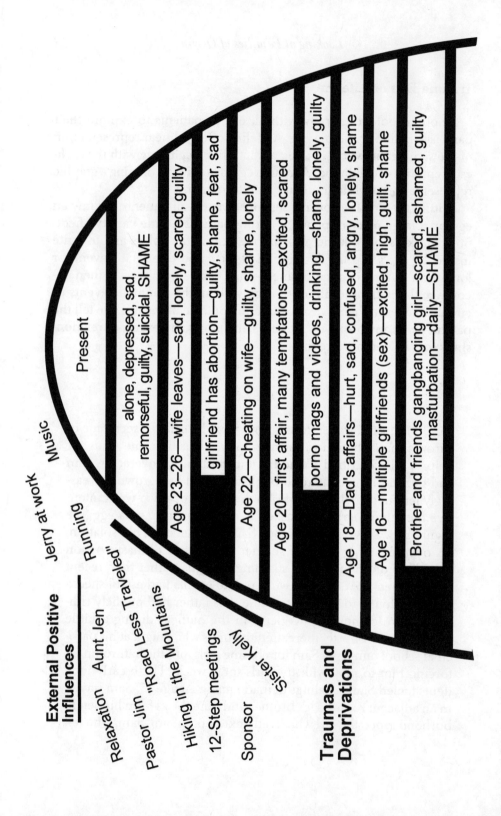

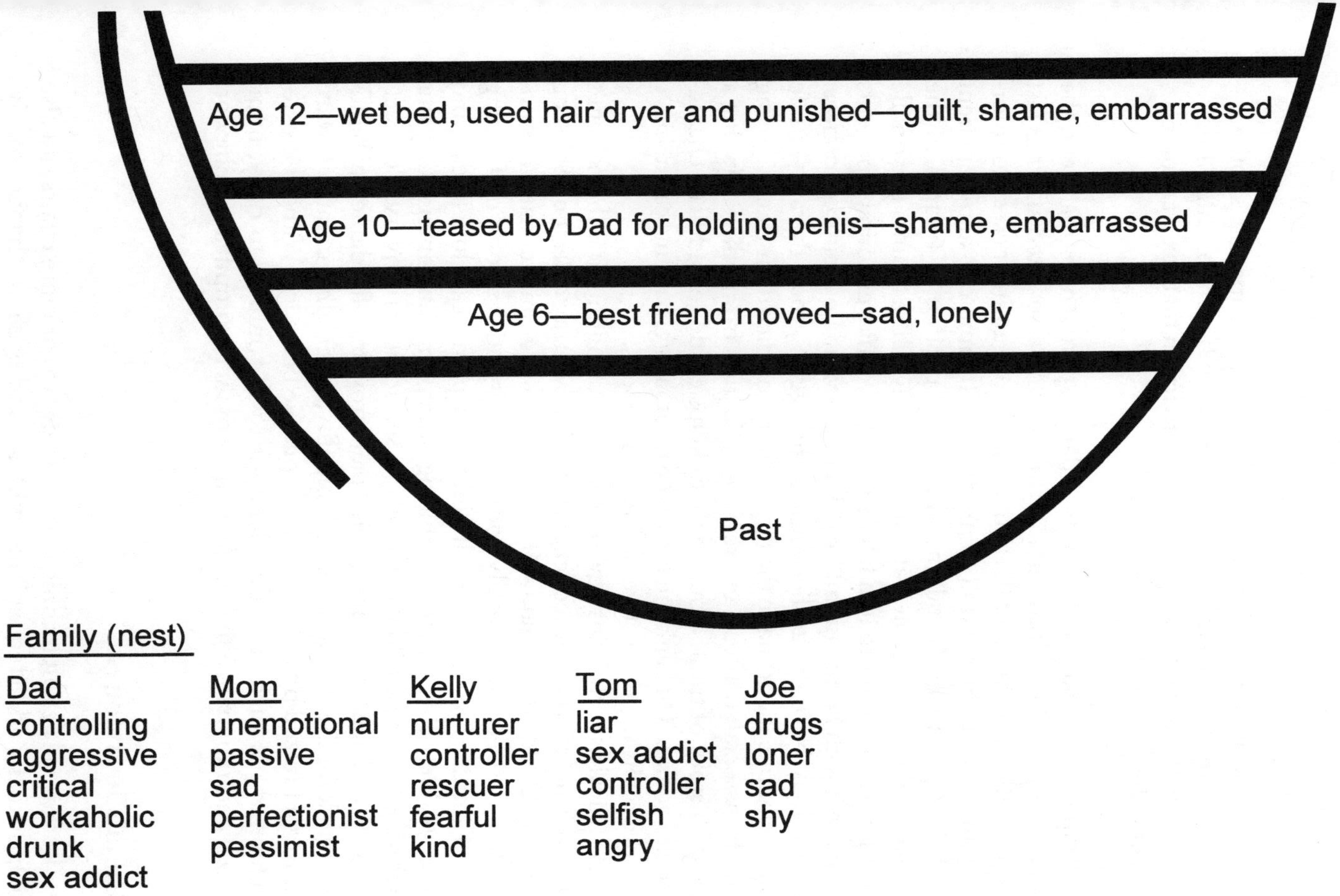

Figure 2.2. Sam's Trauma Egg

Age 12—wet bed, used hair dryer and punished—guilt, shame, embarrassed

Age 10—teased by Dad for holding penis—shame, embarrassed

Age 6—best friend moved—sad, lonely

Past

Family (nest)

Dad
controlling
aggressive
critical
workaholic
drunk
sex addict

Mom
unemotional
passive
sad
perfectionist
pessimist

Kelly
nurturer
controller
rescuer
fearful
kind

Tom
liar
sex addict
controller
selfish
angry

Joe
drugs
loner
sad
shy

scared, ashamed, and inadequate for not participating, soothed himself by masturbating. In treatment, Sam began to realize how this event had helped reinforce his conviction that sex was something dirty, shameful, and covert.

Employed as part of our multimodality approach to treatment, the trauma egg can help draw out information and associated affect as fast as possible. Offering an alternative means of gaining access to information about the sex addict's history, the trauma egg allows patient and therapist to begin talking about the specifics of trauma in the patient's life. We keep the patient's rendering of the trauma egg on file and sometimes refer to it in later sessions. We may encourage patients to share it with family members who might validate their experiences. Or we may have the addict present the egg in group therapy—a safe place where patients have the opportunity to voice their trauma, bring out the associated affect, and receive validation from others. Having a visual history of trauma before them helps erode sex addicts' characteristic denial. Through the use of the trauma egg, patients can achieve a more realistic perspective of their childhoods.

A critical aspect of this new perspective on childhood is the patient's recognition of what our colleague Marilyn Murray calls the "Sobbing Hurting Child" (see Chapter 9). The trauma egg can facilitate the connection between the sexually addicted adult and the Sobbing Hurting Child inside: the bearer of all childhood pain, fear, loneliness, and despair. We believe that recognizing, accepting, and integrating this Sobbing Hurting Child is essential to a sex addict's recovery. Connecting with and validating long-denied pain provides a fundamental building block for the development of empathy, especially empathy toward those victimized by the addict's compulsive behavior. Without the development of such empathy, the addict will continue to deny, minimize, and rationalize the consequences of their compulsive behavior.

Gestalt Techniques

Traditional gestalt techniques involving two or more chairs can also help sexually addicted patients explore—and begin to change—the dynamics of their relationship with their families of origin. Gestalt techniques have many applications in the treatment of sex addicts. Empty-chair exercises can be used to unearth repressed feelings toward living or dead family members; they can help the addict rehearse an upcoming encounter with a family member. Maria, for example, used gestalt techniques to help prepare herself for a family-of-origin session with both of her parents. Combined with role playing in group therapy, the experience helped Maria feel empowered and more comfortable with the imminent meeting. We have found the empty-chair technique useful in establishing a dialogue–ultimately aimed toward integration–among the various aspects of an addict's personality (e.g., the workaholic, the sex addict, and the sober part of self).

Empty-chair techniques can help sex addicts clarify how they see other family members and how they feel toward them. This modality offers patients a safe way to express their emotions, either in rehearsal for an actual confrontation or simply to get them out into the open for the first time. We may use gestalt techniques at any time in the course of therapy. Doing something different can shake things up in a positive way so that the process keeps moving ahead. An important therapeutic aspect of gestalt techniques lies in the directness of the experience for the patient. The empty chair helps the patient focus on talking *to* that person, instead of simply talking *about* the person to the therapist. The impact of the experience is thus more direct and often more powerful.

Letters to Family Members

As with the gestalt techniques, writing a letter to family members provides patients with a safe opportunity to bring out their long-repressed fears and feelings regarding their family of origin. Putting both cognitive and affective material into written words often affords greater room for specificity. It can serve as a catalyst for bringing out unthinkable thoughts and emotions. To underscore the sense of safety and promote an uncensored outpouring of feelings, thoughts, memories, and information, the therapist must emphasize that the patient will not be sending the letter, but rather reading it to the therapist and/or presenting it in a group therapy session.

Through letter writing of this kind, previously repressed feelings can be released. The technique may offer sex addicts their first opportunity to be entirely candid about what they think and feel about family members or other significant persons in their lives. For perhaps the first time, they have the chance to be real about their memories, thoughts, and feelings. Another important benefit is that the patients can hold on to the letter and refer to it as needed. Seeing thoughts and feelings written down on paper invests them with a greater reality. Finally, we always encourage our patients—in addition to expressing both cognitive material and affect—to end the letter with a statement of what they intend to do regarding what they have written. This strategy not only ends the letter on a positive note, but transforms it into a catalyst for action, a force for change in the sex addict's current life.

Some patients have trouble with this freedom of expression. They continue to censor their thoughts and feelings; their defense mechanisms will not allow them to express anything that might be construed as negative. In such cases, a sex addicts' group can help break down resistance. A group of peers can help the addict see that the childhood treatment (s)he describes in neutral or even defensive terms was in fact abusive. They can encourage the addict to be more honest in expressing memories, thoughts, and feelings. Letters revised after having been shared with the group often unlock the affect associated with many memories.

After the letter has been completed, the patient and therapist may consider actually mailing it. As therapists, we discourage the use of letters to family members as a "sneak attack." We consider it irresponsible for a therapist to encourage a patient to dash off a letter to his or her parents without first giving the parents at least the opportunity to have a face-to-face meeting with the patient within a therapeutic context. The family-systems approach requires the therapist to think systemically, to consider the other people involved in the individual patient's circle of family and friends, to recognize that every story has at least two sides. The therapist should try to avoid inviting unintended consequences of therapy, not only to their own clients, but to others in the client's family system.

When the therapist and patient determine that sending a letter to a family member seems both warranted and appropriate, we always have the addict share the letter with the group first, to get feedback from those who have had similar experiences in the past. Group members sometimes suggest revisions to the letter, but their greatest contribution in this context lies in their ability to prompt the addict to explore his or her expectations regarding the letter's recipient. Addicts should prepare for every conceivable response to such a letter, and plan their own response to each possibility in advance. This process will help guard against relapse no matter how the recipient reacts.

FAMILY-OF-ORIGIN SESSIONS

A family-of-origin session, which may be as short as two hours or as long as a full day (or two hours daily for a week), brings other family members together with the sex addict and his or her therapist. A short session should be aimed primarily at further information gathering in the safe setting of the therapist's office. A long session or series of sessions should be aimed at getting secrets out in the open. The other family members should not expect to receive therapy in such a session, but rather to hear the addict's story and to share their own perspective of the patient's childhood.

A family-of-origin session should offer a safe place for confrontation among family members. The safety of the patient is of paramount importance to the therapist. However, to promote the safety of other family members as well, we frequently invite a family pastor or other counselor involved with family problems to attend the session. Prior to such a session, we encourage the sex addict to consider both strengths—that is, what is good about the family—and weaknesses. The patient should understand beforehand that the purpose of the session is not to cast blame, but to focus on healing—that is, to explore the possibility of the family healing by beginning to talk about things that have never been talked about before.

CASE 2-1 *(continued)*

Maria, her husband, their conservative pastor, and both of her parents attended a family-of-origin session in our offices. Maria's sisters declined to attend. After talking about her impressions of the family history, Maria read a letter she had written but never sent to her parents and sisters. She and her mother both cried as she read the letter. Her father reacted defensively, but nonetheless acknowledged the validity of her experiences. He told Maria that they had tried to do the best they could, but finished by saying, "I'm sorry."

Maria's second family-of-origin session centered on setting boundaries between her parents and her children. Maria clearly stated that she did not want her children exposed to their grandfather's rage. She wanted to avoid having them traumatized in the same way she had been. Maria told her father that her children had confided that "Grandpa's yelling" scared them. Maria was surprised by her father's openness to this criticism and his willingness to listen.

Although a family-of-origin session does not benefit every patient, we always find them helpful and therefore try to orchestrate one whenever logistically possible. We have not yet had a family-of-origin session in which our patient's experiences were not validated (although the details sometimes differ from other perspectives). No doubt the willingness of other family members to come at all generally indicates an interest in healing and the likelihood that some, if not all, of the sex addict's experiences will be corroborated. It can be anticipated that some family members, like Maria's sisters, will refuse to attend.) When abuse is validated by other family members, the whole family seems to feel a great sense of relief to have things finally brought out into the light. A family-of-origin session thus can not only further the patient's healing and validate that (s)he is not crazy, but begin to involve everyone in the family in the process of recovery.

Important Note: Such confrontations can be extremely stressful for everyone involved. Prior to even considering such a session, the therapist needs to have worked a great deal with the sex addict, made firm the therapeutic relationship, forged a thorough understanding of the patient's family history, and, above all, established the office as a safe place for the patient.

3

Coordinating the Treatment Team

The Multimodality Approach

In our practice—Psychological Counseling Services in Scottsdale, Arizona—we have developed a therapeutic program for sex addicts and their families that depends on the coordination of a great many people. In designing this treatment program, we operated under the assumption that a disorder as complex as sex addiction demands a multifaceted approach to therapy. It is our conviction that no single therapist—no matter how well schooled, proficient, talented, and compassionate—can provide the range and depth of care that a well-coordinated team of different specialists can. Effective treatment of sex addiction (and its impact on other family members) requires a multimodality approach that includes: specializations in the treatment of addictions, sex offenders, and sexual abuse victims; couples therapy; family therapy; creative-art and other expressive therapies; and sex therapy. And no single therapist can realistically expect to have achieved mastery in all of these modalities, each of which can contribute a different aspect to the recovery of sex addicts and co-addicts.

We believe that part of what makes our practice unique, especially in the treatment of outpatients, is that we have brought together specialists in all of these fields under a single roof. This allows us to provide sex addicts and families with a breadth of therapy that we consider rare even in psychiatric hospitals that treat sex addicts as inpatients. Every one of our sex-addicted patients receives treatment from several therapists, each of whom has a different specialty and a distinct ap-

proach to the disorder. Each patient sees a minimum of three therapists on our staff; many see five or more. In addition, we sometimes
refer sex-addicted patients to either a local behavioral health center or
a halfway house. As our office is located two blocks away from Samaritan, we continue to offer therapy to these patients during their stay in
the hospital programs.

In addition to long-term scheduled therapy, we have also begun
offering a program of "intensive therapy" for sex addicts and their families. Sex addicts and, whenever possible, spouses and other family
members come to us for two to five weeks of treatment. Patients in our
intensive program receive two to six hours daily of individual, couples,
or family therapy—from as many as six staff therapists. In addition,
they participate in two to four therapist-led groups. This program, which
we regard as more intensive than residential inpatient programs, allows the therapists to have a powerful impact on the family system.
The intensive time spent in therapy often facilitates the breakdown of
barriers that may previously have inhibited or blocked progress in the
ongoing therapeutic process.

THE TREATMENT TEAM

Part of our multimodality approach to the treatment of sex addiction
involves pulling together a treatment team. Most, if not all, sex addicts
will benefit from a treatment team that includes the following.

The Primary Therapist: Sex addicts (and, in most cases, their spouses)
need individual therapy that focuses in-depth attention on their specific problems and challenges (Earle & Crow, 1989). Although we
strongly recommend individual therapy for both the sex addict and
the spouse, we do not necessarily use the same therapist for both partners. The one-on-one relationship established between a trusted therapist and an addict or co-addict—that is, the addict's primary
codependent, who may face similar addictive challenges—provides the
safest possible environment for "care-fronting" (Augsburger, 1983) the
patient. This sense of safety encourages the emergence of the many
hidden aspects of a sex addict's history and personality. Individual
therapy can help addicts and co-addicts begin to resolve issues from

past relationships as well as current issues. The trust and safety an addict or co-addict feels within the context of individual therapy can help the patient unearth and express long-repressed emotions. Individual therapy also affords the therapist the opportunity to confront the addict's or co-addict's distorted thinking (rationalization, justification, minimization). Finally, the primary therapist should provide the addict with "edutherapy"—an element of the treatment program that combines therapeutic experiences with didactic lessons—regarding the addictive cycle, the effects of abuse on the addict's victims (to help promote victim empathy), and the improvement of communication skills.

Group Therapists: We view group therapy as perhaps the most essential modality in the treatment of sexually compulsive patients. As secretiveness, dishonesty, and maintaining a facade are critical components of sex addiction, therapy needs to tear down the addict's facade, break open the secrets, and foster a new honesty. Group therapy provides the therapist with the opportunity to encourage the addict to practice open and honest self-examination in the presence of others. As addicts begin to reveal the hidden or repressed sides of themselves, the acceptance by the therapist(s) and other group members helps dissipate the fear that they will be rejected if they let people see them as they really are. Group therapy also gives addicts the chance to develop and practice the social skills that they so often lack. Under the guidance of the therapist(s), sex addicts can learn and try out self-assertion skills, the expression of empathy, the productive expression of anger, and ways to provide appropriate feedback.

Having more than one therapist leading a group offers an opportunity for skilled cotherapists to use the good cop/bad cop approach to motivate further growth and change in sex addicts. For example, in a recent group therapy session for co-addicts, the therapist playing the bad cop role spent several minutes assertively care-fronting Maria's husband, Carter (see Case 2-1). He charged Carter with copping out on therapy, with being stuck and refusing to move forward. The therapist playing the good cop then countered by acknowledging that Carter was going through a lot, not only in dealing with the revelation of Maria's multiple affairs, but also with his wife's emerging anger. Considering how much Carter was handling, the second therapist affirmed that he was really doing a great job. In this scenario, both therapists spoke the truth; both perspectives were valid. Judicious use of the good cop/bad cop strategy can thus help to push addicts or co-addicts to heal further, while still supporting them in their journey.

In our practice, we conduct group therapy for sexual compulsives and also groups for co-addicts. Each group is led by three cotherapists. In most cases, sex addicts and co-addicts attend groups in which their primary therapist serves as one of the group's cotherapists. This setup helps increase the patient's sense of safety within the group.

Addiction Specialist: This may or may not be the patient's primary therapist. However, if the primary therapist does not specialize in addictions we strongly recommend a course of treatment administered by another therapist trained and experienced in therapy for addicts. The sex addict needs to understand and identify how the concept of an addictive cycle applies to his or her own patterns of compulsive behavior. Recognition is the key to interrupting and ultimately breaking away from these compulsive patterns. Without this new understanding, any efforts at developing a relapse-prevention plan will prove ineffective. An addiction specialist can also focus insight on how the addiction has taken control not only of the addict's behavior, but of his or her thoughts as well. The addiction specialist can increase an addict's awareness of the way in which distorted thinking patterns (rationalization, justification, minimization) serve to protect not the addict, but the addiction itself.

Couples Therapists: Sex addicts involved in primary relationships require couples therapy aimed at exploring the dynamics of the relationship, fostering improved intrarelational communication, and developing true intimacy. Especially when each partner sees a different primary therapist, we use two cotherapists in couples therapy whenever possible. Again, this strategy contributes to the sense of safety felt by both partners, a safety that enhances openness and thus increases the therapeutic value of couples sessions. The couples therapist can focus attention on the roles each partner has played—or continues to play—in the development and maintenance of the central dysfunctions in the relationship. Only when both partners take responsibility for their own actions can the dynamics of the relationship begin to change.

Family Therapists: As mentioned in Chapter 1, concentrating all therapy on the sex addict means that the family is ignored or relegated to second place. All of the family's focus remains on the addict in recovery, just as it once did on the addict in his or her addictive cycle. Ultimately, this serves the interests of neither the addict nor the family as a whole. From a family-systems approach, the addiction of one family member promotes or intensifies dysfunctional relational patterns in every other close family member (Black, 1981; Marlin, 1987; Wegscheider-Cruse, 1981; Woititz, 1983, 1985). Exploring dysfunctional patterns and helping create new family dynamics that depend on healthy boundaries, awareness of emotions, and open communication will strengthen the family as a whole and each one of its members. The altering of the family dynamics not only will contribute to the addict's recovery, but it may help break the generational cycle of addiction and co-addiction.

Child Therapists: Frequently, even in sex addiction cases that do not involve incest, the children of the addict suffer from such severe psychological damage that individual therapy is warranted. Because their identities are so closely linked to their developing sexuality, adolescents in particular often experience the revelation of their parent's sex addiction as devastating to their conceptions of family, sexuality, and self. We therefore recommend psychological assessment of all children of sex addicts to determine the appropriateness of individual intervention.

Specialists in the Treatment of Sexual-Abuse Victims: In cases of incest, the victims *always* require therapy aimed at relieving guilt and shame, correcting false attributions of responsibility, heightening self-esteem, and reintegrating dissociated parts of self (whether affective, experiential, or cognitive). A therapist who specializes in such treatment for victims is essential when the sex addict has committed incest. However, sex addicts themselves can also benefit from the intervention of such a therapist. As sex addicts more often than not suffered sexual abuse as children, a specialist in treating victims can help them resolve some of the unresolved issues from their own childhood: issues that gave birth to cognitive distortions and often helped initiate the patterns that would later become the addictive cycle.

Creative-Art or Expressive Therapists: Sex addicts are so often dissociated from affect that they cannot identify and express it without the intervention of modalities that allow and encourage them to access and release their emotions. Art therapies and sand-play therapies (see Chapter 11) can offer new avenues to express emotions; these therapies are particularly effective in accessing consciousness of any trau-

mas that the addict may otherwise, consciously or unconsciously, regard as unspeakable. Gestalt therapies utilizing two or more chairs and
letter-writing exercises can help focus the addict's attention on the honest
expression of affect. Psychodrama (called focused action therapy, or
FACT, in our area) also offers a dynamic alternative that allows sex
addicts (or co-addicts) to safely express the affect associated with current difficulties, or with unresolved issues from the past.

Sex Therapists. Sex addicts, of course, need sex therapy aimed at eliminating the sexual compulsions through which they have victimized
themselves and others. Yet sex addicts almost always need sex education and sex therapy at a much more basic level as well. Sex addicts
(as most co-addicts) not only have little or no notion of sexual relations
as anything but a source of individual physical pleasure, but they often
lack basic knowledge of sexuality, sexual functioning, and human sexual
response. After other modalities have helped the couple begin to deal
with relationship issues outside of the bedroom, sex addicts and co-
addicts require a basic sex education and sex therapy aimed at identifying and resolving any co- or preexisting sexual dysfunctions, recognizing the spiritual dimension of healthy sexuality, and appreciating
and achieving sexual intimacy.

In addition to members of the professional staff, we often include
others in the treatment team. If the addict has an ongoing and healthy
relationship with a member of the clergy, we will often invite that person to facilitate and support the spiritual aspects of recovery. In cases
involving criminal sexual offenses, the treatment team must take care
not to exclude probation officers, attorneys, and judges, all of whose
actions will have an impact on the individual and family in therapy.
We sometimes invite probation officers to family sessions to assess, for
example, the appropriateness or inappropriateness of returning into
the home a sex addict who has committed incest. Finally, 12-step groups
and 12-step sponsors complement the work of the treatment team, but
we generally regard such self-help groups as separate entities. Most sex
addicts find enormous strength in such groups, and we do recommend
them highly.

In developing a customized treatment plan for the individual addict
and his or her family, the primary therapist also needs to make clear to
spouses and other co-addicts that, although they can serve as indis-

pensable members of the sex addict's *recovery* team, they are not part of the *treatment* team. As the primary people to whom addicts must make themselves accountable, co-addicts can play an important role in the relapse-prevention team. They can help establish boundaries, resolve to honor no more secrets, and help maintain the sobriety contract by holding the addict accountable and clearly stating—and following through with—the consequences that will ensue if the contract is broken. The co-addict can support and encourage the individual in recovery. But co-addicts are not responsible for ensuring that the addict recovers, for psychoanalyzing the addict, for overseeing or controlling the care of the addict, or for providing sex therapy to the addict. Co-addicts should be encouraged to support their partners' recovery and to participate in their own recovery programs, but should be discouraged from any attempt to manage their partners' recovery.

Important Note: Patients receiving multimodality treatment from more than one therapist *must* sign a release expressly recognizing and consenting to the intention to share information among all therapists in the practice. The patient has a legal and moral right to know the conditions under which information revealed within the therapist's office will be shared with others. The treatment agreement that we have each new patient sign includes in the confidentiality clause a statement of policy regarding our treatment-team approach: "It is accepted practice at PCS for staff to consult periodically on certain cases."[1] If a patient will be receiving treatment from another therapist outside our office, we ask that (s)he sign a separate release authorizing consultation and sharing of information with that therapist as well.

CASE 3-1

Upon intake, David, a 34-year-old man who molested his eldest stepdaughter over the course of eight years (see also Case 1-1),

---

[1] This clause also identifies all other conditions under which we will no longer be bound by the guarantee of confidentiality. These include situations in which the patient represents a threat to self or others or if the patient files a lawsuit against any of the therapists. Also, we clearly state that it may be necessary to share information with the patient's insurance company in order to obtain reimbursement. Finally, this clause indemnifies us from any breach of confidentiality made by another group therapy member.

was already receiving group therapy from a therapist outside our practice and had for several months been regularly attending Alcoholics Anonymous (AA) meetings. Dr. Bill Harnell administered a plethysmograph, psychological testing, and other assessment tools and helped David prepare a genogram. When David violated a boundary (and court order) by visiting his youngest daughter, Brittany, in the child's home, David's primary therapist, Dr. Ralph Earle, strongly advised that he enter the day program at Samaritan Behavioral Health Center. While in the day program for three weeks, David continued inhospital sessions with the primary therapist.

After leaving the day program, David's program consisted of aftercare provided by the hospital, individual therapy, group therapy led by our staff, AA, and Sex Addicts Anonymous. His wife, Ellen, and victimized daughter, Jenny, were also participating in Samaritan's aftercare program and seeing David's primary therapist for individual therapy. For a short time, all five family members also attended family therapy led by the primary therapist. However, after consulting with the psychiatrist who treated them at Samaritan and the aftercare therapist, we decided to discontinue Jenny's participation in family therapy until she had worked through the individual issues associated with being a victim of her stepfather's abuse. We modified this plan to hold two distinct bimonthly family sessions: one with Ellen and her three daughters (what David's parole officer referred to as "the intact family," the four family members still living together in the home); one with both parents and the two younger daughters.

Shortly thereafter, we added Dr. Roxanne Witte, a specialist in working with victims of sexual trauma, to our staff at PCS. Dr. Witte met several times with Jenny and her father (victim and victimizer) to help them deal with the real pain caused by the trauma. For the next year, Dr. Witte provided individual therapy on a weekly basis to Jenny and later couples therapy to Jenny and her fiance, Frank, himself a victim of childhood sexual abuse. David and Ellen (the parents) saw Dr. Earle for couples therapy. Because we recognized the need for Jenny to have an advocate in family therapy, Dr. Witte joined Dr. Earle as a cotherapist during these sessions. David discontinued individual therapy but continued to attend a group for sexual compulsives led by our staff. Finally, Ellen and Jenny began seeing Dr. Witte for mother/daughter therapy.

Two years after David first revealed his incestuous behavior and turned himself in, his stepdaughter Rebecca, who insists she was never sexually abused by him, attempted suicide with an overdose of Tylenol. (Whenever possible, everyone in the family should receive therapy. Neglected before therapy due to her father's addiction and her mother's workaholism, Rebecca felt ignored a second time by therapy that focused primarily on her parents and her sister.) At this point, Dr. Witte began treating Rebecca. As a result of the suicide attempt, the county parole board halted the family's gradual progression toward reunification. We consulted with David's parole officer and invited her to sit in on several family sessions before reviewing the prospects for family reunification.

After two and a half years of therapy, the court-supervised progression—which began with David's joining the family for dinners or afternoons at home (always in the presence of his wife), moved on to occasional overnights (under strict guidelines), and then moved up to three nights a week at home—approached full-time reunification. Tension increased, especially in the relationship between David and Ellen. While continuing marital therapy with Dr. Ralph Earle, Ellen began to focus on communication issues in individual therapy with Dr. Marcus Earle, who had led a couples communication course that Ellen had taken with her husband. At this time, after violating a provision of his reunification contract by going to the front door (i.e., out of his bedroom) in his pajamas, David resumed individual therapy with Dr. Donald Hall, a colleague in David's sexual compulsives group and a specialist in sex addicts and sex offenders.

BENEFITS OF THE MULTIMODALITY APPROACH

To date, David and his family have seen five therapists on our staff (in addition to several others outside our offices), each suited to a different need that one or more family members had at the time. Having a number of specialists under the same roof—couples therapists, family therapists, victims therapists, addiction specialists, sex therapists, and others—has allowed us to customize treatment modalities to the individual needs presented to us by our patients. A diverse staff allows each member to provide therapy in the area with which (s)he feels most comfortable.

Having a variety of therapists on staff allows a practice to treat every case as unique, to take a situational approach to therapy that provides the therapy each patient needs at any given stage of life and recovery. In our practice with sex addicts, we sometimes deal very little with issues from childhood, and yet, at other times, we need to deal intensely with what Marilyn Murray (1991) calls the patient's pool of pain, the unresolved issues related to childhood trauma. In either case, we have inhouse staff to provide just what the patient needs.

The multimodality approach we practice also affords a great deal of flexibility in dealing with treatment issues. The breadth of our staff enables us, for example, to design specific programs that address the needs of sex addicts who are suicidal or of those who have committed sexual offenses. It also allows therapy to change direction as necessary. For example, if sex therapy triggers traumatic memories, the sex therapist can either handle the crisis immediately and then refer it to the primary therapist for follow-up, or the therapist can immediately consult with the primary therapist, who in our practice can usually be found in the same building.

Changing therapists within the practice can move treatment to focus on a new issue and can also prevent the patient from forming an intense dependence on a single therapist. In considering whether to switch therapists, however, we apply this critical criterion: Do we reasonably anticipate that this patient will do as well or better with the new therapist? If the answer is No, we will not make the change. In switching therapists to focus on individual issues, we take care to avoid causing the patient to feel abandoned, carefully explaining our rationale and ensuring that it is understood and accepted. We regard it as supremely important that such a change does not erode the therapeutic gains made in terms of the sex addict's self-esteem and ability to trust.

The aim of our program for sex addicts is integrative in many respects. In integrating many treatment modalities, we attempt to facilitate healthy change at several levels simultaneously. Often, these levels complement and reinforce one another. The addict can be working on improved communication skills with the primary therapist, for example, while, in the same week, working together with the co-addict in sex therapy. Or the patient who is learning about the addictive cycle in the context of individual therapy may then have the cognitive distortions that propped up that cycle confronted in group therapy. The ultimate treatment goal for the addicts is itself integrative, for it involves discovering or recovering dissociated parts of self (e.g., traumatic affect or victim empathy) and integrating these various selves to achieve a balanced, healthy, whole person.

From a family-systems approach, in which the family itself is regarded as the patient, we also aim toward integration, both in treatment modalities and in the family as a whole. Having more than one therapist involved in treating family members individually allows more than one therapist in the room during confrontations between the victim and victimizer, or between addict and co-addict. This is critically important because each patient needs to have established a rapport and sense of safety with at least one therapist in the room during any couples or family therapy session involving sex addiction—especially in any session that brings together a victim and victimizer. Prior to her first session with Dr. Witte, Jenny told us she felt ready and capable of confronting her incestuous stepfather (see Case 3-1). When actually seated with her father in the therapist's office, however, Jenny felt alone, unsupported, unprepared, and overwhelmed by anxiety. Recognizing this discomfort, Dr. Witte asked David to leave the room and spent the remainder of the session building a base of trust and rapport with Jenny. By slowing down the process, Dr. Witte offered Jenny the time and support she needed to confront her stepfather more productively a week later. This experience taught us not to arrange for any confrontation between a victimizer and his or her victim unless the victim's primary therapist will attend the session or the victim reports feeling safe and comfortable with the therapist who will attend. When each person has his or her own individual therapist present in a couples or family therapy session, it maximizes the perception of environmental safety for both patients. This mutual sense of safety can facilitate greater candor and thus accelerate healing.

In constructing our therapeutic program for sex addicts and their families, we have tried to develop (and continue to develop) the most comprehensive treatment possible. We add new therapists to our staff based on our perspective of what our patient population needs that we cannot currently provide effectively. In the past two years, for instance, we have welcomed a therapist who specializes in the treatment of victims, one who has expertise in treating sex offenders (victimizers), yet another who specializes in eating disorders (a common pathology among co-addicts and children of sex addicts). Still, we recognize that we do not have the expertise to handle everything, and we frequently refer issues to other mental-health professionals. We have no psychiatrist on staff, for example, and so until recently, when we added an addiction specialist, Michel Sucher, M.D., to our staff, we referred out for medication. We also send patients outside our offices for psychoneurological testing.

The key to using a multimodality approach successfully is coordinating the treatment team. The case manager and the primary therapist are both responsible for keeping track of all aspects of a particular case, which includes planning and monitoring the treatment modalities employed and evaluating the progress of the overall treatment program. Having several people looking at the same case from different angles helps keep the evaluation of progress honest. In weekly staff meetings, we encourage everyone to become involved in brainstorming cases. In this context, we share information on cases, discuss strategies, explore options, and suggest therapies for the addict and other family members. Any disagreements on the direction of therapy are then resolved through consensus. At all times, however, as we have emphasized throughout this chapter, the client's safety and security remain the highest priority. For this reason, in making all treatment decisions and adjustments in therapy programs, we first consider how the change will affect the patient's safety. Whenever the therapist compromises the patient's safety, the healing journey rapidly grinds to a halt.

Teamwork and coordination among therapists have proved most effective in our treatment of sex addicts and their families. By having each therapist focus on the issues or dynamics with which (s)he feels most comfortable, we offer customized treatment that can quickly and efficiently unearth and resolve critical treatment issues. In every aspect of treatment, sex addicts and co-addicts thus receive specialized care that speeds family recovery.

4

Eliminating Deviant Behavior

Identifying the Cycle of Deviance and Addiction

As with any addiction, perhaps the most difficult challenge facing both therapist and patient is the prevention of relapse (see also Chapter 10). For the sex addict, compulsive sexual behavior has been *the* defense mechanism used to "handle" stress, anger, and unexpressed fears and feelings. No matter how or when the individual's compulsive sexual behavior began, the addiction has taken on a life of its own by the time a sex addict seeks treatment. Turning to addictive behaviors has become automatic and habitual, the immediate response not only to internal or external stressors, but to pleasures or successes as well. Troubled by personal failures or the world's injustice, the addict feels (s)he deserves the transitory compensation provided by the addictive behavior. Elated by a personal success or triumph, the addict chooses to celebrate and reward him- or herself by supplementing that high with the one provided by sexual compulsions.

Because this reliance on addictive behaviors is automatic and unthinking, depending much less on conscious choice than on ingrained habit, one of the critical elements of relapse prevention involves bringing the elements of the automatic addictive cycle into conscious awareness. Sex addicts in recovery need to identify their personal cycles of deviance and addiction and pinpoint the triggers; that is, both the internal and external sources of stress that prompt the flight response and subsequent escape into addictive behaviors. Increasing self-awareness by identifying the idiosyncratic "red lights," and even the "yellow lights," that signal descent into the addictive cycle will allow addicts to recognize these signals in the future and make new choices about how to respond. To halt the addictive cycle, sex addicts need to begin to look at the little things in their lives, the details that might at first glance seem inconsequential, but have actually served as triggers or permission givers. In encouraging such insight into self, we empower our patients, allowing them to move away from the unexamined life (a life that Aristotle judged as not worth living) and make new choices about where they will go and what they will do with their lives.

In our practice, we use "edutherapy" to teach sex addicts about the addictive cycles detailed throughout this chapter. After developing an understanding of the general model, recovering sex addicts then combine it with their expanding knowledge of themselves in order to determine how the model fits their patterns—how it applies to their lives. Sex addicts at this stage must undertake a thorough and sober examination of their lives in order to identify their unique patterns of deviance and addiction. As understanding and prevention are two very different things, once the addict understands the old cycle of addiction, (s)he will still need to develop new cycles to replace the addictive cycle or the "offender cycle." (For more on relapse prevention, see Chapter 10.) However, recognizing and understanding old patterns of behavior is a necessary step toward changing those patterns.

MODELS OF THE ADDICTIVE CYCLE

As already mentioned, no single model of the cycle of sex addiction can capture all of the elements of every individual's unique pattern of sexually compulsive behavior. We introduce our patients to three different models of the addictive cycle. The first, developed by Dr. Patrick Carnes in his groundbreaking work, *Out of the Shadows: Understanding Sexual Addiction* (1992), provides a useful introduction to the patterns of sexually compulsive behavior (see Figure 4.1). Carnes begins with the sex addict's belief system, based on messages learned through the family of origin and other childhood experiences, a belief system that influences the way in which the individual views her- or himself and the world. Carnes identifies four core beliefs common to sex addicts:

1. Self-Image: I am basically a bad, unworthy person.
2. Relationships: No one would love me as I am.
3. Needs: My needs are never going to be met if I have to depend on others.
4. Sexuality: Sex is my most important need.

These beliefs generate impaired thinking, cognitive distortions that influence the addict's interpretation of reality and response to it. This includes the employment of such defense mechanisms as denial, rationalization, minimization, justification, blaming, and excusing. Impaired thinking leads into the addiction cycle. Carnes conceives of the addiction cycle as a four-step cycle that starts with preoccupation, the trancelike obsession with seeking out sources of sexual stimulation or automatically sexualizing almost anyone or anything. Ritualization, a set of rigid behaviors that precedes the sexual act, intensifies the preoccupation and increases arousal. Many sex addicts get a greater high from

Figure 4.1. Carnes' Sex Offenders' Cycle.*

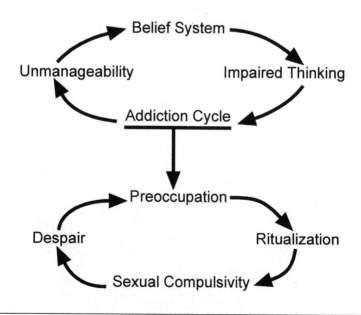

*(Reprinted with permission from Carnes, 1992, p. 15).

the preoccupation and ritualization than from the sexual act itself. The compulsive sexual behavior, experienced as inevitable and uncontrollable following preoccupation and ritualization, is next. This subcycle ends with despair and hopelessness in the face of powerlessness. The only way the addict knows to relieve this despair is a return to sexual preoccupation. This self-perpetuating addiction cycle, and the need to cover up and keep secret sexual behaviors, contributes to the sex addict's sense that life is unmanageable. This unmanageability reinforces the belief system that set the cycle in motion in the first place. Thus the wheels keep on turning and the cycle continues until the addict's life becomes so unmanageable that (s)he is forced to seek help.

Another model of the addictive cycle we introduce to our patients is the sex offender's cycle (see Figure 4.2), developed by Laren Bays and Robert Freeman-Longo and presented in the second of their valuable Sex Offenders' Studies (SOS) workbooks: *Why did I do it again? Understanding my cycle of problem behaviors* (1989).

Figure 4.2. SOS Sex Offenders' Cycle.*

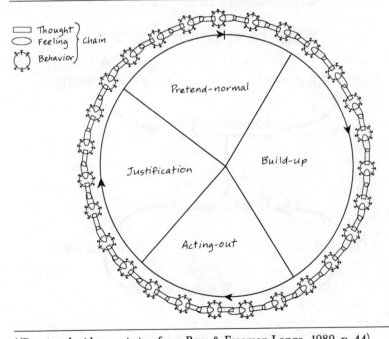

*(Reprinted with permission from Bays & Freeman-Longo, 1989, p. 44).

The SOS cycle begins with normal, everyday life and addicts' feelings about themselves and their lives (anger, boredom, depression). The buildup phase corresponds to Carnes' stages of preoccupation and ritualization. It includes fantasies about sexual pleasure; sexual arousal; the heightening of sexual interest or obsession, often through the use of pornography; planning the sexual offense; and, finally, commitment to making those obsessive fantasies a reality. The acting-out phase is the sexual offense itself. The justification phase involves a wide array of defense mechanisms—including denial, promises to never do it again, rationalization, excuses, anger, and minimization—used to ward off fear, guilt, self-hatred, feelings of failure, and depression in the wake of acting out. The cycle then returns to the pretend-normal phase: The sex addict denies having a problem, hides (from self and others) any evidence of the problem, pretends everything is all right, and returns to normal, daily routine (Bays & Freeman-Longo, 1989).

The SOS workbooks and the SOS sex offenders' cycle serve as important elements of our edutherapy program. The books not only help familiarize our patients with patterns of addictive behavior and the basic elements of addictive cycles, but also encourage and explicitly guide self-examination with regard to how these patterns and cycles apply to their own lives.

CASE 4-1

David, a sex addict and sex offender who molested his stepdaughter (see also Cases 1-1 and 3-1) thousands of times according to the police report prepared after his confession, was given the assignment to write about his deviant cycle and present it both to his therapy group and to his family (in the context of a family therapy session).

Buildup Phase: "I would have feelings of inadequacy, lonely, feel worthless at times. Ellen was always working. What she did was more important than me. But Jenny thought I was important. She would listen to me. She took me serious. I would think about being alone with Jenny and figure out a time. I had gotten Ellen...to work all the time.

Rebecca and Brittany had been programmed to leave me and Jenny alone. I would try and be home alone with Jenny or I would be with Jenny after she came home at nite and everyone else was asleep. At nite I would...use...my alcoholism to get Ellen to drink which would insure she slept sound."

Acting-Out Phase: "When Jenny and I were alone I would talk to her like my wife not my daughter. I spoke sexually. I talked about my work, I listened to her day. All the time fondling her breasts or hugging her inappropriately or rubbing my self up against her. I would try to get under her shirt or in her pants, at which time she would say *no!* I would be pouty until the sexual feeling went away."

Justification Phase: "After the sexual feeling would go away, I would feel guilty and sorry for what I did. I would tell Jenny I was sorry. I would tell myself it wouldn't happen again. I would do extras for Jenny to make up for it. Buy her gas for the car. Be nice to everyone."

Pretend Normal Phase: "Things would go along normal and then I would start thinking about everything I did for Jenny and rationalize how she liked to be fondled or she wouldn't want to be with me all the time. Ellen is always at work. The cycle would repeat."

We find the model developed by Carnes and the one outlined by Bays and Freeman-Longo extremely useful in educating and treating sex addicts. In addition, our colleague Paul Simpson has developed a new model of the addictive cycle that adds more detail to (and thus may provide deeper insight into) the phases that build up to the sexually compulsive act. Like Carnes' model, our model (see Figure 4.3) begins with a belief system. The *pool of mistaken beliefs* shared by most sex addicts includes:

- Leftover childhood survival beliefs (many of which are maintained and acted upon although they no longer function to promote survival)
- Feelings of inadequacy that are also deeply rooted in the self-image formed during the addict's childhood

Figure 4.3. Paul Simpson's Model of the Sex Addiction Cycle.

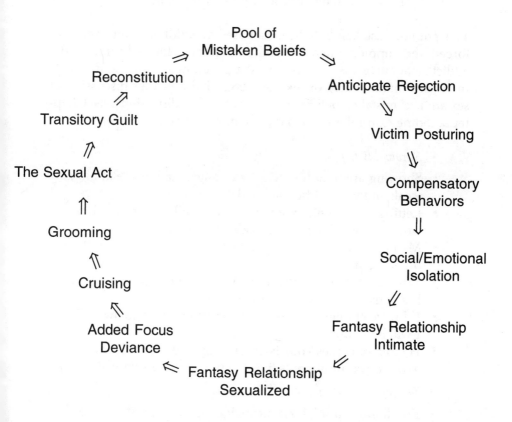

- Beliefs that block or prevent intimacy—dysfunctional beliefs about relationships chiefly learned through childhood observations of the way parents or other important adults interacted or how they modeled behavior in relationships
- Dysfunctional beliefs about sex, frequently based either in misinformation (often taught in an effort to control sexual behavior) or in an almost complete lack of information.

This pool of mistaken beliefs, most based in childhood but later reinforced and supplemented by adult experiences filtered through the addict's cognitive distortions, lays the groundwork for the development and maintenance of sex addiction. (For a further discussion of sex addicts' mistaken beliefs and other cognitive distortions, see Chapter 5.) Some examples of each type of distorted belief follow.

- *Survival Beliefs*
- Showing any emotion (e.g., fear, anger, sadness, elation) is weak and will not be tolerated.
- Letting anyone else know my needs will only make things worse (by leaving me vulnerable to them).
- My needs are never going to be met if I have to depend on others (Carnes, 1983).
- Whenever a group of people gets together, something bad happens (so stay away from groups).
- If I have enough money, all my problems will go away and I will be happy.
- Happiness comes from external things and generally involves avoiding commitments (i.e., the potential for betrayal).

- *Feelings of Inadequacy*
- I'm dumb, stupid, lazy, incapable, incompetent.
- I am basically a bad, unworthy person (Carnes, 1983).
- "I hate myself," Maria (see Case 2-1) admits. "Most of the time I don't feel like I'm a very nice person."
- I don't know the answer (especially if being asked to explain or justify behaviors). Besides, no answer is good enough: I've already been tried and convicted (throughout childhood).

- I'm obsessed with sex. (This negative message about sexuality often stems from rigidly religious upbringings.)

- *Intimacy Blockers*
- No one would love me as I am (Carnes, 1983). I must therefore never let anyone know me. I cannot allow myself to be vulnerable to rejection and abandonment by others.
- Hurt, disappointment, or fear of losing my partner are *never* to be expressed in a way that leaves me vulnerable to my partner or directly lets my partner know how deep-ly I care. (They can only be expressed as criticism and anger—based on an assumption of the other's negative intent.)
- Anger is never productive so it must be stuffed. (This hidden anger is transformed into rage, then usually expressed in passive ways, including victimizing others and other forms of revenge. If the anger arises due to perceptions of sexual rejection or betrayal, then revenge may take the form of sexual acting out. The need for revenge [among men] may be tied to spouse, mother, or other women perceived as sexually abusive.)

- *Dysfunctional Beliefs about Sex*
- Women don't like sex and will only give it in exchange for a generalized right to control a man.
- Women/girls don't want sex before marriage. (See above.)
- Only bad girls have sex. Or as Maria puts it, "[My sisters and I were] made to feel really guilty and made to feel like we were sluts for even thinking about boys."
- A boy is not a man unless he has lots of sex with lots of partners and protects himself from getting emotionally invested.
- Sex is my most important need (Carnes, 1983).
- Boys/men have to be ready for sex at any time.
- A husband should be eager for sex all the time.
- It is a wife's obligation to provide her husband with sex on a regular basis and to satisfy his fantasies.

PHASES OF THE CYCLE

Anticipating Rejection

The sex addict's conviction in his or her own inadequacy leads to the next phase in the cycle: *anticipating rejection.* For most sex addicts, this becomes a self-fulfilling prophecy. This dynamic, described in detail in *Come Here, Go Away* (Earle, 1991), may also lead to anticipatory flight—I'll run away before you reject me.

CASE 4-2

Mark, a sex addict in his mid-30s, used pornography compulsively and engaged in chronic masturbation, voyeurism, and sex with anonymous men in bookstores. Shy and uncomfortable with both men and women, Mark had extremely poor socialization skills. Although he demonstrated heterosexual orientation, he had had sexual intercourse with only one woman in his life. Believing that, "If she gets to know me, she'll reject me," Mark would launch an anticipatory first strike with any woman he dated. He would phone her and tell her, "I'm no good for you." In forcing her hand, Mark made the anticipated rejection a self-fulfilling prophecy. Having achieved some sobriety through therapy, Mark still anticipates rejection and is tempted to fall back into his old routine with new girlfriends. Both the therapist and the group are helping him to practice changing his self-talk, encouraging him to believe, "I am good enough."

Victim Posturing

The self-fulfilling prophecy of anticipated rejection leads the addict into *victim posturing.* Feeling unfairly rejected, the sex addict labels those from who (s)he wants acceptance "unfair," "self-righteous," "hypocritical."

Recall David's description of how he would react when Jenny would say No to his sexual advances: "I would be pouty." David had a long history of pouting and anger when not being seductively abusive. Having declared bankruptcy eight years earlier, just before he began abusing his stepdaughter, David was angry at himself, but even angrier at his family for not helping him out of the financial hole he had dug.

Many sex addicts adopt a similar victim stance, blaming others for their own problems. Convincing themselves that their difficulties are someone else's fault allows them to avoid owning responsibility for their own actions. Many sex addicts have comorbid addictions to alcohol or other drugs, which can likewise take the fall for their pervasive sense of inadequacy. Whenever anything bad happens in their lives, they react by thinking, "This is being done *to* me," rather than "This is a consequence of what I've done." In many cases of sex addiction, this victim posturing may have an antecedent in childhood abuse. Treatment must therefore focus on dealing with past victimization, owning the past and letting go of it in order to live more fully in the present (see Chapter 9). The addict must recognize that as an adult, (s)he has choices and options that were not available in childhood, and that (s)he must therefore take responsibility for actions based on those choices. The addict thus needs a fundamental change in cognitive structuring, a change that can result from feedback provided by the therapist and other members of therapy groups.

Compensatory Behaviors

Believing intimacy to be impossible for them (due to feelings of worthlessness and the consequent anticipation of rejection) and feeling victimized by others, sex addicts adopt *compensatory* behaviors designed at the very least to gain attention, and often to satisfy their grow-

ing preoccupation with control and/or revenge. These motives replace (or get blurred in with) intimacy as a goal.

Maria, who had a long series of extramarital affairs (see also Case
2-1), adopts a victim stance in describing her relationships with
men: "For as long as I can remember I have been put down,
condescended to, and basically treated [badly] by men." She
describes her relationship with her bosses and other authority
figures in similar terms. This assessment dates back to her childhood experiences with her father, an intimidating, abusive, rageful,
dominating alcoholic who saw himself as "king of the house." In
addition, she felt betrayed when her father broke his promise to
provide financial support for her college education. After watching her mother submit to her father's abuse, experiencing it herself, and feeling victimized by other men, Maria sums up her attitude toward men in this way: "Men...are pampered and lazy and
get three times more pay than I do and I work a hell of a lot
harder than they do.... I hate men, I hate their attitudes, I hate the
way they treat women, I'd like to beat every single one of them
up" Maria gets back at men through the exercise of her sexual
power: flirting, seducing, and playing with men's minds (a common dynamic among female sex addicts).

Compensatory behaviors provide the basis of the facade that universally characterizes sex addicts' presentation. Looking good com-
pensates for the sex addict's perceived character deficits. Sex addicts
become skilled "impression managers": projecting a superficial image
through dress, appearance, and demeanor that belies their self-image.
They may construct a facade of niceness, friendliness, personability,
sensitivity, and/or nurturing. Alternatively, they may dress seductively
to compensate for feelings of personal and sexual inadequacy with
overt demonstrations of sexual power and control. We have treated
both men and women, for example, who would wear short shorts and
no underwear, so that their genitalia were visible. They may engage in
staring, leering, or verbal come-ons that establish the illusion of a con-

nection with another person. The sex addict in recovery needs to identify this kind of objectification of self (whether through facade or through sexual objectification) as part of his or her ritual, an essential element of their addictive cycle. The sobriety contract that the sex addict prepares must identify and make the addict accountable for such behaviors.

Isolation

Whether or not the sex addict succeeds in getting attention and surrounding him- or herself with people, (s)he feels *social and/or emotional isolation.* The addict feels unknown and unwanted at an important deeper level. For the addict knows that what other people find attractive or engaging about him or her is not the real person, but only the facade, the veneer of personability or seductiveness. Although their own fears of abandonment and rejection cause them to keep people at a distance except on a surface level, sex addicts increasingly hurt from their self-imposed isolation and want to escape it.

CASE 4-3 *(continued)*

Maria described the isolation she feels in her marriage to Carter. "I have a problem relaxing enough to have sex with my husband. I worry that I won't be in a sexual mood on a frequency that will make my husband happy. I use my defenses to push my husband away from me. I am afraid for him to be close to me." In describing her sexual and emotional isolation from Carter, Maria demonstrates how one stage of the sex addict's cycle leads to another. She first voices some mistaken beliefs about her own personal inadequacy and the sexual "duties" a wife "must" perform. The combination of these beliefs leads to her anticipation of her husband's rejection. Finally, to protect herself from this rejection, she isolates herself and keeps him at a distance.

The guilt and shame that follow compulsive sexual behavior—and the need to maintain secretiveness—only add to the sex addict's isolation. Overcoming social and emotional isolation is a difficult task for the addict in recovery. For the only way to know they are loved on a deeper level than their surface charm is to make themselves vulnerable to significant others, to open up their secret(s) in an appropriate way. Being honest with themselves and their spouses (or significant others) is the best way to prevent relapse into compulsive patterns of behavior—and it is the hardest part of recovery.

Fantasy of an Intimate Relationship

Lacking real intimacy, the sex addict may seek refuge from isolation through the *fantasy of an intimate relationship*. This fantasy may or may not involve a real person. It may involve a specific person perceived as uniquely able to meet the sex addict's intimacy needs, or perhaps an entire subgroup of people who are uniquely able to do so (e.g., professional colleagues, children, prostitutes, gay men, lesbians, married men, CEOs, professional women, close platonic friends). David, for example, (see Case 4-1) admitted feeling more "emotionally married" to his stepdaughter than to his wife: "I would talk to her like my wife not my daughter." The fantasized unique connection replaces the more involved, more difficult, apparently impossible reality of intimacy, and thus it provides momentary relief for the pain of isolation. This fantasy relationship usually involves no real commitments and is very ego-enchancing.

CASE 4-4

Larry, a sex addict in his mid-20s, collects pornography involving children. Although he never acted out sexually with children, Larry was obsessed with fantasies about being part of a family. Ultimately, Larry set out to make this fantasy a reality. He met a family at church and insinuated his way into their lives, simulating a real connection and constantly fantasizing about life as a member of that family. He even went to church camp with them. He took part in all family rituals, watching the children get dressed, helping them brush their teeth, and so forth. Initially, Larry did not see this as a fantasy; he felt he actually was becoming part of the family.

In treating this aspect of the cycle, the therapeutic movement takes the sex addict from initial denial (as exemplified by Larry) to owning the fantasy to deciding what to do about it. We find it useful to encourage the sex addict to apply the "two-second rule"—which controls fantasies by limiting them to two seconds—to both nonsexual fantasies and sexual ones.

Fantasized Sexual Relationships

From fantasies of intimacy, the sex addict moves on to *fantasized sexual relationships.* This fantasy replaces the fantasized intimacy that the sex addict no longer regards as attainable in a real-life, committed, adult relationship. This fantasy relationship is perceived as the one place where sex can finally be truly satisfying and can fill the void the sex addict feels in his or her life. For some sex addicts, this relationship with a fantasized mate is the only relationship pure enough for sex, in other words, they can only have sex with someone perfect, someone who meets all of their needs. This perspective is not based in the reality of the person or the object's realistic ability to meet those needs. Indeed, sometimes the fantasy is not even close to the reality of the person (e.g., celebrities, strangers, or prostitutes).

Often the sex addict's fantasy is not even remotely realizable. One of our patients, for example, obsesses constantly about having sex with actress Julia Roberts and will rent or see any movie featuring her in order to spark his fantasies. Others may have more plausible fantasies, although they remain just that.

CASE 4-5

Pete, a sex addict in his early 30s, had obsessive sexual fantasies involving his boss. Although he never acted upon it, Pete was distracted and ineffective in all of his business meetings with her because he could not stop sexualizing her.

Eventually, the addict becomes fixated on sexual fantasies. The fantasies of sexual relationships dominate their thinking.

CASE 4-3 (*continued*)

"I would fantasize most of my day about men and the way I'd feel with men and this fantasizing would take up 95 percent of my day," Maria confessed. "I was paying much less attention to my husband and kids and I was [constantly] planning the next seduction. I literally had no attention span. My fantasies were controlling my thinking so much that I [couldn't] get any work done. When my children would interrupt one of my fantasies I would get mad at them. I can't believe all the years I've wasted on fantasizing."

The recognition of patterns of sexual fantasizing is a necessary precursor to doing something about it. The two-second rule can help rein in sexual fantasies. Addicts need to develop a plan to get out of fantasy and back to reality. The question becomes, what do I have to do to limit my fantasy to two seconds? Therapists and group members who have dealt with their own obsessive fantasy lives can help the addict come up with a list of healthy behaviors (telephone calls, prayer, taking a walk) that can help cut short sexual fantasies.

CASE 4-5 (*continued*)

In business meetings with his boss, Pete now applies the two-second rule, trying to set aside fantasies by becoming task oriented within the context of the meeting's agenda. If that doesn't work, Pete excuses himself to get a cup of coffee or to go to the bathroom, a deliberate break that allows him to put his thinking into a different place.

Focus on Deviance

As the attraction of this fantasy grows with rehearsal (masturbation), the desire to make it a reality grows. Along with this desire comes an *added focus on deviance*. Sometimes this involves an increased recognition by the sex addict of its deviant nature. Although no sex addict would actually use the word "deviant" until in therapy, most do see their sexual behavior as "illicit," "taboo," "forbidden," or "naughty"– something they themselves believe they should not be doing.

CASE 4-6

Dan, a minister who chronically masturbated, kept all of his sexual behavior on a level of fantasy: pornography, phone sex, topless bars. Even when he met with prostitutes, he would never do more than talk about sex, send them away without paying, and mastur-bate by himself. Yet he regarded even this no-contact sexual be-havior as something illicit. As he drove his car through the pros-titution district, circling around a block several times, he would tell himself, "I shouldn't be doing this" or "I can't believe I'm doing this."

Moving increasingly toward the "taboo" increases the addict's shame and further lowers self-esteem. Yet the added focus on deviance also adds another powerful element to the addictive cycle: an emphasis on not getting caught. The more the addict engages in the behavior with-out getting caught, the more powerful a sense of control (s)he feels. This brings a heightened adrenalin rush triggered by the idea of get-ting away with something forbidden, a rush that equals or even sur-passes the sexual high. David, for example, (see Case 4-1) acknowl-edged that he felt more aroused by the power and control that were manifest in his incestuous molestations than by any sexual high. The thrill of getting away with illicit behavior is especially powerful for the sex addict who is preoccupied with control issues.

Cruising

In order to turn fantasy into reality, sex addicts will spend hundreds upon hundreds of hours *cruising*: looking for potential object(s) or victim(s) with whom they might act out their fantasies. In addition, the countless hours of cruising tend to heighten feelings of arousal. Cruising takes many forms. It might involve driving or walking around looking for sexual objects or victims, studying their habits, and studying the environment for ways to minimize risk of detection. More often, however, it involves more subtle behaviors that may address both respectable and sexually deviant goals. The addict's choice of career, work setting, hobbies, clubs, churches, or activities may allow the cruising to go virtually unnoticed and imbue his or her actions with genuine, honorable motives while denying the existence of sexual motives to self and others.

CASE 4-7

Jack, the minister of a large church, a sex addict who had dozens of sexual affairs, would cruise by looking over his congregation and making eye contact while shaking hands after the service or even while preaching. He also would sexualize attractive women as he offered pastoral counseling.

CASE 4-8

Fred, a business consultant, would use his profession as an opportunity to cruise. At seminars he led, he would approach women and proposition them during coffee breaks.

Grooming

After fixing on a sexual object (or a sexual victim), the sex addict will begin the *grooming* phase. The sex addict aims to groom him- or herself, the sexual object or victim, and any other relevant persons (e.g., the co-addict, the victim's parents) in such a way as to minimize suspicions and simultaneously maximize the potential for fulfillment of the addict's deviant fantasies. As with cruising, grooming comes in many different forms.

CASE 4-6 (*continued*)

Dan would verbally assault his wife, creating arguments either as an excuse to go out or just to intimidate her and make her question her own perceptions. He might then groom himself by rationalizing that he was really going into a strip joint to use the phone or use the bathroom.

CASE 4-7 (*continued*)

Jack, a personable minister, groomed his parishioners through pastoral counseling. An excellent impression manager, Jack gave off an air of friendliness, offering himself as a good, available listener—especially for attractive parishioners. After listening and counseling, he would encourage them to talk about sex, and sometimes progress ultimately to intercourse. In this way, Jack groomed and cultivated a harem within his parish.

CASE 4-1 (*continued*)

David would groom his stepdaughter by "protecting" Jenny when she misbehaved or got a bad grade at school. He promised not to tell Ellen (Jenny's mother), but there was always a price to pay: He would molest her or masturbate over her. He then often warned Jenny that if she ever told anyone, he would go to jail. David's grooming ritual also allowed him the opportunity to fondle her virtually every Friday and Saturday night. Jenny was told she had to wake her parents whenever she came home late at night. Ellen, a workaholic, would be tired and—through David's grooming of her—often would have several drinks after coming home. She would seldom wake for more than a minute, allowing David to go into Jenny's room and sexually molest her. He also groomed Jenny's sisters, treating Rebecca and Brittany with anger and coldness in order to get them to go to their rooms, leaving him alone to abuse Jenny.

The Sexual Act

Fantasy, cruising, and grooming pave the way for *the sexual act* itself. The sex addict often experiences the sexual act as "uncontrollable" or "beyond the point of no return." Due to the ritualistic rehearsal of the act through fantasy, the sexual act itself may feel automatic and un-stoppable to the addict. The addict may be very surprised that (s)he is actually doing the act that has thus far been restricted to fantasy. Caught off guard by their own actions and how automatic they feel, sex ad-dicts often experience the entire incident as spontaneous, as if they are not really in control of themselves or responsible for what they do.

CASE 4-9

Bill, a traveling sales representative whose sexual activities had previously centered on voyeurism, occasional exhibitionism, and masturbation, fantasized constantly about having sex with the women he spied on. One night, after peeping for a while at a woman through her bedroom window, Bill casually tried the door and found it open. As his fantasy seemed to be turning to reality, he walked into the woman's home "like I was in a trance." When the woman saw him and screamed, Bill ran away. For Bill (unlike many sex addicts), crossing this new line to more deviant, more dangerous behaviors was a wake-up call. He immediately sought us out for therapy.

Transitory Guilt

Immediately after the sexual act, the sex addict may experience *tran-sitory guilt*, shame, anger, fear, and diminished self-esteem. David (see Case 4-1) admitted to feeling "guilt and remorse afterwards. I would hate myself. I would tell her I would not do it again and say I'm sorry." And at that moment, he would truly not want to do it again. Maria (see Case 4-3) echoed David's feelings, saying, "I came to hate myself so much that no matter what I did, it didn't make me feel any better about myself. I worried for the last six months what was wrong with me."

The addict's thinking becomes desperately confused in the wake of the sexual act. The addict may try to convince her- or himself that, "It almost didn't happen" or "Really it was hardly sexual." Or (s)he may attempt to ease guilt by sharing it with the sexual object or victim—" *We* can't keep meeting like this" or "If they didn't have those damned enticing ads, I wouldn't have called." Despite such denial, minimization, and/or justification, the addict almost always feels guilty and vows that it won't happen again ("even though I didn't *really* do anything and wasn't really responsible and it was someone else's fault anyway").

Reconstitution

To help ease the guilt and shame that follows the sexual act, the sex addict focuses on *reconstitution.* Because the addict believes (and society often reinforces) the notion that a sex addict is a bad person, being a good person is viewed as incompatible with being a sex addict. In the reconstitution phase, the sex addict sets out to deny the addiction by proving to her- or himself and others that (s)he is indeed a good person (so how can [s]he possibly be an addict?). The refashioning of the sex addict's image (to self and others) may involve such things as becoming a model spouse and parent, volunteering for the fire department, experiencing a religious conversion, and/or joining AA and admitting to alcoholism or drug addiction.

CASE 4-1 (*continued*)

David describes himself as a Santa Claus type, a nice guy. He would offer Jenny special treatment after abusing her, and several times promised her a bicycle, which he never actually gave her.

CASE 4-3 (*continued*)

Maria explained how she would reconstitute herself in her relationship with her husband after having sex with another man. "I

make love with my husband because I feel guilty many times,"
she acknowledged, "because I don't want to hurt him and I don't
want him to hurt me by saying that I don't make love to him very
much and that in that way I'm an inadequate lover."

CASE 4-7 (*continued*)

Jack, a minister who crossed sexual boundaries with several parishioners, would offer tearful confessions of his sins to his wife.
He would then pray to God, asking for forgiveness. In this way,
Jack bought "cheap grace," without doing anything substantial to
change his behavior.

In rebuilding their facades, sex addicts believe that if they make
these simple, superficial changes, they will no longer be guilty and that
they will not repeat their deviant behaviors. In actuality, reconstitution
does little more than relieve guilt feelings—while often simultaneously
grooming self and others for the next sexual ritual (as David clearly
did). This surface approach allows the sex addict to avoid having to
face the awesome task of changing deeply rooted survival beliefs, relinquishing sexual fantasies, and accepting full responsibility for the
pain (s)he has caused. Undertaking cosmetic surgery (as opposed to
major surgery) thus protects the cycle by covering up its existence.

Sex addicts in recovery (especially, but not exclusively, during the
early stages of treatment) often present this type of reconstitution in
initial therapy sessions. Engrained patterns of behavior do not immediately cease with the onset of therapy. Although the therapist can
effectively point out that these surface strategies skirt the real problem
of addiction, members of group therapy can often offer powerful testimony that helps cut through the denial these diversionary tactics demonstrate. Comments like, "I wish it were that easy" or "I've said the
same things in the past, I hope it works for you" starkly confront the
emptiness of such attempts at reconstitution.

The reconstitution phase, as well as all the preceding phases of the
addictive cycle, reinforces or supplements the pool of mistaken beliefs
regarding survival, self-worth, intimacy, and sex. And this just sets the
cycle of addiction spinning out of control once again.

In familiarizing themselves with all three models of addictive cycles, both patients and therapists should keep in mind that no single model, no matter how comprehensive, can include every element of every sex addict's pattern. In order to customize treatment to the unique needs of the sex addict, therapists need to take care not to try to fit one individual into another's profile. Approaching each sex addict as a distinct individual will not only heighten the effectiveness of therapy for the patient, but will also help prevent therapist burnout by keeping his or her creative juices flowing.

The therapist will find that the sex addict in treatment will offer less resistance if (s)he too understands the limitations of psychological models. In order to recover, the sex addict needs to say the words, "I am a sex addict." Simply using these words helps to overcome lifelong resistance to self-examination and to change. For this reason, the sex addict needs to understand that just because one or two elements of an addiction model do not seem to fit his or her life does not mean that the whole cycle fails to apply. Although the general principles of a good model will apply broadly each patient will, for example, need to identify his or her own unique triggers. In addition to pinpointing the elements of the cycle that do apply to their lives, sex addicts should also be encouraged to identify any elements that don't seem to be included in the model. Used properly, models of addictive cycles can thus help initiate a continuing, lifelong process toward increasing the addict's understanding of her- or himself. As David (see Case 4-1) marveled after applying models of addiction to his own life, "It's amazing how much more honest you become."

In combination with individual therapy, group therapy, couples therapy, family therapy, family-of-origin work, and self-help groups, we use both edutherapy and bibliotherapy to help sex addicts identify and break away from their deviant cycles. (Recommended Reading on page 261 provides a list of books that we suggest sex addicts and their families read.)

Identification of the sex addict's unique personal cycle of addiction requires a real commitment to the work of recovery. Recognition does not take place all at once; rather, it comes as a dawning, as the rolling back of a fog, as the sex addict progressively cuts through denial and rationalization to look at him- or herself and life honestly. The process involved in identifying the addictive cycle is the first stage of the sex addict's self-assessment, the "searching moral inventory" suggested by the fourth of AA's 12 Steps. As the sex addict begins to identify more and more elements in the cycle (e.g., staring or leering = fantasy relationship, sexualized), (s)he can then begin to develop appropriate rules or guidelines to interrupt the cycle (e.g., the two-second rule, tools that enable individuals to take charge of their fantasies, rather than the other way around).

As indicated throughout this chapter, therapy groups comprised of other sex addicts are particularly effective in the process of pinpointing elements of an individual's addictive cycle. The group may point out previously unrecognized elements. Early in recovery, for instance, many sex addicts dismiss the continuation of leering or masturbation as "no big deal"—despite the fact that the leering initiates or the masturbation is accompanied by obsessive fantasies of the addict's temporarily discontinued compulsive behavior. Group members who have already been through the process of identifying the addictive cycle will help the addict to recognize this type of minimization, rationalization, or other insane—i.e, delusional—thinking (see also Chapter 5).

By focusing on the individual's addictive cycle, group members can also help tighten his or her sobriety contract (see Chapter 10). They can help define elements for inclusion that go beyond the sexually compulsive behaviors themselves. A sex addict's sobriety contract should cover not only sexual behavior, but any other behaviors that might contribute to the cycle for instance, poor self-talk, isolation or withdrawal, self-pity, and feeling hungry, angry, lonely, or tired (HALT, an acronym widely used in AA and other 12-step programs).

CASE 4-1 *(continued)*

In addition to prohibiting any sexual behaviors involving his stepdaughter, David's sobriety contract includes a variety of behaviors and types of thinking to avoid. These include a promise to avoid victim-posturing (the "poor me" attitude) with Ellen, and a promise not to pout or to withdraw in his relationship with her. David's sobriety contract also includes a positive commitment to do certain things that advance recovery and help keep him away from the addictive cycle. These include continuing involvement in groups, talking to people on the phone, and taking responsibility for his own behaviors, for example, self-examination and full disclosure regarding any reversion to former patterns.

Real change and relapse prevention depend on the clarity of the sex addict's understanding of the cycle: how (s)he did what (s)he has done. The addict needs to develop a continuing and growing understanding and identification of the unique elements of his or her addictive cycle in order to recognize them when they occur. Only by increasing awareness in this way can the addict hope to interrupt the course of the cycle through the institution of healthier behaviors (e.g., contacting a therapist or sponsor). We acknowledge that insight alone will not change a sex addict's behavior or break the addictive cycle. Relapse prevention requires a combination of insight and accountability. But without insight, the sex addict will never change.

5

Correcting Cognitive Distortions
Helping the Sex Addict Develop
New Ways of Thinking

As the cycle of sex addiction begins and ends with a pool of mistaken beliefs about self, sexuality, relationships with others and the world in general, correcting these cognitive distortions is critical to the success of any treatment program. The attitudes and nonsexual behaviors that build up to compulsive sexual behaviors are founded on the underpinnings of cognitive distortion. A change in any one of the core beliefs that provide the foundation for the compulsive behavior will therefore help to bring down the whole house of cards that we call sex addiction. Changing beliefs will lead to changed attitudes and changed behavior. For example, the sex addict who begins to believe that (s)he is *not* "a bad, unworthy person" will no longer automatically anticipate rejection and will thus have little need for victim posturing. These changed attitudes will then diminish the need for compensatory behaviors and reduce withdrawal and isolation. Because our thoughts and attitudes greatly influence our behavior, correcting the sex addict's cognitive distortions will contribute significantly to breaking the addictive cycle and preventing relapse (see also Chapter 10). Conversely, unless sex addicts confront their own delusions, they will make little progress in recovery and will likely relapse before long.

From the very beginning of therapy aimed at correcting cognitive distortions (and thus altering addictive–or contributory–behaviors), it is essential that the therapist emphasize concepts of health and wholeness while using words like "sick" and "powerlessness." Both the therapist and the patient need to be comfortable using the word "sickness" for sex addiction. The choice of this word affects the whole system: The disease concept of sex addiction necessarily implies that the individual is not a bad, unworthy person, but rather a valuable person with a serious illness. It simultaneously affirms the existence of positive parts of the person and establishes a target of putting the sickness in remission and achieving wholeness and balance. To achieve and maintain this balance, both patient and therapist need to celebrate the healthy, functional parts of the addict while at the same time dealing with the dysfunctional aspects of their personality and behavior. To achieve complete recovery, the sex addict must focus on the entirety of self, not just the part of self identified with compulsive sexual behavior and its damaging results.

Certainly, to overcome denial and effect lasting changes in thought and behavior, sex addicts must begin by acknowledging to themselves and others: "I am a sex addict." This is the critical first step of recovery: admitting the existence of a problem that has made life unmanageable. At the same time, sex addicts in recovery need to see beyond the label represented by this diagnosis. Just as the person who learns (s)he has cancer is not defined solely as a cancer patient, the sex addict's primary identity is not defined by the addiction. Especially in the early stages of recovery, sex addicts often need their therapist's and/or their therapy group's help to understand that although sex addiction is part of who they are, it does not represent the totality of who they are. Sex addicts need regular reminders that in reality they are good people who have committed destructive, perhaps even horrendous, acts.

This strategy goes to the very heart of cognitive restructuring: changing the sex addict's bottom-line, core belief that, "I'm a loser, I'm worth less than nothing." Unless the sex addict can learn to affirm that, "I'm a good person who has done these bad things," (s)he will not get far into recovery. Sexually compulsive behavior springs from poor self-image and other cognitive distortions. Without changing the core belief, the addict will almost certainly continue to revert to patterns of compulsive behavior.

More than anything else, true growth and change spring from building up the recovering sex addict's self-esteem. With the support and guidance of their therapists, sex addicts need to work on changing their self-talk: what they say, think, and feel about themselves and about the world in which they live. In time, the ability to maintain sobriety will in itself augment the recovering sex addict's self-esteem; but sobriety seldom, if ever, makes the addict feel good about him- or herself at first. The stripping away of the veil of denial and the sober reassessment of the addict's past actions deliver crushing blows to self-esteem. The clearer the sex addict's thinking becomes, the more (s)he will have to come to grips with the destruction and injuries the addiction has wrought in his or her own life, the lives of those who love the addict, and the lives of anyone victimized by the compulsive behavior.

CASE 5-1

David, who sought therapy after admitting to his wife that he had been molesting his stepdaughter for the past eight years (see also Cases 1-1, 3-1, and 4-1), felt suicidal when he first began treatment. As recovery progressed and he began to develop victim empathy, he felt even more suicidal, suffering from extreme depression, pain, anxiety, and remorse. In both individual and group therapy, we helped David recognize that in reality he was a good person with deviations in both thought and behavior. While dealing with the destructive aspects of his personality and behavior, we simultaneously focused on the positive aspects of his personality: his intelligence, his charm, his caring. In the past, he had used these talents solely to further seduction or grooming. In recovery, we helped him to recognize these talents and begin to harness them for another purpose. If he had any hope of recovery, it was essential that he began to affirm the positive things about himself, to recognize that he was worth salvaging.

The challenge that all sex addicts face throughout the recovery process involves taking the concept that life is worth living and making it a reality in their lives. They need to recognize and affirm, for perhaps the first time in their lives, that "I am worthwhile. I have value." Affirmations like these are an important part of the healing process. Without this new core belief to sustain them, sex addicts will find the burden of adult responsibility, the accountability for their past, present, and future actions, overwhelming.

Recovery does not follow a steady, upward progression. Sex addicts may slip, experiencing a partial or total relapse, they may face a court date that imposes legal judgment on their compulsive sexual behaviors, or they may simply receive a blow to their self-esteem in the course of typical, everyday experiences. In such situations, poor self-talk can lead to a full-blown reversion to compulsive behaviors, a return to the addictive cycle. Facing sentence in court or being passed over for a job promotion, for example, can quickly revive mistaken beliefs about self that initiate anticipated rejection and victim-posturing. For this reason, it is critical that the therapist help the addict to balance these blows to self-esteem with affirmations of positive characteristics.

DISTORTIONS AND DEFENSES

The cognitive distortions of sex addicts go beyond the core beliefs outlined by Carnes and the pool of mistaken beliefs considered in Chapter 4. The sex addict's cognitive distortions involve not just beliefs, but entire ways of thinking. Most addicts, for example, have extremely rigid, compartmentalized thinking. Extremely judgmental (except when it comes to their own compulsive behavior), their way of thinking does not allow for any nuances or shades of gray. People (and their actions) are either good or bad; no middle ground exists.

The sex addict also depends on a wide array of cognitive distortions that protect the patterns of compulsive behavior by warding off (or regarding as impossible) change. Chief among these defensive ways of thinking is, of course, denial. That addicts can deny that their compulsive sexual behaviors pose a problem as the addiction erodes or destroys their marriages and families, depletes their savings, threatens their health, interferes with their ability to concentrate at work, results in their firing, or even lands them in jail represents a gross cognitive distortion. Yet regardless of the cost to the addict, denial safeguards the addictive behaviors.

The other defensive ways of thinking also serve to deny—and thus protect—the addiction despite the cost to addicts and the people close to them. The addict's repertoire of defenses (and some examples of each) includes the following:

Rationalization: "Just this once, and then I'm through" or "I think I'll stop in this topless bar to use the bathroom." David (see Case 5-1) convinced himself that Jenny actually liked the "extra" attention he gave her. Early in therapy, he described his fondling of his stepdaughter as more of a "loving" relationship than a physically aggressive one. He also told himself that if she came home when he was there alone—or if she woke him up when she came home late at night (a family rule)—then she must want his sexual advances.

Justification: "I deserve this. I've had a really hard time lately" or "I deserve this. I've been so good." David used the strain in his relationship with his wife to justify his sexual advances to his stepdaughter: "Ellen doesn't understand me and doesn't really care. Only Jenny really understands me."

Minimization: "I'm not hurting anyone." David more than once told Jenny, "It could be worse, I could rape you." This defensive distortion often becomes manifest in group therapy, with members new to the group favorably comparing their own behaviors with those of other members of the group.

Excuses: "I wouldn't have done it if my spouse hadn't made me so angry" or "I got fired, so I was depressed. Anybody else would have done the same thing in my situation."

Shifting responsibility (i.e., blaming the victim): "Anyone who dresses that way wants me to..." or "If a child doesn't want to have sex with me, all (s)he has to do is say No." David constantly told himself that if Jenny didn't say No, she must have meant Yes. In other words, he fancied that it was Jenny who was in control of the abuse scenarios.

Each of these types of distorted thinking protects the sex addict from shame, guilt, and any sense of responsibility for his or her actions. To keep the sex addict locked in the cycle of addiction, these cognitive distortions perpetuate themselves. The addict will dismiss or distort any new, potentially corrective information, accommodating every aspect of behavior, perception, and experience to the prevailing belief system. Thus, distorted thinking allows the sex addict to avoid any perceived need for change so that the addiction may continue uninterrupted.

CASE 5-1 (*continued*)

After more than a year in therapy, David came up with the following list, which he described as "10 lies I used to tell myself."

David's Distortions

- I drank too much. That's why it happened.
- Jenny wakes me up at night when she comes home. She must want me.
- Ellen is always working. Then all she does is talk about work. She doesn't care.
- I don't ask Jenny to ride along with me, but she always asks to come along. She must like to be alone with me.
- Ellen drinks too much. She will just fall asleep when we go to bed.
- Jenny calls me into her room.
- Jenny leaves her door open when she is getting dressed.
- All Ellen talks about is money. That's all she cares about.
- Work really sucks. Of course Ellen's not here to talk. Jenny is. She'll listen.
- Jenny makes me feel young. I don't have to worry about all those responsibilities Ellen wants to talk about.

TOOLS AND TECHNIQUES TO TRANSFORM THINKING

To confront and correct cognitive distortions in the context of individual and group therapy, we use a number of different tools. The first centers on traditional talk therapy: We create a safe atmosphere, which encourages the sex addict to talk openly and honestly, allowing us to find out for ourselves how and what the addict thinks about her- or himself and the world. Getting sex addicts to talk about what they perceive, think, believe, fear, and feel will inevitably bring out cognitive distortions—and therefore provide the therapist with the opportunity to correct them. When using talk therapy to unearth cognitive distortions, the therapist must stay alert and focused on what the addict is saying. Whenever the therapist hears the sex addict voice a cognitive distortion, it calls for immediate intervention. The therapist has a fundamental responsibility not to let anything slip by. A therapist who fails to correct a patient's cognitive distortion unwittingly reinforces and validates it for the addict. However, no one person—no matter how skilled, trained, and attuned—can catch all of a sex addict's cognitive distortions. This is another reason that a team approach to treatment, utilizing several therapists and groups, has a significant advantage over a single therapist. Indeed, we regard it as very risky for a therapist who treats sex addicts not to consult with another therapist. The more ears that listen, the more cognitive distortions will be caught, and the faster the healing process will progress.

Upon hearing a cognitive distortion, a therapist should immediately repeat what (s)he thought (s)he heard and explore with the patient where that belief or type of thinking may lead in the course of the addict's life. How does this statement of belief meet the addict's needs? How will this belief or way of thinking influence the addict's day-to-day life? Immediately challenging mistaken beliefs and distorted styles of thinking accomplishes two critical therapeutic goals: it catches, confronts, and corrects specific cognitive distortions, and it teaches sex addicts how to listen to themselves, to catch these distortions themselves when they hear the words come out of their mouths. Through the therapeutic process of correcting cognitive distortions, sex addicts thus learn the skills they need to correct their own thinking, to challenge and change their ingrained thought patterns and beliefs.

CASE 5-2

Henry came to us under duress. His fiancée Suzanne, was ready to call off their engagement if he did not consent to therapy. Henry had begun frequenting strip clubs and topless bars at age 12. He wanted to continue this behavior after his marriage and initially convinced his fiancée to agree to those terms. But Suzanne ultimately told him she couldn't marry him if he expected to continue going to topless bar several times a week. In his initial sessions, Henry clearly believed that he would always be the way he was, that he not only couldn't change, but didn't really want to change. He resisted the notion that his behavior had anything to do with his fiancée, or that his "fun" had any impact on his relationship with Suzanne. Henry denied both the personal despair and the pain it caused his fiancée.

The therapeutic process of looking at his denial and rationalization helped make clear his "sick" thinking. Henry realized that acting out actually caused him more grief than happiness. He also came to appreciate that what Suzanne was requesting was both fair and reasonable and that anyone who truly cared about him would ask him to do the same. By this time, Henry not only wanted to change, but recognized that he *had to* change. Individual (and group) therapy gave him a safe place in which to identify and alter his cognitive distortions and begin the process of change.

Another tool we use in exposing cognitive distortions is bibliotherapy, especially the use of workbooks that encourage sex addicts to identify and explore specific beliefs they have about themselves, about others, about sex, about honest communication, and so on. A number of workbooks are available for sex addicts or sex offenders in recovery programs. Recovery Publications publishes two excellent workbooks on the 12 steps of AA and the Sex Offender Series published by the Safer Society Press has proved useful in treating both offending and nonoffending sex addicts (see Recommended Reading on page 261). We ask sex addicts to complete assignments between sessions and then formally share their insights in the context of both individual therapy and group therapy. After sharing or presenting workbook exercises, the sex addict has the opportunity to receive feedback from both the group and the therapist that often underscores the cognitive distortions brought to light through the assignments.

Exposure to a group made up entirely of other sex addicts in recovery can also serve as a powerful corrective for cognitive distortions. Under the supervision of the therapists, group members provide invaluable feedback that challenges destructive or self-destructive thoughts.

CASE 5-3

Larry demonstrated significant distortions in thinking—rationalizations that allowed him to fraternize with children, and at the same time, maintain an extensive collection of child pornography (see also Case 4-4). Larry insisted that he liked kids and that all he wanted was to get close to them. He claimed that kids would seek him out since their parents would not spend the time horsing around with them that he would. These beliefs were challenged and broken down by both the individual therapist and the group process. In sharing how they themselves had used rationalization to further their addiction, other group members helped Larry look at what he got out of these beliefs. And in examining them more closely, Larry found that he did have some discomfort about rationalizing these "innocent" contacts, which would almost invariably take him into the realm of fantasy and sexual arousal.

Although they lack the mediating influence and expertise of a professional therapist, self-help groups can also prove enormously helpful in confronting and changing a sex addict's cognitive distortions. Rational Recovery groups, although perhaps not as well known as 12-step groups, maintain a tight focus on changing cognitive distortions. Although it does not deal with family-of-origin issues, spirituality, or the emotional side of the sex addict in recovery, the Rational Recovery program can help a sex addict recognize the irrationality of the belief systems that keep the addictive cycle in motion. The Rational Recovery program concentrates on setting rational goals and establishing rational plans to achieve those goals.

Twelve-step groups modeled after that of AA have an excellent track record in helping addicts through their recovery. Like Rational Recovery, Sex Addicts Anonymous, Sexaholics Anonymous, and Sex and Love Addicts Anonymous all raise questions about the sex addict's core beliefs. The 12-step program emphasizes that the addict be honest about who (s)he is. The "fearless moral inventory" mandated by the fourth step encourages the type of thorough self-examination that can often bring cognitive distortions to light. Also like Rational Recovery, the 12-step groups provide the addict with a new sense of connectedness, a network of equals for the person who feels "lonely all the time" (Earle & Crow, 1989). Often functioning as the addict's first "healthy family," such groups offer a system of peers "care-fronting" one another. In helping the individual addict realize that (s)he is not terminally unique, that others share the same or similar difficulties, both 12-step and Rational Recovery groups can significantly reduce the addict's shame base.

Twelve-step groups differ significantly from Rational Recovery groups, however, in their emphasis on dealing with spirituality as a resource for healing. This distinction centers on the first three of the 12 Steps: (1) admitting powerlessness; (2) fostering a belief in the possibility of healing through a Higher Power; and (3) turning the addict's will and life over to the care of this Higher Power. Rational Recovery groups view the notions of powerlessness and faith in a Higher Power as antithetical to their emphasis on personal empowerment and the correction of cognitive distortions—that is, making rational choices to achieve rational goals. Rational Recovery does not acknowledge the essentially paradoxical nature underlying these three steps—that admitting powerlessness and giving up control can actually empower the sex addict to change for the better (just as abstinence from sex can actually improve a couple's sexual relationship). With the first step, the sex addict acknowledges that what (s)he is doing to control the behavior isn't working. With the second step, (s)he recognizes the need for help. With the third step, the addict admits *powerlessness* to change alone, and yet, at the same time, the individual emerges as *the* catalyst for healing—by seeking help outside her- or himself. This process thus involves the correction of a fundamental cognitive distortion: giving up grandiose notions of personal power to control the compulsion.

CASE 5-4

Jack, an evangelical minister who had dozens of affairs with parishioners (see also Case 4-7), suffered from distorted religious beliefs and cognitive distortions relating to God. He feared a vindictive God, a God who was "out to get him." At the same time, Jack viewed religion as a fix and believed in a magical God. He believed that if he prayed enough and read the Bible enough, God would cure him. Yet prayer alone apparently wasn't working for him. He would always end up doing whatever felt good.

Although Jack found 12-step programs invaluable to his recovery, he describes Rational Recovery in almost religious terms, as if it were a born-again experience. Given the ideological disparity between the two programs, Jack is unique in having found a way to combine them. Yet we believe Jack has discovered an important strategy for recovery from sex addiction: that an individual *can* integrate the rational and the spiritual, and indeed *must* in order to maximize the possibility of recovery. A good 12-step program does help to change distorted thinking, but does not focus on it to the extent that a Rational Recovery program does. At the same time, however, we believe that it is seldom enough just to change the addict's thinking. By simultaneously pursuing the goals outlined in the 12 steps and those embraced by Rational Recovery, Jack has found ways to deal both with his powerlessness and with the fact that he has choices.

LIVING RATIONALLY: REPLACING DELUSION WITH REALITY

Treatment to correct a sex addict's irrational belief system begins with the addict's acceptance of the notion: "My life is based in living rationally." All sex addicts we have treated regard this belief as critical to their recovery. What does it mean for a sex addict to begin living rationally? It requires the addict to leave the delusions and defenses that have fueled or protected the addictive cycle behind and to form a new set of beliefs and attitudes, a new set of rules and principles to live by. In order to give up long-held delusions and defenses, the sex addict must first identify them (with the help of the therapist(s), group therapy members, and peers in self-help groups). As they begin to develop a thorough understanding of where they are now, recovering sex addicts can simultaneously begin the work of changing the present and the future by discovering and embracing new beliefs that will lead to a healthier self, a self in recovery. By altering their thinking and choosing to live rationally in accord with their new beliefs and attitudes rather than the old delusions and defenses, sex addicts will make great progress toward changing their behavior.

CASE 5-4 *(continued)*

Jack, the minister who had had sexual affairs with his parishioners, had participated in edutherapy, group therapy, and individual therapy for several months. He had already made significant progress toward recovery, working on changing his self-talk and correcting many cognitive distortions. Jack recognized that to be real, to live rationally, to recover, he needed to assess more thoroughly his beliefs, weeding out the ones that didn't work in terms of recovery. Taking a hard-nosed look at his "stinking thinking," Jack asked himself, "Okay, then, what are my delusions?" On his own, Jack developed the following tool to help guide him through recovery. He came up with a list of his delusions and underneath each one noted an affirmation that examined the delusion under a more realistic light, a new belief that would help free him from addiction to live more rationally.

"A Few of My Favorite Rationalizations"

1. "'I admit that I am powerless over my addiction' means that I am not responsible for my acting-out behavior."[1]
Response: "I am a sex addict. That means that I can't take that first drink. I am responsible, with God's help, for not taking that first drink today."

2. "I don't act out as much as I once did or as much as other sex addicts."[2]
Response: "If I continue to act out at this level, there is a good chance I will escalate in the future. Besides, I don't want to be controlled by lust on any level."

3. "I deserve the attention of women and sexual fantasy is my way of getting it."[3]
Response: "What I deserve is peace and serenity. And that can only be found inside of myself, not from the approval of women."

---

[1] This rationalization is common among sex addicts early in recovery. It deals with one of the foremost paradoxes of recovery, the apparent paradox between powerlessness and choices.

[2] Both of these attempts to minimize are typical of sex addicts, who often perceive themselves as "terminally unique." Many sex addicts point to what they're *not* doing as a way of justifying or minimizing what they *are* doing: "What I'm doing is no big deal; at least I'm not doing what (s)he's doing." Group therapy is a great equalizer in this respect. In groups comprised solely of other sex addicts, nobody is intrinsically better or worse than anybody else (even though certain behavior may be worse).

[3] This is typical of sex addicts, who think they are somehow special. Jack's response offers an affirmation important both for sex addicts and "relationship" addicts.

4. "I deserve the immediate gratification of lust."[4]
Response: "I deserve the satisfaction that comes from growing up and facing life as an adult. One important step toward maturity is learning to delay gratification."

5. "It's not right that I should be denied something that feels so good."
Response: "I am more interested in experiencing long-term serenity than any momentary rush, only to be followed by hours and hours of torment."[5]

6. "All men lust after women. It's only natural to look at women. Its only natural to look at women"[6]
Response: "What other men do doesn't have any bearing on me. I admit that I am a sex addict. I am allergic to lust. I, therefore, give up my right to practice lust."

7. "Lust is my way of coping with insomnia, boredom, etc."[7]
Response: "That's absurd. Lust doesn't even work. I am learning better skills for coping with life's difficulties."

8. "The only way to get this out of my mind is to give in to it."[8]
Response: "Ridiculous. The only way to get lust out of my mind is to stop feeding it."

------

[4] This might be described as a universal cultural belief (although more universally held by men than by women in the general culture) taken to extremes in the addictive belief system.

[5] Not all sex addicts experience what Jack describes as "nagging torment," yet all experience doubt, uneasiness, or discomfort.

[6] This too reflects a generally held cultural belief. Indeed, therapists should help sex addicts understand that it *is* natural for heterosexual men and women to look at and appreciate the beauty of members of the opposite sex—while at the same time recognizing that *not* everyone then proceeds to objectify, groom, and endlessly fantasize, as sex addicts typically do. The affirmation that follows echoes the recovering alcoholic's recognition that (s)he cannot justify his or her own drinking by saying that, for instance, everyone has a drink after work.

[7] For the addict, this is true; this has been the coping strategy. What follows is the realistic appraisal that this strategy fails. Learning more effective and appropriate coping strategies provides the thrust of all cognitive-behavioral therapies and all programs aimed at training addicts to improve their social skills.

[8] A common justification for giving in to the compulsive urge is to rid oneself of the obsession. Addicts commonly persist in this delusion even after acting out hundreds or thousands of times.

9. "I will die if I can't do it."[9]
Response: "I may have to endure some unpleasantness for a while, but it will be worth it. On the other hand, I will most certainly die if I keep on acting out."

10. "I'm not hurting anyone."[10]
Response: "What about me? I'm someone and I'm very important. Lust hurts me emotionally, physically, socially, financially, and spiritually. It also hurts my wife by depriving her of my love."

11. "This is the last time."[11]
Response: "Yeah, sure. That's what I said the last time and the thousand times before that. I have a better idea. Why not make last time the last time?"

12. "I've tried everything to quit and nothing works. So why try and fight it?"
Response: "The truth is that I have made countless half-assed efforts in order to rationalize my continued acting out. I think I will cut the excuses and not use (act out) today."[12]

13. "Maybe if I can just get this out of my system...."[13]
Response: "Nice try, but the only way I can get this out of my system is by starving it out."

---

[9] This is not an uncommon feeling, shared by 30 to 40 percent of the sex addicts we've seen. These addicts feel that they won't survive, that they can't make it without their compulsive sexual behavior. Often, this is literally and figuratively true: Many addicts are suicidal, especially when stripped of their compulsive behaviors. An enormous challenge facing addicts in recovery is learning how to live with gray, with ambivalence, with shades and context, learning how to endure the difficulties that life brings to those who remain clean and sober.

[10] This represents another minimization typical of sex addicts. In recovery, sex addicts must acknowledge that even nonvictimizing behaviors hurt themselves and hurt others by interfering with their ability to be intimate.

[11] This expresses a universal sentiment among sex addicts, one that indicates their illusion of control. If the behavior is sufficiently out of character, a sex addict might tell him- or herself this the very first time. In any case, this conviction tends to build as the addiction progresses.

[12] Not all attempts to quit are "half-assed"; some people make wholehearted efforts and still fail. When previous efforts to control the compulsion on their own fail, however, sex addicts need to try something *different*—i.e., looking beyond themselves for help.

[13] Another justification typical of sex addicts, very similar to delusion #8.

14. "I'm such a disgusting pervert and loser that it's only natural for me to act like one."

Response: "It's true that my behavior has been disgusting, but that has nothing to do with my value as a person. I am a person of great worth, a creation and cherished child of God. I owe it to myself to behave with dignity."[14]

15. "They obviously want me to lust after them since they are dressed like that."[15]

Response: "I refuse to become involved in judging the intent of others. I also refuse to be enslaved to the habit of lusting after women, regardless of their manner of dress."

16. "God has never given me any sensation that comes close to replacing what I get from lust. So how can I give this up?"[16]

Response: "I have recently experienced a sensation of serenity that is not only exhilarating, but lasting as well. I can't give this up for anything."

17. "I just won't tell anyone. What they don't know won't hurt them."[17]

Response: "It may not hurt them, but it could kill me. My sobriety can only continue if I practice rigorous honesty."

---

[14] In writing this, Jack has accomplished one of the fundamental goals of cognitive therapies: reconciling odious past behavior with true vision of the self. This affirmation marks a significant turnaround in Jack's self-talk, transforming his self-image from worthless loser to valuable person.

[15] Again, this statement reflects a common cultural assumption, which sex addicts carry to extremes.

[16] This belief, universal among sex addicts, reflects the fact that the high, the adrenalin rush, that accompanies the satiation of lust is indeed extremely powerful. Sex addicts find it very difficult to give up the intensity of that high. To do so, they must answer the critical question posed earlier in this chapter: "What am I giving this up *for*?" Because it's hard to market serenity as a kind of high on a par with the high the sex addict has experienced through acting out, both the therapist and the patient need to acknowledge that in adopting the long-term view, the sex addict will suffer a very real loss. Even in the context of an intimate relationship, the recovering sex addict may never again achieve the kind of illicit high delivered by compulsive sexual behavior.

[17] Like delusion #10, this attempts to minimize the consequences of the sex addict's behavior by ignoring the neglect or indirect harm done to others, as well as the harm done to oneself.

18. "God will forgive me afterwards. So why not one more time?"[18]
Response: "I know that God would forgive me. But I don't intend to submit myself to the hellish torture of guilt, self-hatred, and despair following even one more episode of acting out."

We have chosen to include Jack's list of delusions in complete detail because we believe that the tool that Jack developed on his own will help all sex addicts in recovery. Every sex addict we see could benefit from doing this exercise as a homework assignment. The exercise explicitly promotes change from cognitive distortions to a more rational belief system. In setting out positive motivations as part of the response to recognized delusions, sex addicts who do this exercise will formulate their own answers to questions regarding both the reasons for change and the goals of change. In putting delusions and more realistic assessments side by side, the exercise outlines ways that sex addicts can begin to change their thinking. And as we indicated earlier, identifying and correcting delusions play a huge part in both rational recovery and relapse prevention.

---

[18] Magical beliefs such as this one are very ecumenical; that is, sex addicts of all faiths use such beliefs as a way of handling their addiction. Yet as Jack notes in his response, even if a person believes (s)he is bound for heaven in the afterlife, addiction creates a hell on earth.

6

Developing Alternatives
Communication and Social-Skills Training

In our first book on sex addiction, *Lonely All the Time: Recognizing, Understanding and Overcoming Sex Addiction, for Addicts and Co-Dependents* (Earle & Crow, 1989), we suggested that to the list of four core beliefs identified by Patrick Carnes (1983) a fifth should be added: "If I have to depend on my social skills to get close to anyone, it will never happen." For most sex addicts, this belief actually reflects the reality of their situation. As a rule sex addicts do lack the social skills needed to get close to others. The dynamics of communication in the context of both individual and group therapy allows sex addicts to practice certain fundamental skills—honesty, self-examination coupled with disclosure to others, and empathy. But for most sex addicts the deficit in communication skills is so great that practice inside the therapist's office is not enough. In order to achieve intimacy in their lives, they need a more formal program designed to improve communication skills.

The first and most significant step toward improving communication comes with finally getting the secret of sex addiction out in the open. The pervasiveness of this secret has previously made open communication impossible. Bringing the secret out sets the stage for the sex addict and co-addict to communicate about it, to deal openly as a couple with a major issue. In this early phase of recovery, the therapist can help the couple draw up a contract for communication. The contract may set down procedures governing their communication, but it should focus above all on a mutual commitment to honesty. Both partners need to pledge to tell no more lies and to keep no more secrets.

COUPLES COMMUNICATION SKILLS

For the recovering sex addict, improvement of social skills begins with one-on-one communication. Relatively few couples today communicate well, whether sex addiction is involved or not. However, since sex addicts by definition have an intimacy disorder, communication is always a problem in their relationships. When recovering sex addicts have a significant other, we strongly encourage both partners to improve their communication skills by taking a couples communication course or undergoing couples communication training with on-staff therapists. Sex addicts, and their partners, can then apply these skills in other relationships in a wide variety of settings: work, social gatherings, classes, etc.

Both married and unmarried sex addicts in recovery need to improve their social skills and habitual patterns of communication. We have found that each situation has advantages and disadvantages in terms of changing communication patterns. Unattached sex addicts in recovery may lack immediate opportunities to practice their new or improved communication skills, but may actually have more freedom to remake themselves entirely, to experiment with and practice these skills in a wide variety of relationships and situations. Sex addicts who are married or involved in long-term relationships may have more opportunities to improve their communication skills directly, but they also have more history, more baggage, and more established patterns, all of which may interfere with attempts to change the dynamics of communication in the relationship.

CASE 6-1

After returning home on a full-time basis, David had an especially difficult time dealing with his lingering shame and guilt over his past incestuous behaviors (see also Cases 1-1, 3-1, and 4-1, and 5-1). These feelings became particularly intense in the context of the continuous time he now spent with his wife Ellen. For David and Ellen, the occasion of their reunification seemed the best time

to begin a couples communication course. After more than two
years in treatment, both had achieved sobriety in relation to both
alcohol and sex. Both had changed greatly, which caused increasing tension in their communication. According to David, Ellen
had become more direct and more emotionally expressive, making it more, rather than less, difficult for him to communicate with
her. In living with each other seven days a week once again, the
deficits in their communication skills came to the forefront of their
relationship. In their two years of separation following the disclosure of David's molestations of Ellen's oldest daughter, the only
threat of divorce had come from Ellen immediately after the revelation. Now that they had reunited, however, arguments began
to lead to threats of divorce on both sides. Clearly, in addition to
working out the new relationship dynamics, both David and Ellen
needed to learn how to communicate with each other and to
handle their anger more effectively.

These early arguments centered most often on the issue of
David's compliance (or noncompliance) with the rules and boundaries for reunification and probation that had been established by
the courts and by themselves in conjunction with their therapist.
Whenever Ellen observed some breach of these boundaries, David
would react quickly and defensively, effectively ending the communication as soon as it began. With their therapist's support,
encouragement, and guidance, David began to share with Ellen
how the rules and regulations governing his conduct in the home
and within the family constantly reminded him of his past offenses and tended to put him into a shaming cycle. He explained
that his sharp defensive reactions sprang not from anger at her,
but from anger at himself and what he had done. This shame and
anger interfered with his ability to communicate openly with her.
Ellen in turn told David that she felt enormous pressure in trying
to balance the role of being his "keeper," that is, the enforcer of
compliance with the rules of reunification, and the still-evolving
role of being his partner. David began to appreciate the difficult
position in which Ellen found herself in their relationship. After
dealing with this immediate source of conflict, the therapist suggested that Ellen and David enroll in a communication skills
course.

Learning to Speak

The first challenge of couples communication involves learning to speak, to assert one's impressions, thoughts, feelings, desires, and intentions in a way that transmits the message accurately instead of raising a listener's defenses. On the continuum from aggressiveness to passivity, most sex addicts would be placed at one of the extremes. They may be entirely passive, seldom expressing a thought or feeling to others. Or they may be aggressive to the point of rage: hostile, angry, dumping on others, intimidating, or patronizing. In recovery, sex addicts need help with transforming their passivity or aggression into appropriate assertiveness. Because sex addicts have trained themselves to be devious and secretive, to stuff rather than share their feelings, straightforwardness must be learned anew. For this reason, we often complement couples communication training with assertiveness training. (Recovering sex addicts who are not involved in intimate relationships need this kind of assertiveness training just as much as couples do.) Sex addicts need to learn that they have a right to be honest with themselves and to relate honestly to others.

A critical component of assertiveness training (and couples communication) involves learning to communicate from the "I." The sex addict's earlier communication patterns may have relied on statements that disown any responsibility for the thoughts or feelings conveyed by attributing them to anonymous others (e.g., "What you did might make someone think..." or "It might help us if..."). Alternatively, the sex addict might have displayed overresponsible, controlling communication patterns, speaking for other people or telling other people what they think or feel or how they should behave. The first approach depersonalizes and thus devalues the message; the second depersonalizes and devalues the other people. By contrast, "I" statements own personal responsibility for the individual's own perceptions, thoughts, feelings, desires, and behavior. This approach to communication demonstrates respect for oneself and the other person.

In teaching individuals how to assert themselves and in training couples to communicate more effectively, we employ a program developed by Sherod and Phyllis Miller and detailed in *Talking and Listening Together* (Miller, Miller, et al., 1991). The program uses two mats on which the fundamental protocols of their talking and listening program are outlined. We have found that these mats offer our patients visual and tactile stimuli that valuably complement the auditory aspect of communication, thereby accelerating the learning process.

The first mat, utilized by the speaker, depicts the five aspects of speaking about an issue through what Miller and Miller call the awareness wheel. The awareness wheel map encourages the speaker to explore all the aspects of an issue that (s)he might want to communicate:

- Sensory data (What have I seen and heard related to this issue?)
- Thoughts (What do I think is going on?)
- Feelings (How am I feeling about this issue?)
- Wants for self, other(s), and us (What do I want for myself? For the other person(s)? For both of us?)
- Actions, past (What have I been doing?), and current (What am I doing?), and Future (What will I do?) (Miller, Miller, et al., 1991)

By using the awareness wheel, couples can communicate their feelings, desires, and thoughts more effectively. Moving from spot to spot on the mat while addressing each different aspect of the issue at hand can help the speaker remain grounded instead of spinning off into side issues, broad generalizations, or attacks. It helps the speaker to bring out emotions and desires and intentions as well as facts and impressions.

Expressing Anger (and other Emotions)

Sex addicts and co-addicts tend to have most difficulty with the area of the awareness wheel marked "Feelings." Most sex addicts and co-addicts in recovery need to learn, often for the first time, how to express their feelings—especially anger—appropriately. As a rule, both have adopted a lifelong strategy of suppressing feelings and keeping secrets. Neither partner may have ever dealt with intentions or past actions. They may have no experience in bringing out their thoughts and feelings about their relationship and the significant issues that confront them either individually or as a couple. Indeed, the couple may never have dealt openly with any major issue.

One of the primary challenges in improving communication skills centers on the appropriate expression of anger. Without exception, sex addicts in recovery must face the challenge of handling unresolved anger. This unresolved anger may stem from a wide variety of sources: anger about the neglect or abuse endured in childhood, anger because their behavior is not normal, anger that they have to live by the same rules and regulations as others (or that they have to live by even stricter rules and regulations than others), anger toward God for not relieving the pain in their lives, or anger at previous therapists who focused on depression and excused their sexual compulsions or didn't hold the addicts accountable for their sexual behavior. Sex addicts can seldom handle anger productively and often don't even recognize their own anger. The unresolved, often unexpressed anger leaves sex addicts full of rage. This bottled up rage demands an outlet, often finding it through indiscriminate raging at others or through compulsive sexual behaviors. For this reason, anger management, learning to handle anger constructively, must be a significant focus of therapy with sex addicts. In recovery, sex addicts need to be taught new skills and to be helped to identify and augment any skills they already have.

Expressing anger constructively begins with recognition of anger. We help teach sex addicts to become increasingly aware of the physical symptoms of anger (e.g., a knot in stomach, flushed face, rapid heartbeat and rapid breathing, clenched fists). Recognition of anger is also aided by thinking about anger in a new way. Sex addicts probably will never be anger free, but can begin to learn to deal with anger in such a way as to avoid harming themselves or others. To begin this revision in thinking processes, the addict must begin to acknowledge that anger, especially maladaptive anger, as a compensatory emotion. That is to say, the expression of violence or rage is a way for many people (and especially addicts) to avoid the primary emotions that underlie their expressions of anger. Two primary emotions that underlie anger are pain (if you don't believe this, try to remember what you said or felt the last time you stubbed your toe) and fear. The experience of these emotions can be traumatic because both contribute to a sense of powerlessness and vulnerability that causes one to feel out of control, helpless, incompetent, and hopeless. Children learn quite early in life that they can quickly gain false feelings of competency or control by dominating others. We call them false feelings because the feelings of competency or safety are generated from an external, as opposed to an internal, focus, and it is precisely that external focus that causes so many problems for people who habitually resort to anger as a means of controlling their environment.

An external focus, or locus of control as it is often called, prevents one from introspection (looking inside one's self) to experience fully whatever emotion exists at the present moment and keeps attention focused on others, which can allow a person to feel victimized by events or other people. Once the personalization distortion (a common cognitive distortion among addicts) is in place, the anger/rage/violence cycle has been activated and a person can go through this whole cycle, from victim posturing to rage or violence, in the blink of an eye (See Figure 6.1, The Anger Cycle). This rapid progression is possible because this cycle is a chain of thoughts and behaviors that become habituated or automatic. Once this cycle has been habituated, no thought is given to the discreet components of the cycle and often the individual reports that nothing is recalled but the blinding rage he or she felt. Any conception of how they got to that rageful place is no longer available to them.

The component parts of the anger cycle begin with the *event*. Nearly anything can trigger this cycle. Experiences, emotions, situations that develop, even exposure to another's difficulties can constitute the event that begins the anger cycle.

Following exposure to the activating event, one lapses into the *victim posture* that we discussed briefly above. In this stage the events appear to be personal attacks or insults and malevolent intent is assumed on the part of the actor.

Negative expectation builds on the victim's posturing by contributing a kind of cynicism to the evaluation process. In this stage one may assume that since the past has been difficult or painful, the future will no doubt be the same. The victim believes that there are few options to choose from in dealing with the events to date, and feelings of helplessness greatly increase causing a concomitant rise in subjective discomfort or anxiety.

By advancing to the *avoidance* stage of the cycle, the individual is making his or her first attempt to deal actively with the activating event and usually this is in the form of withdrawal and/or isolation. "Forgetting" and denial become more pronounced defense mechanisms in this stage and substance abuse and other addictive behaviors may become more florid. Some individuals who wish to cultivate their external focus will develop such toxic behavior that people will avoid them, and they will continue to bemoan and criticize others for a lack of concern or consideration.

Figure 6.1. The Anger Cycle.

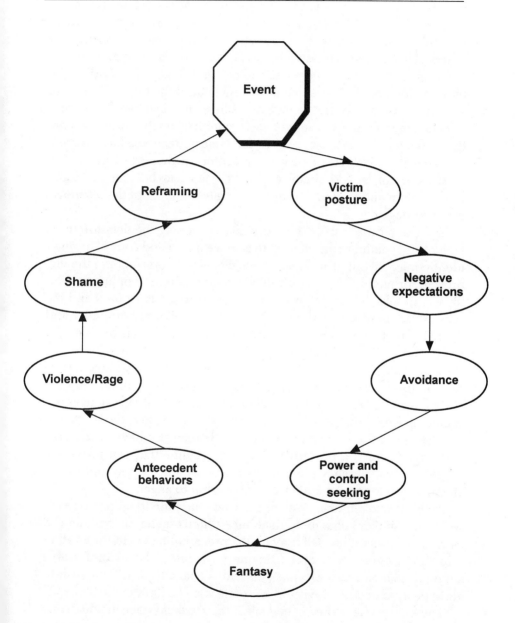

When avoidance has failed to control the discomfort an individual is feeling, the next step is to advance to the *power and control seeking* stage. In this stage, behavior is manifested in a passive-agressive manner and the individual is seeking a sense of competency by controlling others. This passive-agressive behavior does a relatively good job of masking fears, pain, helplessness and poor self-image. It is fairly common for the person to plateau at this stage until the time when he or she can no longer control thoughts, feelings, or subjective discomfort.

When that binding of thought and emotion through power and control seeking fails, *fantasy* begins. In the fantasy stage one has a torrent of "what if..." fantasies that usually center on themes of increasing power, control, and domination. Often the fantasies become more and more violent and lead to the more concrete planning of the *antecedent behaviors* stage.

In the antecedent stage the individual is refining the decision to be violent and continues the attempt to achieve power and control through identifying a victim (usually someone even less powerful than the victimizer), providing him- or herself with a rationalization or justification for victim selection and future action. Opportunity is scouted and the objectification of the victim is undertaken. A failure of empathy and the belief that the victim is nothing more than an obstacle or an object to be used for the victimizer's purposes is common. Once in this stage, the *violence/rage* stage is inevitable. By embracing the cognitive distortions in this phase, the victimizer has crossed the point of no return.

By engaging in rage and/or violence, the individual experiences tremendous feelings of power and control, not to mention the discharge of other unpleasant emotions that he or she may also have been experiencing. There is a powerful rush of adrenaline that can provide a "high" and encourages the use of rage or violence again and again, thereby developing an addictive relationship to anger.

In the *shame*/remorse stage of the cycle the individual promises to avoid any similar behavior in the future. Often the shame experienced is so intense that it in itself may be the precipitating event for another trip through the anger cycle. Shame is an intensely uncomfortable emotion that can also incapacitate and is characterized by a wish to disappear, to become invisible, or to die (Lewis, 1992).

The final phase of the anger cycle is the *reframing* stage in which one attempts to rationalize behavior by identifying provocations or threatening behaviors in the victim that justified or elicited the rage or violence. Often the victimizer concludes that his or her behavior was a "minor overreaction" and won't happen again, so there is nothing to worry about.

We also encourage sex addicts to monitor their management of anger in order to identify the personal conditions that increase the likelihood that they will manage it poorly (HALT—hungry, angry, lonely, tired). Dealing in a therapeutic way with unresolved anger from the past diminishes a significant portion of the rage a sex addict feels. Correcting cognitive distortions (see Chapter 5) can also transform associated affect, including feelings of anger. But unless sex addicts learn new ways of handling anger on their own—outside the therapist's office—they will refill the storehouse of rage as quickly as therapy empties it. For this reason, we help our patients to develop new strategies that will allow them to dump their anger in healthy ways without depending overly on the therapist's intervention. These strategies might include punching pillows, keeping a journal, biofeedback or hypnosis aimed at increasing relaxation, and relaxation and centering techniques or exercise.

Case 6-2

Gus, a recovering alcoholic and sex addict, would drink and womanize whenever he was angry. In recovery, Gus found a place to talk about his anger. In group meetings, he can safely blow up, sounding off and getting feedback, with nothing to lose. When he can't get to a meeting right away, he goes horseback riding or does other exercise as a way of dissipating the energy invested in anger. By releasing some of this energy beforehand, Gus has found he can express his anger in more constructive ways directly to those with whom he is angry.

Once recovering sex addicts have learned how to manage anger rather than letting anger manage them, they can put to better use their improving assertiveness and communication skills. This growing mastery allows sex addicts to harness anger and use it to fuel change rather than let it eat them up.

Learning to Listen

The second mat used in Miller and Miller's program details the five stages that they define as the listening cycle.

- Attending–demonstrating caring and interest in the other person and his or her experience by maintaining focus, eye contact, and occasional supportive touch, and tracking the other's verbal and nonverbal messages
- Acknowledging–demonstrating acceptance, understanding, affirmation and *empathy* for the other person's experience, message, and feelings in addition to what they're saying
- Inviting–showing interest in and value for the other person by actively encouraging the speaker to share more information when (s)he pauses or seems finished, rather than jumping in with an immediate, often defensive, reaction
- Summarizing–demonstrating understanding and accurate reception of the message by providing evidence of *shared meaning,* or providing the opportunity for the speaker to correct or clarify what the listener heard in an attempt to arrive at a shared meaning
- Asking open questions rather than either/or questions, yes-or-no questions, or why questions–gathering more information to clarify or check the accuracy of the listener's observations or interpretations, not to challenge the message imparted by the speaker (Miller, Miller, et al, 1991)

Together, the two mats reinforce the two fundamental tenets of good communication: that the speaker is the sole authority on what the message is and that the listener is responsible for giving feedback that demonstrates awareness and understanding of that message. Both addicts and co-addicts tend to be poor listeners. They may attempt to control or lead the discussion in the direction they want instead of following what the other person has to say. They may judge every statement as it comes out instead of listening for the whole message. Or they may be so busy preparing a response that they cannot possibly pay full attention to what the speaker is saying.

CASE 6-1 (*continued*)

Shortly before they began taking the couples communication course, Ellen opened one session by complaining about a "discussion" she had had with David a few days earlier. Ellen had been sharing a story with David about something that had happened to her at work. As soon as David thought he had grasped the gist of what she was saying, he cut in with a story about something that had happened to him in the past, preventing Ellen from finishing her own story. Ellen had then immediately confronted him with his poor listening behavior, and David reacted by pouting and becoming mean, cursing at her. In session, Ellen said that she was tired of being told she was wrong whenever she expressed her feelings. The exchange had left her feeling "overwhelmed and hopeless and angry."

Using the awareness wheel and the listening cycle can quickly help improve the communication patterns of a couple in recovery. Like David, most sex addicts (and co-addicts) are not skilled listeners. The mats designed by Miller and Miller helped David to focus on what Ellen said rather than on what he wanted to add to the discussion. Only after demonstrating that they have arrived at a shared meaning should the speaker and listener trade places on the mats, thereby affording the other person an opportunity to offer feedback by sharing his or her own observations, feelings, thoughts, wants, and intentions related to the issue(s) at hand.

Our staff teaches couples communication during four weeks of 2 1/2-hour sessions. Throughout the course, we assign specific homework designed to implement and practice changes in communication behavior. For example, we might ask the couple to write out what each appreciates about the other and then share the written thoughts with each other over dinner. Or we might ask the couple to write and read letters to each other as a means of establishing better listening patterns. Hearing an entire letter forces the person to listen to everything the other person has to say without interruption or objection. Only after hearing the whole piece does the listener have a chance to consider it and respond with how (s)he perceives and feels about what the other had to say. Such assignments reinforce the very specific behavioral modifications taught through the communication course.

Improving communication patterns takes a lot of work, so both partners must be willing to put in the time and effort required. For this reason, we do not encourage the initiation of couples communication training early in treatment. Although suggestions on how an individual addict (or co-addict) might improve the quality of his or her communication should be made throughout the course of therapy as specific issues arise, the course as a whole will provide more significant and lasting benefits if both partners have achieved a foothold in sobriety first.

The primary goal of applying new communication skills within a marriage or long-term relationship is to have as few issues as possible become problems. Improved communication patterns establish a framework within which a couple can quickly and productively deal with issues as they come up. If the sex addict slips or relapses, for example, (s)he knows to communicate this quickly to his or her partner. If the couple operates within this framework, the co-addict, in turn, will listen completely to what the addict has to say before responding. Both partners thus have the opportunity to deal with a slip as fact, that is, acknowledging that it really happened, that the addict really did it. Both partners get a chance to share their thoughts and feelings about the slip (e.g., "that's not acceptable behavior"). Really hearing (perhaps for the first time) the co-addict's feelings about his or her sexual behavior helps the addict to develop sincere victim empathy. Then both partners have the opportunity to share what they want (e.g., "I don't want you to do this again"). Finally, both get to state what they will do about the issue (e.g., the addict and co-addict actualize previously agreed-upon consequences of a slip and the measures intended to prevent recurrence). Recovering addicts and co-addicts who make this framework, and the goal of shared meaning, a part of their day-to-day lives will transform the dynamics of their relationship, moving from an almost complete absence of communication to good communication.

EXPANDING THE CIRCLE OF IMPROVED COMMUNICATION

Often, the introduction of improved communication methods will have an impact on communication within the entire family system. Improved family communication encompasses the same tools as couples communication, extended for practice within the larger framework of the family. Mutual respect, communicating full awareness (through observations, thoughts, feelings, wants, and behavior) of the way an issue affects each individual speaker, listening skills, and the quest for shared meaning provide the basis for productive family interaction, just as they do for a couple.

CASE 6-1 *(continued)*

After Ellen's daughter Rebecca attempted suicide, David and Ellen—at the urging of their family therapist, Roxanne Witte—began to conduct regularly scheduled family meetings every week. At these meetings, everyone in the family had a chance to bring up any concerns, issues, or problems and discuss them with the rest of the family. Both parents and children report that this somewhat formal structure allowed them to open up discussions among family members in a way they had never done before. Everyone in the family knows that they will have the opportunity to air their concerns—and that the other members of the family will listen to them.

Jenny, Ellen's oldest daughter, and her new husband Frank, (like Jenny, a survivor of sexual abuse), have also been influenced by her parents' improved communication. The younger couple borrowed materials that had been given out in the communication workshop. Honesty, boundaries, respect, and problem-solving skills were—and to some extent still are—problems in their relationship. Jenny tends to deal with fears or hurt feelings by becoming aggressive, whereas Frank reacts by withdrawing, becoming angry, or trying to laugh them off. Both have agreed to work on becoming more direct with their feelings and needs and to try to focus on themselves rather than trying to force the other person to agree with them. Dr. Witte has used specific homework assignments to change incrementally the couple's communication. For example, Frank once agreed not to lie and not to complain more than once about preparing bottles for their new baby, while Jenny agreed not to disparage his family and not to call him stupid. By working in this very structured, behavioral way, the couple can alter the most problematic behaviors quickly—even before looking at the underlying personal issues and emotions that may have caused them.

As these cases demonstrate, a change in the communication style of a couple can affect and improve communication in the whole family. The mats used by couples trained according to Miller and Miller's program can also be used by the entire family, allowing everyone a chance to express the facts as they see them and their thoughts, feelings, and desires regarding a particular issue. Young children seem particularly receptive to the concept of using the awareness-wheel and listening-skills mats to guide both speaking and listening. Not only do children think it's fun to use the mats, but it also gives them a sense of control and autonomy to be able to pull parents onto the mats to communicate.

CASE 6-3

Tim, a recovering sex addict, and his wife, Lily, had let an argument get out of hand. Their voices got louder, their words harsher, and their tempers increasingly out of control. Suddenly they stopped at the sight of their four-year-old son dragging their communication mats into the room. The boy looked up at them and asked, "Could you please use these?"

The primary therapist or family therapist has an important role in reinforcing the skills learned through couples communication training. Couples sessions or family sessions afford the therapist the opportunity to monitor the communication style used by individual family members. The therapist can then take some of the new terms learned by the family (e.g., shared meaning or procedure setting) and make sure that everyone understands these concepts in their own words. By encouraging everyone in the family to bring these new communication skills into practice within the session, the therapist can reinforce their application outside the office as well. In this way, sex addicts and their families can begin to incorporate couples communication skills into their family dynamics.

In addition to employing new communication skills within the context of family life, we encourage our patients to apply them to other social situations. Since these skills are new to most sex addicts, we often suggest that they experiment with them in the safe environment offered by therapy or self-help groups. This practice in improved communication skills is, of course, of particular importance among recovering sex addicts who have no spouse, significant other, or family of their own.

Such practice often begins in the relationship between a recovering sex addict and his or her sponsor. We believe that every sex addict in recovery needs a sponsor, another sex addict who has achieved a greater degree of sobriety. The sponsor becomes a friend and peer to whom the sex addict can turn for understanding and support. Prior to pursuing recovery, most sex addicts have no or few real friends. Heterosexual sex addicts tend to have no close friends of the same sex, and their friendships with people of the opposite sex have more often than not been disguised grooming for fantasized (or actualized) sexual liaisons. For this reason, we believe it makes sense for a heterosexual sex addict to have a sponsor of the same sex. It promotes the development and deepening of a relationship based on communication and shared intimacy rather than on physical attributes. (Similarly, homosexual sex addicts might benefit more from a relationship with a sponsor of the opposite sex than from one of the same sex.) For heterosexual sex addicts, forming healthy same-sex friendships—developing social comfort with people of the same sex—represents a huge change.

Recovery programs can also help sex addicts begin to form friendships. Going through pain and recovery together creates a powerful bond between people. Given this, groups and members of hospital programs often help create extended families for sex addicts in recovery.

CASE 6-3 (continued)

Valerie and Charles, a much older couple in recovery, took Tim and Lily under their wing, functioning as surrogate parents, or grandparents, for the younger couple. Last year, the two couples vacationed together in Mexico.

We often encourage couples groups and family groups to get together once a month or so outside of our offices: to play, to socialize, and to talk seriously about what's happening in their lives. Such surrogate families often provide the first loving, caring environment the sex addict has ever known. For the first time, sex addicts and co-addicts discover what it's like to have healthy social relationships.

As recovering sex addicts become more comfortable with their new communication skills, we encourage them to make practical use of their training in real-life situations, in other words, those outside the therapist's office or recovery groups. We often suggest involvement in other groups not connected with either therapy or 12-step programs. The recovering sex addict needs to explore and maximize his or her own potential for connectedness. We strongly support recovering sex addicts' involvement in outside activities, and the development of friendships outside recovery programs. (For unmarried sex addicts, this means dating in addition to less intimate group activities.)

CASE 6-4

Dana, a recovering sex addict, had been sexually abused by her stepfather during childhood. This molestation had established a pattern of secretiveness and isolation in her life, a pattern that well served the disease. For Dana, who did not have the skills needed to connect intimately with others, the only sense of intimacy she had ever known was purely sexual. In recovery, we encouraged Dana, who loved the outdoors, to become involved with the Sierra Club. Through such activities as group hikes, Dana began establishing healthy friendships based on common interests. Recovery and increased involvement in this community have helped Dana to create a healthy balance in her life.

Improved communication skills and activities that appeal to outside interests help recovering sex addicts become integrated into a community, establishing a long-absent feeling of connectedness with others. In addition, structured participation, requiring a certain amount of time and commitment, leaves the recovering addict less "downtime," fewer empty hours to fill—hours that were once spent thinking about or acting out sexually compulsive behaviors. Making a commitment to do something (almost anything) with other people thus helps maintain balance in a recovering sex addict's life.

7

The Family of the Sex Addict

Assessing, Treating, and Recreating

Assessing and treating sex addiction must include assessment and treatment of family members. Just as most alcoholics do not "play out their drama alone" (Wegscheider-Cruse, 1981), neither do sex addicts. Because sex addiction, like alcoholism, does affect the entire family, therapy must center on the unhealthy adaptations of the family system in addition to those of the individual. Since the "core experiences of psychological trauma are disempowerment and disconnection from others" (Herman, 1992), the primary goal of family treatment must involve restoring the connection with self, others, and Other while empowering the true self. Intervention and interruption of the "family connection" (Schneider, 1988) is needed for recovery of the family as a whole, but this connection may or may not be broken completely. The unmasking of sex addiction and co-addiction may lead to recovery and restoration, including individual growth, marital growth, family growth, and clarification of boundaries; but it may also lead to family dissolution, *even if every individual in the family is sincerely pursuing recovery.* In working with families of sex addicts, our philosophy promotes reunification whenever possible—but never at the expense of any individual within that system. Truly successful treatment of sex addiction does not end with the mere cessation of the addict's compulsive behaviors, but rather with the growth and enhancement of the entire system, and of each individual member of that system.

Important Note: To be able to offer therapeutic value to clients, a therapist must have done his or her own work first. Working with sex addicts and their families can be demanding and draining. To help others overcome or remake their childhoods, the therapist must already be able to distinguish his or her own self and object representations—that is, "the sum of the intrapsychic images of the self and of significant others, as well as the feelings associated with those images," along with the capacities for action in the environment guided by those images (Masterson, 1988). Unless therapists themselves have undergone therapy, they may find that working with a client who has similar problems triggers unresolved issues of their own. Conversely, however, the mental health, growth, and recovery of the therapist will better enable that therapist to assist a client in attaining similar stages of growth.

TREATMENT OF THE FAMILY

Our treatment plan for sex addicts and their families, both adults and children, consists of three phases: assessment and the establishment of rapport; communicating, accepting, and integrating; and creating and empowering the true self. These phases, however, do not necessarily happen sequentially, but rather overlap in the course of this progressive transformation. Moving through these phases, the work of family recovery from sex addiction and co-addiction often seems overwhelming both to family members and to therapists. Yet during difficult times in therapy, therapists and patients do well to remember to approach recovery one step at a time, individually and gently—to view recovery as a process rather than as an event, as a journey rather than as a destination.

The Initial Phase: Assessment and the Establishment of Rapport

All family members undergo a comprehensive initial evaluation. Assessment must take into account all levels of the individual's functioning: physical well-being, emotional stability, mental health, developmental stage, family history. As part of our initial assessment, we try to pull together all professional reports or summaries prepared outside our offices, take a family history, interview family members individually, and administer any psychological testing we deem appropriate.

We also often find it helpful in the assessment of family functioning to undertake activity assessment, examining family dynamics through the modalities of art or sandplay or through directed or nondirected play (see Chapter 11).

Establishing rapport with clients takes time and effort. Both adults and children in addictive households have difficulty trusting anyone. For many years, everyone in the family—including the youngest of children—has invested their energy in maintaining secrets, protecting and preserving the family facade, and/or keeping others at a distance, even pushing them away. Overcoming these defenses with each family member will usually not happen in the first session. In most cases, the building of trust and relinquishing of defenses will proceed in fits and starts: three steps forward, two steps back. Most family members will demand that the therapist demonstrate again and again that (s)he can be trusted and that (s)he will not neglect, reject, or abandon the patient. Therefore, the most effective means of facilitating rapport and establishing a connection with members of addictive families involves simply providing a safe, protected, and supportive space and demonstrating unconditional acceptance of the child or adult. At the same time, the therapist must work to establish, maintain, and teach appropriate boundaries with the patient, sometimes a difficult challenge with this population. This process of building and maintaining rapport within the context of appropriate boundaries, essential as a foundation for more intensive work, will continue throughout the course of therapy.

Central Phase: Communicating, Accepting, and Integrating

The central phase of treatment focuses on increasing all family members' self-awareness, consciousness, insight, and acceptance of every aspect (both positive and negative) of themselves, and their ability to express themselves honestly to themselves, and then to others. Not surprisingly, addicts, co-addicts, and other family members (adults and children) can find this phase especially challenging, strenuous, and sometimes painful or frightening. In the early stages of therapy, most are still bound by the three rigid primary rules of the dysfunctional family: "Don't talk, don't feel, don't trust" (Black, 1981). For this reason, this phase almost always entails psychological or interactional detours and roadblocks along the way. The therapist must not slight or ignore these diversions or obstructions, for they indicate the patient's or family's need to slow down and confront areas where they feel stuck or blocked by repression. Therapists must patiently move at the client's or family's pace rather than at their own. Child therapists often express this guideline as "letting the child lead and the therapist follow." This strategy applies just as critically to therapy with adults. At the same time, however, it is important that the therapist keep the process going and not allow the client or family to dictate recovery.

Since they never experienced any other childhood but their own (parts of which may have been repressed), most addicts, spousal co-addicts, young children, and adult children do not regard their family history as dysfunctional, traumatic, inappropriate, abnormal, or even out of the ordinary. As a result, everyone in the family will benefit from didactic edutherapy aimed at teaching what *is* normal, appropriate, and healthy behavior. Edutherapy combines therapeutic experiences and complementary didactic teaching, or, learning new concepts and applying them to life. We initiate edutherapy in the first sessions with sex addicts and their families. Some of this education must by necessity take the form of didactic lectures, followed by a discussion that allows clients to raise any questions they might have. We have found, for example, that treatment progresses more smoothly and rapidly the sooner sex addicts and all co-addicts (adults and children) come to understand the process of sex addiction. Family members need to understand how sex addiction progresses and how it determines the dynamics of family systems. Educating family members about co-addiction, enabling behaviors, and the rules and roles in addictive families can prompt recognition of their own dysfunctional patterns of thinking and behavior (see Chapter 4). Finally, as part of their education about the process of sex addiction, sex addicts and their families need to appreciate the concept of recovery from both sex addiction and co-addiction as an ongoing, day-to-day process that lasts a lifetime. Given that the possibility of relapse to either addictive or co-addictive patterns is intrinsic to this concept, sex addicts and co-addicts also need to familiarize themselves with relapse-prevention plans and begin to develop their own.

Many sex addicts and family members join self-help groups modeled on the 12-steps of AA: Sex Addicts Anonymous, Sexaholics Anonymous, Sex and Love Addicts Anonymous, Recovering Couples Anonymous, Co-dependents of Sexual Addicts, S-Anon. In the therapeutic context, we support and complement this involvement with a thorough exploration of the 12-steps as part of our edutherapy program. Often, this education and experience in the 12-steps and how they might apply in a therapeutic way to patients' lives lead to transformational examinations of how spirituality can provide a road to individual growth and family recovery.

Two other critical aspects of this edutherapy phase involve developing an understanding of emotions and how to express them and learning communication skills. Sex addicts, co-addicts, and their children are often so dissociated from their emotions that awareness of feelings must begin at a very basic level. We provide families with handouts, for example, listing "feeling words" (e.g., contented, safe, frustrated, upset, outraged, anxious, embarrassed, depressed) grouped into five major categories: happy, angry, scared, confused, and sad. With young children, we use a list of emotions that illustrates the expression of each feeling with a cartoon face. These simple tools help members of the sex addict's family to begin to become aware of and identify their own feelings. This identification lays the groundwork for sex addicts and co-addicts to experience, own, and communicate their feelings.

As a first step, we may ask either adults or children to draw a symbol of a feeling and begin to talk about it. The emotion chosen and its description often yield personal insight that can help launch a fuller exploration of that individual's feelings. With very young children, we may use colored squares of construction paper, asking the child to name the color and identify any feelings or associations related to that color. Such simple but necessary beginnings allow children (and adults) to find the words needed to verbalize emotions. It also gives them permission to feel and to accept their own feelings without judgment. In addition, it provides a way for patients to dissipate some of the energy associated with their unexpressed feelings, which diminishes the power of these emotions over the individuals and frees them from being helpless victims of their own emotions.

The ultimate goal of edutherapy that concentrates on emotional awareness is to allow sex addicts, co-addicts, and their children to begin "handling" their feelings in healthy, direct ways rather than re-pressing them and/or expressing them in displaced, unhealthy ways. We encourage patients to learn how to deal with their feelings accord-ing to a five-step progression:

1. Increasing awareness, decreasing dissociation—knowing that they are feeling something.
2. Examining and identifying—exploring layers of feelings and giving the feeling(s) a name.
3. Differentiating between past and present—determining how much of their feelings comes from the past and how much from the present.
4. Accepting the feeling—giving themselves the right and per-mission to feel what they feel without judgment.
5. Empowering—taking appropriate action based on personal values, religious beliefs, lifestyle, and so forth, as detailed in "feeling journals" and discussed in sessions with their therapists.

Mastering the steps involved in handling their current feelings pro-vides the foundation for the later work of acknowledging and accept-ing the trauma(s) and/or neglect of their childhood—and any associ-ated affect. In this way, such mastering also offers a fundamental stepping-stone for the development of victim empathy.

One of the case challenges of this phase requires the therapist to help addicts or co-addicts "sort out" the traumas or deprivations in their lives. Sorting out involves recognizing and beginning to under-stand, as much as the individual can, the reality of what has happened and how events have affected attitudes, feelings, and behaviors. For the sex addict, this sorting-out process must encompass, in addition to the traumas and deprivations suffered, those inflicted through their compulsive behavior, the formation of victim empathy.

Both children and traumatized adults often lack the words to de-scribe their experiences or to express their feelings. The deeper the emotions and feelings are repressed, the more distanced they become from conscious memories and personality, the less likely that individu-als will find the words needed to express them. Most often, people experience the feelings associated with childhood trauma and/or deprivation as overwhelming; they lock their unexpressed emotions inside their minds, bodies, and spirits. By putting the trauma, neglect, event, or affect into words or some other form of expression, the recovering sex addict or co-addict can transform them from the inside (unconsciousness) to the outside (consciousness). The process of feeling, communicating, and sorting through events then dissipates much of their energy and control over the individual. This process can free the individual to begin healing.

Both education and therapy play essential, complementary roles in healing and recovery from family sex addiction. When didactic teaching is combined with therapeutic experiences (including therapy itself, particularly expressive modalities; exercises or experiments in healthy living; practicing improved communication skills in the home or in social settings), positive changes come faster, have more impact, and last longer. These changes move patients from this phase to the final phase of therapy: the ongoing process of recovery.

Final Phase: Creating and Empowering the True Self

Sex addicts, co-addicts, and their children share a sense of powerlessness over their lives. Among adults, feelings of helplessness and powerlessness, along with an image of themselves as victims reflect a distorted view founded in childhood, when the overall sense of powerlessness was, for the most part, warranted. While addicts and adult co-addicts may feel that they are powerless to stop the cycles of addiction and co-addiction, children truly are trapped: intrapsychically and physically. Dependent upon their parents or other adults for care, children have little power. They cannot, for example, choose to leave the family at an early age. In recovery, young children of sex addicts offer vivid testimony of this helplessness in their art work: Self-portraits often feature weak hands or no hands (see Figure 7.1). The lack of hands symbolizes helplessness, children's essential dependence on the mercy of others coupled with their inability to reach out and connect with those others.

Because children feel and truly are (at least to some degree) powerless, the therapist must help them recognize the assets, positive characteristics, and limited power that they do have. When we work with

Figure 7.1. Self-portrait Without Hands.

children of sex addicts, we often try to empower them by offering them the opportunity to choose their own therapeutic modalities: art, play, games, talk. If they have created a work of art, we again offer them the option of sharing it or not sharing it with their parents. We discuss power as a positive attribute (rather than a license to abuse), and emphasize that with power comes responsibility. And we help children relate how it feels to be powerless in a situation. We ask how they feel when they are helpless. We carefully explore exactly who and what might serve as resources for them when they find themselves powerless in a certain situation. The therapist can help children develop resources and plans to protect themselves in such situations and encourage them to ask for help whenever they need it.

CASE 7-1

Tommy's father, a sex addict, heaped verbal abuse on his son, constantly demeaning him and putting him down. Tommy had been treated as a scapegoat for anything that went wrong, both at home and in school. In therapy, we explored Tommy's feelings of powerlessness in the face of his father's abusiveness. In the course of a discussion held in a children's support group, Tommy was delighted by the expression "like water off a duck's back." Thereafter, in verbally abusive or demeaning situations, Tommy began to exercise his power to visualize. He saw himself as a duck with the water (his father's harsh words) falling off his back and rippling into a pond until they disappeared. Through this method, Tommy learned how to deflect his father's abuse—not to deny it, but simply not to take it in. (This image and experience became so important to Tommy that in his teens he gained local recognition as an expert carver of wooden duck decoys, which he sold first to neighbors and then to the local hunting store.)

These same strategies, adjusted for developmental and age appropriateness, can also facilitate individual growth and recovery among adult co-addicts and sex addicts. With adult addicts and co-addicts, however, one of the chief challenges of empowerment involves helping patients understand and appreciate that they are not only worthy of treatment, but that they deserve it. Although the focus on empowering the recovering addict or co-addict does not come until the final phase of treatment, the issue of "worthiness" must be confronted immediately, beginning at the initial meeting with the patient. If the individual does not first feel worthy of recovery, (s)he will not accept that (s)he has any power to change.

The process of creating and empowering the true self involves defining and refining the meaning of "self" (the whole self) and all that the word implies. In the context of this redefinition, the process also entails taking responsibility for one's own behavior. As a rule, neither sex addicts nor co-addicts have a clear sense of self; so much of their self has been denied, given away, or held hostage. As a result, sex addicts and co-addicts suffer from severe attachment disorder issues (clinging or bolting). Relationship problems with extremes of idealization (projection) and disappointment are common. Sex addicts and co-addicts alike are often unable to connect to healthy relationships because of conscious or unconscious rage, fear, shame, guilt, lack of trust, and lack of clarity in their emotions. For this reason, therapists must focus a good deal of work with recovering addicts and co-addicts on reclaiming (or claiming for the first time) the true self and letting go of the false self that has developed through roles, rules, and defenses in addictive family systems.

In *The Search for the Real Self,* James Masterson describes two types of false selves: the borderline, who displays a deflated false self; and the narcissistic, who presents an inflated false self. Both "are rooted in defensive selves and poorly developed egos and live in a world bounded by their projections" (Masterson, 1988). In working with addicts and co-addicts, much of the recovery work must concentrate on deflating the addict's narcissistic self while simultaneously inflating the co-addict's borderline self. The therapist must help addicts and co-addicts see beyond the false selves in order to define and refine the meaning of the true self.

After recognizing their own facades (their false selves), addicts and co-addicts need to work on discovering and expressing the true self. Often, patients in recovery describe the lack of self as a void, a deep hole, an empty feeling. One co-addict, just beginning therapy, described this selflessness when she said, "I have a deep yearning in a place within me to go home, but I feel like I won't find anyone or anything there." Before beginning therapy, many addicts and co-addicts have no real sense of who they are. They have identified with and become the scapegoat or hero, or whatever role they played out in the family system. Sex addicts have lost their selves to the addiction, living out lifestyles that often contradict their personal values, morals, and ethics. The addiction itself becomes the addict's identity. Co-addicts surrender their selves, focusing so much energy and attention on the needs and wants of others (especially those of the sex addict) that they become unaware of, or unable to express, their own. Entering the therapist's office for the first time, one of our co-addicted clients referred to herself more as an object than as a self, asking, "Where do you want me?"

The first step in the process of redefinition and refinement involves patients in recovery answering basic questions that help them define their true self: Who am I? What do I want? What do I need? What are my values? What are all the parts that contribute to the whole self: physical, mental, emotional, spiritual, sexual, creative, secret, negative, positive? What are my hopes, desires, goals? Where do I find meaning in my life? Taking a multidimensional approach, the therapist thus encourages patients to look at themselves afresh. In redefining themselves, patients begin to plot out a personal course for their individual recovery.

CASE 7-2

Bess, the daughter of two addicts and ex-wife (after 21 years of marriage) of an alcoholic, had married her current husband, Andy, simply because he stimulated her sexually. Repressed sexually prior to her second marriage, Bess admits that their sexual relationship was the only "good part" of the marriage. By convincing Bess that she was shut down, "frigid," and a "prude," Andy–a sex addict–had talked her into experimentation with a variety of sexual behaviors that she felt were wrong. In accepting his acting-out behavior, she questioned her own values as being old-fashioned. In this way, she rationalized that their sexual activity was normal. In recovery, Bess found it helpful to distinguish between her false self and true self by representing each side as a jigsaw puzzle and then labelling the pieces (see Figure 7.2).

This exercise yielded a symbolic personal inventory that highlighted both the strengths she needed to develop further and the aspects of herself she wanted to overcome. She began to regard her life, values, and behavior as lying on a continuum rather than in stark, rigid, either/or terms.

In defining the self, addicts and co-addicts need to examine the belief systems that prompted them to create the false self. Co-addicts and addicts often have similar belief systems, in part because both usually come from dysfunctional family backgrounds and in part because co-addicts become so enmeshed in addicts' lives that their beliefs and behaviors begin to parallel those of the addicts. Children then absorb these beliefs from both parents. In general, these beliefs include regarding oneself as worthless, flawed, invalidated, unacceptable, needy, and undeserving of happiness or love. Because both addicts and co-addicts believe love must be earned and feel unworthy of love, they have a profound fear of abandonment. Both overcompensate for feelings of powerlessness and helplessness through the delusion that they can control and manipulate the behavior of others.

Uncertainty or the absence of any awareness of limits and boundaries also contributes to the unclear sense of self characteristic of all members of sex-addicted families. In defining the self, both adults and children therefore must clearly distinguish between what is mine and what is not mine. The application of this distinction to physical space, emotional issues, behavior, and problems within the family will help define healthier boundaries than they have known in the past. Each family member can then begin to take appropriate responsibility for personal behavior, emotions, and problems while disavowing responsibility for what belongs to someone else. (The principle of detachment introduced by Al-Anon and echoed by such self-help groups as COSA and S-Anon provides valuable guidance as a tool for living in recovery.)

The next step in the process calls on the recovering addict or co-addict to redirect and refine the self to reflect new definitions. If, in the process of defining self, an addict discovers, for example, that (s)he is creative or spiritual or prefers solitude, (s)he must next ask: How can I more fully express and experience these parts? What kind of creative activity do I choose to engage in? How do I nurture my spiritual aspect? When and how can I find the necessary solitude?

Defining and refining the self will, generally for the first time, produce congruency in the individual's life. When the sexual part of self is either repressed or acts out through compulsive behavior, a large part of the self becomes incongruent with the whole person. And this incongruency ultimately comes at the expense of other, neglected parts of self, for instance, spirituality or creativity. The sexual self must be integrated (made congruent) with the rest of the individual's true self. For only when we are "firmly grounded in a strong, real self can we live and share our lives with others in ways that are healthy, straightforward expressions of our deepest needs and desires, and in so doing find fulfillment and meaning" (Masterson, 1988).

SPECIAL ISSUES IN THE TREATMENT OF CHILDREN OF SEX ADDICTS

Children in sex-addicted families cannot escape being affected by the distorted and unhealthy behaviors and attitudes of their parents. The adaptations that become prevalent in such families include lying, depression, and flattened affect (Greenleaf, 1981). In addition, the generalizations that Janet Woititz (1983) observes in reference to adult chil-

Figure 7.2. Pieces of the Puzzle of Self.

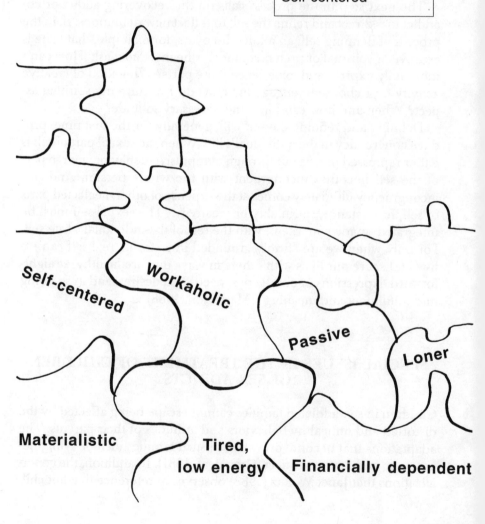

FALSE SELF

Financially dependent
Tired, low energy
Materialistic
Workaholic
Passive
Loner
Self-centered

Self-centered

Workaholic

Passive

Loner

Materialistic

Tired,
low energy

Financially dependent

TRUE SELF

Spiritual
Creative
Active
Energetic
Compassionate
Sensitive
Bright

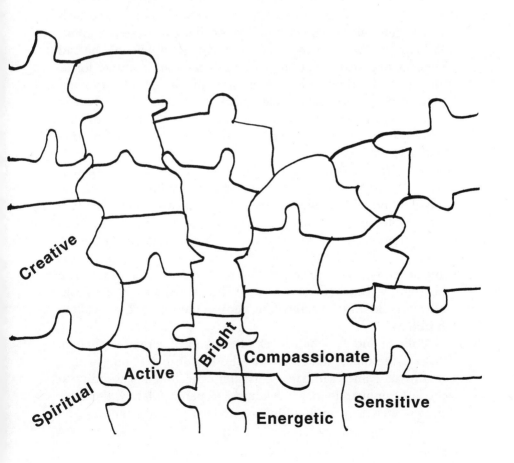

dren of alcoholics also apply to family members of sex addicts. Indeed, such issues as the question of normalcy, lying, seriousness, difficulty with intimacy, and feeling different seem more prevalent and more intense among this population. Children of sex addicts also seem to experience greater devastation in terms of self-esteem, sexual self-acceptance, and spirituality.

CASE 7-3

William is a prominent business, community, and church leader in a small Midwestern town. He is also a sex addict who has had a string of long-term strictly sexual relationships with men across the country, as well as hundreds of anonymous sexual encounters with men in "adult" bookstores. His double life led to such severe guilt that seven years before receiving treatment from us, William had broken down and confessed to his wife that he had been having sexual liaisons with both men and women for as long as she had known him. After his confession, William sought help from a Christian counsellor who, regarding it solely as a matter of sin, advised him to read the Bible, pray, and avoid doing it again. Still, William had been unable to stop his compulsive sexual behavior.

Tina, William's wife, suffered from severe bouts of depression and anxiety following her husband's confession. Heeding the advice of both her family pastor and the Christian counsellor (advice reinforced by William), Tina felt that she could not talk to anyone about her husband's sexual affairs. Angry about being "forced" to keep the secret, she began to turn to eating to comfort and soothe herself. She continued to take care of her home and her family, but both family and friends saw her as emotionally volatile and unstable. The family identified Tina as "the problem."

William and Tina had six children, four of whom we treated. Nancy, the oldest daughter, was the first in her family to seek treatment. Nancy came to see us after cancelling her wedding at the last minute due to severe attacks of panic. Clearly, the prospect of marriage profoundly scared her. Nancy's success (she married less than a year later) in a one-week intensive with Marilyn Murray inspired her mother to seek treatment. This therapy led to discovery of her husband's sex addiction (neither William nor Tina had ever heard of sex addiction prior to therapy). In the months following the disclosure of their father's sex addiction, the three other daughters also sought therapy. The two boys, the oldest in the family, have not yet received therapy of any kind.

Wayne, the oldest, had been viewed by the family as the problem child or scapegoat. Throughout his adolescence and early adulthood, he had had loud fights with his father and got deeply involved in using alcohol, other drugs, and sex to bury his pain.

Adam, the family hero, absolutely shuns therapy. The mirror image of his father, Adam is totally cut off from his own emotions. Stoic and uptight, Adam has become extremely successful financially.

Leslie, who had always been the family rabble-rouser, constantly confronting her parents and siblings, sought therapy for an obsessive-compulsive disorder. Leslie suffered from a paranoid obsession over the possibility that her husband, a corporate consultant, might be having an affair. She had severe attacks of crying and sobbing.

Holly had always been the family's "smiling sunshine." After Tina's breakdown seven years earlier, Holly had given herself the job of keeping her mother happy. From preadolescence, she had essentially raised herself and her younger sister. (The four other children were all at least five years older than Holly.) Holly suffered from bulimia.

Cristy, the youngest, was considered a problem child by her parents and a spoiled brat by her siblings. At age 16 (less than a week after her oldest sister had become the first in the family to seek therapy), Cristy had gone on a rampage: tearing apart her room, destroying furniture, bedding, and clothes, and throwing a chair and various personal objects through her second-floor window. After a brief hospitalization, Cristy began undergoing intensive therapy as well.

As this case clearly demonstrates, the family "secret" of sex addiction and the dysfunctional dynamic between the sex addict and the co-addicted spouse affects everyone in the family. At least three children in this family (Wayne, Nancy, and Leslie) suffered from severe sexual anxieties or sexual disorders as adults. One (Holly) developed an eating disorder, as her mother had before her. None of the children had learned the social skills needed to form intimate relationships. All of the children have difficulty expressing emotion appropriately or constructively.

That children of sex addicts often become sexually confused themselves should not be surprising. Like their parents, children of sex addicts generally receive either no sex education at all or an inappropriate one. Damaged by inadequate or nonexistent sex education, these children seldom develop healthy sexual attitudes and behavior. For example, sex addicts—and often their partners, too—equate sex with love and acceptance. Children who absorb this belief will invariably experience sexual confusion. In addition, due to the intense sexual excitement of their parents (whether repressed or expressed inappropriately), the children of sex addicts can become eroticized. Any form of sexual abuse, whether overt or covert, can create unconscious fear, restriction, and rigidity related to sexuality. Children may begin to regard themselves as sex objects—and by extension to regard others as such. Conversely, they may shut down sexuality altogether. This sexual confusion often makes it essential that the children receive special coping and social-skills training. Throughout the treatment process, the therapist therefore needs to focus on emotional signals and distortions that may arise from violation and invalidation.

As sexual identity plays such an important part in defining a person's whole identity, children of sex addicts also experience identity confusion. They tend to define themselves exclusively according to the rigid roles they play in their families: roles such as family hero, scapegoat, lost child, and mascot (Wegscheider-Cruse, 1981). When a parent is a sex addict, the family system seems even more closed, the secrets more closely guarded, and the rules and roles even more rigid than in other addictive family systems.

The secrets of parents cannot help but prove destructive to the child. No matter how deeply hidden or repressed by their parents, these secrets affect children. Secrets creep into every aspect of family living, creating high levels of psychological stress, pressure, and tension. The energy focused on keeping secrets does not allow children to be fully alive or fully present. Not allowed to live the lives of children, they are merely able to exist.

Children may not even be consciously aware of the family secrets, but these secrets seldom escape the unconscious. "The greater part of the psychic life of the child lies in the unconscious" (Wickes, 1988). And the younger the child, the more the unconscious life contributes to the sum total of the personality. In therapy, secrets are often revealed through play or art. In many cases, children assume that something is wrong with them or that they bear responsibility for the sense of discontent they detect in their family. Children see themselves as the center of all their experiences, the center of their universe. As such, they take on a sense of responsibility for everything that goes on inside the home. For this reason, children of sex addicts can often assume a parentified role toward siblings and even toward their parents. They give up childhood in an attempt to control inappropriate interactions, which they do not recognize as having little or nothing to do with them. They become extremely serious, finding it hard to relax, to play, even to be. (Other children, seeing this strategy fail, sometimes go in the other direction, becoming highly irresponsible and preoccupied with immediate gratification through play, sex, or other activities.) Yet all attempts to control family problems and adapt to the unhealthy dynamics of the family system inevitably fail. Combined with long-term deprivation on all levels—physical, emotional, psychological, and spiritual—this "failure" causes the child to feel inadequate and disconnected from the family, and from friends, community, and society in general. Unmourned losses, grief, and deprivation manifest themselves in low self-esteem, inchoate fears, anxiety, hopelessness, and depression. Fortunately, when the unconscious life of the parent is examined and resolved, the problems of the child *sometimes* vanish (Wickes, 1988).

Denial of the problem not only preserves the addictive cycle, but also inculcates children in the practice of dishonesty. When spouses in denial adapt to the lies of the sex addict and lie themselves in order to protect their partners and the family image, children too learn to lie as an adaptive response. Indeed, lying becomes such a habitual response that children in these families often spontaneously resort to lying before they even consider the alternative, telling the truth.

Similarly, denial of the feelings associated with the problem also preserves the addictive cycle—and keeps all family members blocked or stuck in the closed and rigid family system. Through a combination of parental modeling, parental restrictions, and the fear of repercussions, children learn to repress and harshly judge their own affects. Denial thus flattens affect and thereby retards the personal growth and development of every member of the family. Indeed, a child who is denied permission to feel or whose feelings are seldom (if ever) validated feels invalidated as a person. Refusing a child the right to feel means stripping him or her of the right to be.

Together, these attributes—lying, secretiveness, low self-esteem, flattened affect, sexual confusion, identity confusion—make intimacy a frightening, next-to-impossible prospect for children of sex addicts. Thus, the parents' intimacy disorder gets passed down to a new generation of potential addicts and co-addicts. Many children of sex addicts develop attachment disorders, for example, that will become manifest in their later relationships with spouses and children. As Alice Miller (1986) has noted, "Whatever one doesn't get from one's parents—respect, honesty, trust—one demands at emotional gunpoint from one's own children." The therapist must attend to all of these issues in order to interrupt the intergenerational cycle of addictions.

TREATING THE "INNER CHILD"

As Beverly James concludes in *Treating Traumatized Children*, strong parallels exist in the treatment of traumatized children and work done with adult victims of childhood trauma (James, 1989). This does *not* imply that we should treat adults as children, but it does suggest that similar treatment modalities will facilitate the treatment and recovery of both populations. This parallel depends upon the recognition and acceptance of a part inside every adult, a part that various clinicians have labeled the divine child archetype (Jung), the inner child (Bradshaw, 1990; Whitfield, 1987), or the Original Feeling Child (Murray, 1991). Jung, for example, suggested that not only does the child archetype provide a significant link to the past, offering a picture of forgotten episodes from childhood, but it also exists in the present and has the potential to evolve toward independence in the future (Jung,

1968). Yet to achieve this full potential, an individual must unearth and resolve these forgotten episodes. Therapy with sex addicts, co-addicts, and their children must therefore include inner child and actual child work; each member of the family has an inner child sorely in need of healing, an inner child or actual child damaged by repeated trauma or persistent neglect, an inner child or actual child plagued by the issues detailed in the previous section.

Therapists working with any sex addict or family member must address the healing of this injured part. We cannot overstress the importance of helping the child or adult to reexperience—or to experience for the first time—the trauma(s) and/or deprivation(s) of childhood. If the therapist cannot help children—and adult children—to experience and express the pain resulting from childhood trauma or neglect, healing will be incomplete. Many adults who have already gone through treatment and recovery programs remain stuck in recovery; they still cannot feel whole or function fully. They may have, for example, stopped drinking, but escalated compulsive sexual behaviors. Or they may have renounced compulsive sexual behaviors only to turn to compulsive eating in an attempt to fill the internal void, the emptiness inside that so many sex addicts describe. We believe that the saying "no pain, no gain" has some truth when applied to the treatment of sex addiction. However, experiencing the pain does not mean wallowing, blaming, or staying stuck in that pain. Instead, addicts (and their family members) need to uncover or discover, experience, accept, integrate, and heal their pain, traumas, and/or deprivations.

Intervening, treating, and healing childhood wounds in adults or children does not mean merely helping the client to repeat the story, talk about the pain, and intellectualize or understand the situation and the motives (or the addictive behaviors) of the one(s) who inflicted the pain. The therapist must also confront defense mechanisms (denial, rationalization, minimization, projection, intellectualization). Confrontation must take place in a safe place and be carried out in a supportive way. The therapist may choose to employ either direct or indirect (symbolic) techniques. Art therapy or other expressive therapies (see Chapter 11) can offer avenues of metaphorical expression that navigate around and through defense mechanisms, allowing the patient to express feelings while channeling and dissipating energy.

CASE 7-4

June, the 12-year-old daughter of a sex-addicted father and an alcoholic mother, could not speak negatively about her family. June had shut down emotionally and invested all her energy in protecting the image of her family. Asked to draw a picture that represented her family, however, June drew a big black tornado (see Figure 7-3). After having created this drawing, she became able to talk more explicitly about her family's depressive and stormy state.

Trauma may have affected the children (or the now grown-up parents) covertly or overtly on many different levels: cognitively, physically, emotionally, spiritually. For this reason, treatment and recovery from family sex addiction demands multidimensional strategies, encompassing a holistic approach that addresses issues of body, mind, and spirit.

As Tom Robbins suggested in one of his popular novels: "It's never too late to have a happy childhood." In addition to exhuming the pain of childhood, therapists need to help members of sex-addicted families, both children and adults, to rediscover—or discover for the first time—how to be childlike. This does not mean reinforcing childishness—for example, the addict's tendency to disavow adult responsibility and focus on immediate gratification. (One addict in recovery took his family on an extended vacation in Hawaii and returned unable to pay his bills.) Indeed, childish, irrational, or irresponsible behavior must be arrested—by helping the patient establish priorities, examining procrastination, teaching impulse control, and emphasizing responsibility—before childlike behavior can be encouraged. Yet therapy cannot be just about discovering pain without its becoming overwhelming; it must also be about discovering pleasure and establishing balance in life. The therapist must therefore include leisure planning as part of the overall treatment plan.

As Marilyn Murray describes this process, finally connecting with the Sobbing Hurting Child offers the opportunity to reestablish contact with the Original Feeling Child, the child the individual was meant to be (see Chapter 9). The therapist needs to help the patient explore childlike activities, to design and structure time and exercises that will

Figure 7.3. June's Big Black Tornado.

help all members of sex-addicted families to explore this inner child. Creative modalities often encourage just such contact. Art, play, music, sports, and dance can tap into the individual's creativity and spontaneity, helping to release the trapped child part. Only by identifying with and integrating the Sobbing Hurting Child, the Controlling Child, and the Original Feeling Child will addicts, co-addicts, and their children approach wholeness. By providing insight and changes in attitude and behavior patterns that promote healthy coping and living skills, this process can further the integration and balance that will promote and maintain recovery.

8

The Neglected Dyad

The Mother-Daughter Relationship

When discussing incest in the context of sex addiction, we should remember that not all sex addicts become sex offenders; nor do all breach
societal, cultural, and religious taboos and become involved in incestuous relationships with their children. Although incest can occur between any family members, incestuous relationships between fathers
and daughters account for 75 percent of all reported cases; this dyad
also represents the most common type of incest relationship we treat at
PCS. This chapter, therefore, focuses on cases involving sex-addicted
fathers who have had incestuous relationships with their daughters.

THE MOTHER-DAUGHTER DYAD

When sex addiction crosses family boundaries and becomes incestuous, healing the family demands a wide range of interventions. Systemic treatment models suggest treatment not only of the victim and
the victimizer, but of the entire family system. Ideally this would entail
family sessions, marital sessions, father-daughter dyads, mother-daughter dyads, sibling sessions, and family-of-origin work. Sadly, the realities of in vivo treatment are often such that lack of funding limits the
scope of the treatment to providing services for the victimizer and the
victim, and in the most fortunate cases, some family sessions as well.

Anecdotal evidence from our practice supports the conclusion of the few clinicians who have written about the mother-daughter relationship in incestuous families (Hagood, 1991; Hewitt & Barnard, 1986; Scott & Flowers, 1988; Strand, 1990): The healing of the mother-daughter relationship is the most crucial component in the daughter's recovery from an incestuous relationship. However, because few professionals acknowledge the fundamental importance of addressing the mother-daughter relationship in treatment settings, treatment planning seldom gives enough attention to the mother's individual needs or to the mother-daughter relationship. Those rare therapists who do recognize the importance of healing this relationship are hampered by a "dearth of information on actual treatment strategies" (Hewitt & Barnard, 1986).

A Mother's Experience

The disclosure that incest has occurred within a family can have devastating effects on every family member. Most mothers experience intense conflict between their roles as protective parent and supportive spouse. Some women resolve this dilemma by retreating into a surprisingly strong denial that any problem exists at all. Others will choose to side with either the daughter or the spouse and accuse the one not chosen of fabricating a wildly absurd, lurid tale to advance some sort of personal agenda. More commonly, mothers feel highly ambivalent about the situation and their families and strive somehow to preserve the family structure and a sense of togetherness. In any case, regardless of how a woman's defense mechanisms had operated, no matter how illusory her beliefs about herself, her family, and her family's relationships with one another may have been, the disclosure of incest has shattered these beliefs. These women begin to question their own perceptions, judgment, and feelings as though they have passed "through the looking glass": Nothing makes sense anymore.

One mother, who had reported her husband to the authorities after her seven-year-old daughter told her of his sexual victimization, told us, "I felt panicked...literally sick to my stomach thinking, 'Oh no, our life is being torn apart.' I felt like I was in the middle of a stream of water and it was heading towards a waterfall. Then I kind of went into shock. I started to anesthetize myself. What do we need to do here, instead of facing the true reality."

The disclosure of incest between her husband and her daughter often leaves a mother apparently immobilized, unable to take any action. Although this inaction may appear to demonstrate profound denial on the mother's part, it more accurately reflects confusion and ambivalence regarding the many issues and fears that incest forces into the open. Indeed, as Elbow and Mayfield (1991) point out, because confusion is typical of a crisis state, a mother should not be criticized for failing to act immediately to protect her child. Yet all too often, we expect mothers in this state of crisis to make clear, rational, life-altering decisions—choices that we would not expect someone in any other severe crisis situation to make.

A mother must quickly weigh a great number of considerations when faced with the disclosure of sexual abuse in her family, including the potential loss of economic support; issues of loss in general; whom to believe when her spouse denies the child's accusations; anger toward her partner, her daughter, and the legal and child-protective systems in general; and the social ramifications of disclosure. Finally, she must also deal with her feelings about herself.

The issue of financial support frequently comes into play. If the disclosure of abuse ultimately leads to divorce or imprisonment, the mother will find herself a single parent; she may not have employable skills or the earning power to support the family without a major change in lifestyle. Even when the family decides to work toward possible reunification, the victimizer is usually required to live apart from the rest of the family for an extended period of time. Maintaining two separate households places an enormous financial burden on the family.

Issues around loss usually extend beyond economic matters, however. The lost illusion of a happy, healthy family, for example, often leaves mothers shaken and contributes to their apparent immobilization. Loss of self-esteem, well-being, and safety heighten their sense of being overwhelmed. The potential loss of social status and support among friends and family serves to increase a sense of isolation. If the state places the child in foster care for a period of evaluation or because of concerns for her safety, this loss can cripple a mother. Her self-doubt increases, her opinion of her own efficacy plummets, and her sense of powerlessness escalates. A mother will adjust to these losses and potential losses based upon her interpretation of their severity and her own ability to cope.

If the victimizer denies the child's accusations of abuse and the mother has not been consciously aware of its existence, the mother must decide whom to believe: her husband, whom she loves and trusts; or her daughter, whom she loves and must protect. If the victimizer continues to stonewall, the mother must essentially toss a coin, for she has no way of knowing who is telling the truth.

On an emotional level, the mother will feel angry and betrayed because of her partner's breach of familial boundaries. This anger and pain can become overwhelming, especially if the acknowledgment of her child's victimization brings the mother's own previously repressed childhood victimization or neglect into awareness. A legacy of pain from remote or inconsistent parenting or from sexual abuse in their families of origin can become even more acute with the current disclosure. In an attempt to avoid her own overwhelming feelings of powerlessness and victimization, a mother may express anger toward, and attribute responsibility for the abuse to her daughter. Even if she avoids blaming her daughter, however, a mother will almost invariably feel confused, angry, and guilty about her daughter's inability to confide in her or to ask for her help.

The mother of an incest victim must also deal with the intense reactions of family members and friends to the disclosure. If the courts become involved, she must also deal with child-protective services, law enforcement, the judicial system, and even court-appointed therapists, all of whom have their own biases and agendas with regard to how to treat her and her family. Frequently, a mother will feel intensely angry at the agencies and institutions involved, because their power to make decisions that affect her family tends to increase her feelings of powerlessness.

The initial disclosure of incest creates a flurry of actions and emotional reactions. As a mother works her way through the immediate shock and trauma of what has happened, a flood of emotions will wash over her. Most of these feelings will at first focus upon the victim and the victimizer, with little or no thought given to her own feelings. With the aid of therapy, however, a mother will begin to confront her denial and work through her feelings.

Though many mothers feel a sense of responsibility for the sexual abuse because they did not protect their daughter (a notion often inadvertently reinforced by law-enforcement officers, child-protective agencies, and therapists), we have not treated many overtly complicit mothers. Mothers who actually collude with their incestuous partners are rare. Those who do, as Hagood (1991) notes, may avoid their perceptions by blacking out, leaving the home, or becoming suicidal. We believe that most mothers, however, remain, at least on a conscious level, unaware of the sexual abuse prior to disclosure.

Once the incestuous relationship has come to light, many mothers in fact take forceful action to protect their children from further abuse—actions sometimes overlooked by child-protective services or other workers who have the responsibility to protect the child from further harm. The failure of such agencies to acknowledge a mother's protective efforts intensifies her poor self-image and her eroded sense of self-sufficiency. At a time when support from the victim's mother could play a critical role in the child's eventual recovery, this failure serves only to magnify the distance between them.

As therapists, we must take care to avoid automatically blaming the mother for either allowing the incest to occur, or somehow colluding with the victimizer. We would do well to remember that *without the motivation to sexually abuse on the part of the victimizer, the incest would not have occurred.* Yet all too often, a mother gets little support from child-protective agencies, which blame her overtly or covertly for failing to act sooner or more forcefully. As therapists, we must recognize the impossible situation in which the mother finds herself, torn between her love for and allegiance to her husband and her love for and guardianship over her daughter. Without this recognition, we cannot provide the safe, nurturing environment that can become the foundation for the mother's healing.

A Daughter's Experience

A daughter who has been sexually abused by her father must deal with a host of complex issues, the betrayal of trust being the most obvious and paramount among them. However, as Jacobs notes in her 1990 article, the therapist should not ignore "the extent to which the mother becomes the focus for feelings of anger, hatred and betrayal [by] daughters who were abused by their fathers."

CASE 8-1

In her first session with us, Jenny, whose stepfather molested her for seven years, described her mother Ellen as stupid (see also Cases 1-1, 3-1, 4-1, 5-1, and 6-1). She insisted that her mother must have known what was going on. She expressed much more anger at her mother for letting the abuse happen than she did at her stepfather for inflicting the abuse.

Often this issue of anger and betrayal takes on added complexity because the daughter internalizes these feelings and begins to loathe herself. How much a particular incest victim internalizes these emotions may depend upon the degree to which the daughter identifies with the mother. Incest survivors who identify strongly with their mothers may come to "regard all women, including themselves, with contempt.... They identified with the mothers they despised and included themselves among the ranks of fallen and worthless women" (Jacobs, 1990).

The range of feelings that mothers and daughters experience can be conceptualized as existing along a continuum from overinvolvement to underinvolvement. If the mother and daughter have an enmeshed, extremely dependent relationship, the child may feel so responsible for her mother's feelings that she will try to hide the abuse for fear of hurting her (or even killing her, a fear victimizers often nurture and fuel with such statements as, "It would kill your mother to know"). Early in treatment, such an enmeshed daughter may not even be aware that she harbors any anger toward her mother. If confronted with this possibility in therapy, she will vehemently deny her anger. At the other end of the continuum, if the mother and daughter have a cold, distant relationship, the child may remain silent about the abuse afraid that she will not be believed. Or she may worry (and not always without justification) that *she* will be the person ostracized by the rest of the family. Which ever the case, the daughter may also fear that if she speaks out about the sexual abuse, she will break up the entire family constellation, thus adding to her burden of guilt (Hagood, 1991). Threats by the victimizer to do physical harm to her or others may also heighten the daughter's reluctance to disclose.

As mentioned earlier, the degree of maternal support provided to a daughter who has been sexually abused plays a critical role in determining the child's later adjustment. Children who do not receive support from adults upon whom they depend exhibit far more emotional disturbances than children who do receive support (Adams-Tucker, 1982). Regardless of the soundness of the mother-daughter bond, most victimized daughters, especially adult daughters, want to improve their relationships with their mothers. These victims seem innately to know that a healthy relationship with their mothers is a vital component of their recovery. Sadly, however, mothers and daughters seldom discuss their relationship or the incest because both are afraid of the pain and anguish that revolve around the incest. Unfortunately, the fear against which they are protecting themselves not only keeps them from dealing with the incest, but keeps them apart as well.

CASE 8-1 *(continued)*

While in individual therapy, Jenny continually expressed a desire to have some mother-daughter sessions and work on improving her communication with her mother. Shortly after the incest was disclosed, Ellen and Jenny had attempted some mother-daughter work. However, Ellen—feeling unsupported and criticized by the therapist and never establishing a connection with her—discontinued the sessions (although she maintained her involvement in family therapy, couples work with her husband, and a codependency group). About a year later, Ellen and Jenny again attempted mother-daughter sessions, some including Ellen's other two daughters, Rebecca and Brittany. Ellen once again demonstrated an inability to work on these relationships in therapy, this time citing financial difficulties as a reason for discontinuing the sessions. She also admitted to feeling "mother bashed," beat up by the process, as if she did not count as much as her husband, the offender. Besides, she insisted, "I can do it on my own." Clearly, Ellen had not done enough of her individual work at this stage of her recovery to begin looking at her relationships with her daughters.

In the year since this second attempt at mother-daughter therapy, Ellen has had several months of individual therapy. Jenny reports an increased feeling of support and better communication with her mother. Although they have not yet completed their mother-daughter work, their relationship has improved significantly. Ellen may soon show greater willingness to explore the incest itself in more depth and to do the work needed to improve her relationship with Jenny.

Virginia Strand (1990) has identified four characteristics that often manifest in victims of sexual trauma: sexual traumatization; stigmatization; betrayal; and powerlessness. The Strand model is important because she nicely demonstrates how the aforementioned dynamics manifest behaviorally in adults who were sexually abused as children. Not surprisingly, many of these behaviors are consistent with the experience of sex addicts who suffered from childhood sexual abuse. Addressing each of these characteristics is critical to the recovery of the incest victim. Throughout the course of mother-daughter therapy (as well as in individual therapy and in group therapy comprised solely of sexual-abuse survivors), the therapist must help the incest victim to deal with these issues.

Sexual traumatization refers to the inability to enjoy healthy sexual functioning because of the sexual nature of the trauma. This can include confusing sexuality with affection, negative emotional valences attached to sexual feelings, a tendency to form only erotic relationships, sexual dysfunctions, sex addictions, age-inappropriate sexual knowledge and experience (during childhood), and in some cases, the continuation of the cycle of sexual abuse.

Stigmatization indicates the tendency for incest survivors to blame themselves for the abuse, to feel shame or guilt and self-hatred. Often stigmatization manifests as low self-esteem and poor self-image. More severe manifestations include such self-injurious behaviors as self-mutilation, anorexia/bulimia, substance abuse, and suicidal ideation.

Betrayal refers to the shattering of trust experienced by daughters whose fathers have sexually abused them. This betrayal commonly has the result of inhibiting the formation of intimate relationships or other relationships in which trust is a major component.

Powerlessness describes the helplessness and vulnerability a child feels as the result of sexual abuse. As an adult, powerlessness can manifest in mood disorders, dissociative disorders, and personality disorders.

Betrayal and powerlessness, we believe, are intermingled issues. As Jacobs (1990) has observed, a child will often identify with the victimizer in an effort to retrieve that sense of power, and in so doing will develop sympathetic feelings for the abuser and hostility for the mother who not only failed to protect her, but also exhibits the same vulnerabilities and weaknesses that she does—the very things she believes led to victimization in the first place. Thus the sympathy shown toward the victimizer, though it serves to reduce some intrapsychic conflict, is not particularly genuine. The daughter also feels betrayed at a very deep level and as a result may not be able to develop trusting relationships with men. The entwined issues of powerlessness and betrayal leave the abused daughter in an isolated and lonely place, unable to trust men, and unable to get along with women, in whom she invests the same negative qualities she identifies in herself and her mother.

In addition to grasping the traumagenic dynamics addressed in Strand's model, the therapist must also demonstrate an understanding of boundaries in order to change the dysfunctional dynamics of the incestuous family system. Incest distorts or erases personal and familial boundaries. The incestuous family operates in an overly enmeshed fashion that subverts all individual autonomy in favor of a "group think" (or more specifically, a "family think") style that functions solely to preserve family secrets—in essence, a closed family system. In families like these, poor communication abounds. Family members rely heavily upon metacommunications and are overly attentive to nonverbal cues. Family members rarely express individual emotional states in a direct manner. The therapist will see these issues surface in mechanisms of repression, passive-aggressive behaviors, withdrawal, and irrational outbursts of fear and rage that serve to silence or cripple communication. This indirect method of addressing emotions and needs reinforces a kind of magical thinking. Family members assume they know exactly what the other members are thinking and therefore act without real knowledge of the actual needs and feelings being experienced.

As family members do not experience their own autonomy and personal identity, they often incorporate parts of other family members and suffer a kind of role confusion. For example, a father may use a child to bolster his own self-esteem or, as in the case of incestuous families, use a child to meet his own sexual needs. When this happens, what should be appropriate nurturing care from a parent becomes sexualized in an adult manner, setting the stage for the child's later confusion between sex and intimacy.

Often in such families, the child becomes parentified, allowing the mother to abdicate her responsibilities. The child finds herself in the role of surrogate spouse. Jenny (See Case 8-1), whose mother worked 60 hours a week outside the home, reports having taken over responsibility for many household chores—cooking, cleaning, taking care of her younger sisters—from the time she was ten or eleven years old. The therapist must appreciate this role confusion, because the child will need help in sorting out her own sense of identity and appropriate roles for her in order to develop healthy, intimate relationships as an adult.

TREATMENT FOR MOTHERS

We will not describe or summarize treatment methods here for sexually abused daughters, as they are well documented in the psychological literature and well known to practitioners working in the field. Much less has been written about treating the mothers of incest victims. We see this therapy—and particularly, the devotion of attention to the mother-daughter relationship—as an absolute necessity in the treatment of incestuous families.

Ideally, therapy for mothers of incest victims (as for the victims themselves) should begin as soon as possible after the initial disclosure of abuse. Some mothers who find themselves faced with news of a daughter's molestation refuse therapy, however, because they completely deny, both to themselves and to others, that the abuse ever happened. Indeed, some mothers will go so far as to urge their daughters to retract their allegations in an effort to make their problems disappear (Hagood, 1991). For if the daughter's allegations prove true, the mother's life becomes irreversibly altered.

The disclosure of incest forces a mother to endure drastic changes and adjustments, as other authors have detailed (Elbow & Mayfield, 1991; Hagood, 1991; Hewitt & Barnard, 1986). A therapist can help facilitate long-term changes and adjustments necessitated by more immediate concerns. Commonly, the mother finds herself in the position of providing the sole economic support for the family. The reality of suddenly becoming a single parent, with all of the concomitant responsibility, is monumental. The simultaneous loss of support and forced assumption of all family responsibilities can prove overwhelming. Furthermore, if her husband is imprisoned, the mother must make the difficult adjustment to being a prisoner's wife, with all its attendant stigmata.

When these immediate issues arise, a therapist needs a working knowledge of available community support systems: job-training and placement services, child-care services, support groups for single parents, and general assistance programs if appropriate. This is also a good time for a therapist to encourage mothers, when applicable, to get in touch with people and programs at her church. By addressing these practical, day-to-day needs in a therapeutic setting, the therapist provides a "holding environment," an essential component of treatment. By offering support and encouragement—and putting the mother in touch with others who can offer the same in addition to practical assistance—the therapist can often set the stage for her confrontation of the profound psychological issues brought to light by the disclosure of incest in the home.

The mother of an incest victim needs access to these sources of support because, as suggested earlier, social, legal, and even mental-health systems tend to attack a mother's defenses of denial without providing adequate emotional support for her dilemma. Yet as Hagood (1991) notes, it is "necessary for therapists to build the self-esteem of these women and to reflect belief in their ability to grow and change in order to dissipate their ongoing denial." If, in the early stages of treatment, the therapist begins to confront the mother without simultaneously offering support and encouragement, the mother's denial mechanisms will only strengthen and she will become more intransigent in the therapeutic setting. The initial treatment of mothers of incest victims must therefore focus on providing a source of nurturance and emotional support.

For this reason, we regard group therapy in groups comprised of mothers of sexually abused daughters as an essential treatment modality for any incestuous family. In these groups, a new member will find support from women who, not so long ago, went through the same or similar experiences. To hear other mothers tell stories of their disbelief, shock, pain, fear, and denial can be most therapeutic. "What helped me more than anything is the support groups," Ellen (See Case 8-1) acknowledges. "Other women with incest in the family. I find it easier to talk to other mothers with incest. If I had to pick just one thing, it has been the other female support [that has proved most helpful]."

Group therapy provides a useful distance between the mother and the therapist, whom she often perceives as a threatening figure. Mothers of incest victims, however, will not generally be as confrontational in group therapy as members of other groups. Most of the group members are involved in an ongoing crisis state of their own. Having often been abused in some way themselves, they manifest passivity and avoidance of confrontation. Most members also rely on denial as a habitual coping mechanism of their own. Such a group therefore demands the gentle ministrations of the therapist in order to move all members along in their therapy. The group format, in helping mothers to sustain one another during this time of crisis, does offer the opportunity for the therapist to prod them gently to move past their defense of denial. However, the group facilitator must walk a fine line: ensuring that all the mothers in the group feel safe and supported while at the same time providing gentle "care-fronting" to break through their denial systems.

In addition to offering an emotional support system, group therapy also serves a socializing function. Many mothers who face the revelation of incest in their families have, over many years, become extremely isolated. "Every friend or anyone that I would talk about at home, [my husband] would bad-mouth," recalls Ellen. "I fell for it. I don't feel like I ever really had any friendships...other than acquaintances at work.... I was working up to 60 hours a week." Demonstrating poor self-concepts and equally poor assertion skills, mothers of incest victims often become so focused on their partners that they end up socially isolated. Disclosure only tends to increase their feelings of isolation.

Most have had their husbands removed from the home in some fashion; they deeply feel the resulting loss of emotional and financial support. Isolated and confused, a mother often finds that group therapy fosters friendships among members and can sometimes generate social activities that take place outside the group setting.

Finally, group therapy also offers the opportunity for a mother to grow and become stronger on her own, away from the symbiotic relationships so common in incestuous families. Most mothers of incest victims have exhibited dependent behaviors in their primary relationships. They tend to serve as caretakers, over-nurturing their husbands, who often demonstrate passivity and abdicate responsibility in their relationships. This sort of mother or wife has been described as a "dependent person who seeks to ensure her sense of self through a symbiotic attachment to another.... The mother in the symbiotic [relationship] is unable to negotiate an appropriate middle ground between extreme dependency and extreme isolation" (Koch & Jarvis, 1987). Although the classic family setting in which incest occurs involves this kind of dependent-dependent relationship, Stern and Meyer (1980) note two other patterns that frequently occur in incestuous families. In the first, the possessive-passive, the father controls most aspects of family life and the mother submissively and passively acquiesces. The dependent-domineering relationship offers a mirror image of the possessive-passive one, with the husband virtually being ineffectual and the wife dominating. Despite the differences in the dynamics, all of these relationships can be characterized as symbiotic. Mothers in recovery need to begin forming relationships that will allow them to grow in a way that does not depend on another person's behavior, to break away from the symbiotic traits that typically characterize their family relationships. Group therapy nurtures these types of independent-independent relationships.

Once the mother feels safe and emotionally supported within the therapeutic context, the therapist can then begin to address, in both group and individual therapy, such defining issues as the disruption the mother feels in her family, her conflicting feelings about both her daughter(s) and her husband, and her guilt about what happened. The therapist needs to combine gentleness and firmness in confronting these issues, for mothers of incest victims frequently demonstrate a desire to avoid talking about the details of the abusive incident and their feelings about the abuse. Commonly, a mother will initially refuse to acknowledge her anger about the incest itself. During her first months of therapy, for example, Ellen directed much of her anger and energy toward her husband's parole officer and the intervention of court officials and social-service providers. This defensive diversion allowed Ellen to avoid dealing with her feelings about the incest. However, it also created an air of hostility and poor communication between her and the parole officer. This history of antagonism complicated the court-supervised process of reunification two years later. Such a dynamic is not uncommon among mothers of incest victims. Directing her anger toward the intervening agencies (or toward the therapist) supports the mother's defense of denial and, for a while at least, lessens the psychic pain she feels in relation to the incestuous incident.

The mother may also exhibit a similar reluctance to talk about her own sexuality. She may feel as if it were her own sexual inadequacies, her inability to satisfy her partner sexually, that "forced" him to turn to her daughter for gratification. The resulting sexual competition and jealousy toward her daughter, combined with the poignant awareness that her daughter has actually been victimized, often induces overwhelming feelings of guilt and inadequacy.

The mother may feel guilty about not having acted in some decisive manner to prevent her daughter(s) from being abused. In response, we point out that the mother did not wake up one morning and ask for her daughter to be molested. The bluntness of such an approach can help the mother put her sense of responsibility for the abuse into better perspective. This adjusted perspective will play a critical role in her recovery. For if the therapist fails to help the mother reframe her beliefs regarding her own culpability, the patient will find it impossible to move beyond self blame and recrimination to begin identifying the piece of the family puzzle that she actually does represent.

The fact that sexual abuse took place in her home, perhaps for many, many years, without her conscious knowledge, causes the mother to doubt her ability to judge situations and other people's intentions accurately. She feels confused and totally disoriented, as if she has awakened in a world entirely foreign to her. If, for example, she chooses to try and maintain a relationship with the victimizer, she must confront her self-doubt, questioning her judgment, dealing with concomitant guilt feelings, and exploring whether it is "normal" to attempt to hold onto such a relationship. Again, a group comprised of mothers of incest victims can offer a supportive environment that allows women to reexamine "their attitudes toward their husbands and daughters without having to defend their decision to remain in the marriage" (Hewitt & Barnard, 1986). If a group treatment setting is not available, supportive individual therapy can help lessen the mother's confusion about her situation, reduce her level of discomfort, and help her begin to form realistic assessments about herself, her husband, and her children.

The complexity of all the intermingling issues that the mother of an incest victim faces demands frequent treatment contact and multiple therapeutic techniques. In addition to standard, didactic individual sessions and supportive group therapy involving other women in similar situations, we have found that a wide variety of complementary modalities—including art therapy, role playing, assertiveness training, family-of-origin work (mapping and genograms), journaling, and gestalt techniques aimed at improving the client's functioning in the here and now—can facilitate the process of uncovering and resolving the difficult issues. And just as they would in any family in which a sexual dysfunction exists, the treatment modalities of marital, family, and family-of-origin sessions also contribute to a complete recovery of both mother and family. We also urge mothers of incest victims to join an appropriate 12-step support group, such as COSA (Co-Dependents of Sex Addicts) or S-Anon. Finally, we encourage these mothers to go on appropriate retreats, especially those that emphasize restoration and renewal. By taking advantage of all of the above techniques and modalities to address the multiplicity of issues in treatment, the therapist can elicit more assertive behaviors and help reduce dependency. These treatment gains can, in turn, free the mother to become more proactive in managing not only her own life, but her family responsibilities.

Countertransference Issues in the Treatment of Mothers

As suggested earlier, therapists who work with mothers of sexually abused children must guard against negative countertransference with these patients. Our culture tends to assign the duties of protecting the children to the primary caregiver—in most cases, the mother. Thus, "Mother blaming is, unfortunately, a common characteristic of our society and affects mental health professionals as well. It is therefore necessary for clinicians to analyze their own attitudes and emotional reactions to the mother in the incest family" (Strand, 1990). None of us escapes childhood unscathed; many of us are aware of the times when we did not get all the emotional support we needed as children. We must therefore take care to consider that much of the anger and disgust we feel toward the mother who comes to us for treatment may be a product of our own unconscious projection. Remember that if we treat the mother of an incest victim with disdain or hostility, she will react by strengthening her defenses, thereby diluting or even negating the impact of our therapeutic intervention.

The therapist's development of empathy for the mother will profoundly influence the therapeutic outcome. For if the mother can acknowledge the therapist's empathy, her feeling of being understood will lay the foundation upon which all subsequent therapy will be built.

TREATMENT OF THE MOTHER-DAUGHTER DYAD

In reviewing the published literature that speaks to the mother-daughter relationship (Giarretto, 1978; Horowitz, 1983; Jacobs, 1990; Koch & Jarvis, 1987), a single idea consistently stands out: Improving the mother-daughter bond is an essential strategy in treating incestuous families. The mother's involvement in therapy, both on a group and individual level and in sessions with her daughter(s), enhances the victim's adjustment and her ability to make use of the therapeutic intervention.

We believe that in most incest cases, the therapist should meet with mother and daughter together as soon as possible following disclosure. This initial contact should aim toward helping the mother move into a more protective and nurturing role in relation to her daughter, increasing each individual's feeling of self-efficacy, and beginning to foster an alliance between the two. The fears and negative feelings each has about herself and the other are powerful obstacles to recovery. Early sessions will need to address these obstacles in order to begin moving mother and daughter toward more open communication. Once their communication patterns have begun to improve, the therapist can then focus therapeutic energy on the themes of anger, powerlessness, separation, and individuation.

The mother often becomes the target for feelings of anger, betrayal, and even hatred by daughters who have been sexually abused (Jacobs, 1990). The incest victim tends to hold her mother accountable for allowing her to be sexually abused; she may be convinced that her mother knew about the incest and, by not stopping it, colluded in some manner with the victimizer. The daughter often believes she had long ago given her mother all the information she needed to alert her to the abusive situation. Unfortunately, the victim may have attempted to alert her mother in such a subtle way that the communication went virtually undetected after it had filtered through the mother's defenses. She may have felt caught in a double bind: To have been more direct in alerting family members to the abusive situation would most likely have thrown the family into a spiral of decompensation.

Mothers, of course, must deal with their own anger and confusion as well. In most cases of incest, the mother may have harbored negative feelings toward the daughter for some time prior to disclosure (sometimes actually predating the sexual abuse). The victimizing father may have taken advantage of the emotional and/or physical distance these feelings created between mother and daughter; indeed, if no distance existed, he may have attempted to create it in order to further groom the child for abuse. He may, for example, have lavished attention and affection upon the daughter, thereby increasing the child's dependency upon him and greatly decreasing the likelihood that she would tell her mother about the abuse.

CASE 8-1 *(continued)*

Ellen, a workaholic, spent 60 hours or more on the job every week, a schedule that created distance between her and her children. On the rare occasions when she took time off from work, Ellen says that Jenny and Rebecca would both be nasty and ask sarcastically, "What are you doing here?" When she got home after a 12-hour day, she would regularly drink five or six beers, making her even less present and available. David certainly exploited the distance between his wife Ellen and his stepdaughter Jenny in his abusive behaviors. He later admitted that he treated Jenny "better...in a sick way." He promised her a bicycle (although he never actually gave it to her) and generally set himself up as the "nice guy." He agreed, for example, not to tell her mother when Jenny got a bad grade on a report card, thereby increasing the split between Ellen and her daughter. David (an alcoholic himself) routinely encouraged the exhausted Ellen to drink after work, making it difficult for anyone to wake her later. Yet Jenny was told she had to awaken her parents when she came home at night. Her mother's heavy sleep left Jenny essentially alone with her abuser for the rest of the night.

The distance between a victimized daughter and her mother may also have been exploited by the victimizer to set the stage effectively for more coercive measures such as threats of suicide or homicide, punishment aimed at the child, threats of withdrawal of love from one or more parents, threats of expulsion from the family, or family dissolution. These methods of coercion had added impact because the child did not have sufficient confidence in her relationship with her mother to check the accuracy of such statements.

Incest increases the distance between mother and daughter, and disclosure may widen the gap farther. In the absence of therapeutic intervention, this gap may never close. Ann Ferguson (1984) describes incest situations as events that severely impair the mother-daughter bond by forcing the daughter's emotional involvement away from the mother. The resultant effect on the mother is twofold. Not only has her child turned against her, but she must also confront her husband's appalling betrayal of their relationship.

An important therapeutic task in treating the mother-daughter dyad involves helping the mother form a more realistic conception of her anger. Various cognitive distortions may have caused the mother to misperceive and misdirect her anger. As most (although not all) mothers who suffer a breach in their relationships with their daughters have experienced a similar disruption in their relationships with their own mothers, some mothers of incest victims may, for example, have unconsciously projected their feelings of acrimony for their mothers onto their daughters, eventually weakening the maternal bond (Brooks, 1983). The therapist must strive to bring this distortion to light as soon as possible, through the use of genograms and family-of-origin work, so that the mother may begin to separate her feelings about her relationship with her mother from her feelings about her daughter and their relationship.

In a gestalt role-playing session, Ellen participated in an empty-chair piece dealing with her own mother, whom she described as "controlling and cold." Ellen told her mother (the empty chair), "You were never there for me." She identified feeling hurt and angry at her mother's message: "I'm too busy for you. I don't love you." She then recognized that she stuffed these feelings and projected this hurt and anger on to her family. Afterward, she asserted, "I don't want to be like my mother: cold and distant. I open my arms to everyone." She became tearful, saying, "I'm being lost in everyone's needs." She acknowledged feeling overwhelmed when, at age 17, she became a mother, and she talked about the guilt she felt on hearing Jenny (her molested daughter) tell her, "You're never there for me."

By understanding her dysfunctional relationship with her own mother, the mother of an incest victim can work on freeing herself from perpetuating the old dysfunctional patterns in her relationship with her daughter. She can at last see her daughter as the person she really is: not a rival for her role as spouse and parent, but simply a child in need of protection and nurturing.

Once she has recognized her daughter as a child who needs parenting, the mother must begin to examine and improve her own parenting skills. Parents in general feel unsure about their own parenting abilities. These concerns become even more pronounced among women whose daughters have been sexually abused. In recovery, for example, a mother may find it very difficult to set appropriate and necessary limits with her abused child. Given the daughter's recent experiences with her father and the mother's intense feelings of guilt, the mother may want to avoid imposing any demands on the child that might increase the daughter's sense of powerlessness. Improving the mother's parenting skills (and her confidence in those skills) may take place in the context of individual therapy, group therapy, or through referrals to parenting classes in the community. Regardless of the specific treatment modality chosen, however, mothers of incest victims almost always need an education in issues of child development, appropriate consequences for misbehavior, and basic knowledge of the effects of reward and punishment on children.

Although this education can facilitate the process of establishing more appropriate roles for family members, resistance to change remains a powerful force in incestuous families well after recovery has begun. The daughter, for example, may not want to return to a more dependent state; indeed, she may actively resist all efforts to do so, confounding the process of redefining roles. She may challenge, actively or passively, her mother's right to parent, to discipline, or to impose limits on her (and her siblings) regardless of how reasonable and appropriate those limits and discipline may be.

CASE 8-1 (continued)

Less than four months after the family began seeing us for therapy, Jenny moved out of the house. She furiously rebelled against what Ellen insisted were the only two conditions she laid down: that she come home at night and that she help around the house. Ellen's attempt to resume parental responsibilities generated resistance for some time. A year later, in a family session, Rebecca reported that when the three sisters were together they got along fine and that she and Brittany got along with their mother when Jenny was not there. But when all four got together, tension and acting out erupted. Although the younger daughters were less articulate than Jenny, all three of the children clearly resented and resisted Ellen's attempts to change her role.

A lingering sense of betrayal, anger at the mother for her unavailability in the past, and deep abiding pain may prevent the victimized child from being receptive to her mother's attempts to take on appropriate parental responsibility. In families where the victimized daughter has also assumed a parenting role, her siblings may join her in rejecting their mother's attempts to discover a healthier parenting style. The other children may continue to turn to the incest victim for guidance and "parenting."

The therapist in such a case needs to help the mother to see this realistically, dispassionately, as a natural apprehension about the realignment of the family system, rather than as a personal attack or a rejection. This realistic perspective will help defuse her anger at her child(ren), thereby allowing her to remain engaged in the process of establishing a healthier family constellation and strengthening the maternal bond.

The growing bond between mothers and daughters in recovery will be undercut if they do not acknowledge and express their anger toward each other. Mothers and daughters in incestuous families often minimize or fail to deal directly with the anger they feel toward each other. In mother-daughter sessions, the therapist must allow and encourage the daughter to express her anger toward her mother, an experience that empowers the victim. At the same time, the therapist needs to support the mother, helping her to tolerate her daughter's anger without becoming defensive or trying to "fix" it. Once the daughter has externalized her angry feelings and the mother has (with the therapist's guidance) reframed her cognitive distortions, the therapist can focus on helping both of them arrive at a more accurate perception of the mother's role in the incestuous event. This realistic perspective will allow both mother and daughter to begin focusing their anger more appropriately on the victimizer and the way his behaviors have disrupted the family. As mother and daughter examine this family disruption and begin to see themselves and the roles they've adopted within the family in a new light, they will begin to move away from feelings of powerlessness and enmeshment with—or alienation and detachment from—each other. The new bond fostered by this therapeutic intervention can promote movement into healthier family roles; for example, the daughter may feel more comfortable moving back into a child's role and the mother will feel more confident moving into a parental role.

Because it usually carries with it a tremendous negative emotional charge, a discussion of the incestuous events, sexuality, and appropriate boundaries presents one of the most difficult treatment issues for mothers and daughters in therapy together. However, this discussion—because it paves the way for the development of healthy sexual boundaries the daughter will need in order to have healthy, satisfying sexual relationships—should not be avoided. Most parents, even in non-incestuous homes, avoid discussing issues of sexuality with children, because they feel uncomfortable about the subject ourselves or fear exposing children to ideas that they are not developmentally ready to hear. But in order to help repair the damage done to her daughter's sexual image, attitudes, and beliefs, the mother of an incest victim *must* talk about sexual issues with the victimized child (and often with her other children as well, especially those aware of the incest). The therapist can facilitate this discussion through the use of genograms, an examination of messages about sexuality passed on from generation to generation in the family, and input on female roles and boundary issues. Mothers and daughters seldom realize that the dynamics they experience in their sexual relationships result in part from a legacy inherited from their ancestors. By orchestrating these discussions within the therapeutic setting, the therapist can gear the dialogue to developmentally appropriate levels and language while at the same time managing the anxiety inherent in conversations about sex and sexuality.

For mothers and daughters in incestuous families, the successful negotiation of these therapeutic tasks can lay the groundwork for the emergence of a positive experience of being female. Each can acknowledge her own power, her own feelings, and her own uniqueness—as well as the power, feelings, and uniqueness of the other. This mutual respect and self-respect will allow the natural developmental process of separation and individuation to get back on track. The mother and daughter can, for the first time, offer nurturing support to each other, rather than remaining rivals in a competition that knows no winners.

9

The Victim-to-Victimizer Dynamic

Inner Child and Family-of-Origin

Therapies

Sex addicts who victimize others generally have a history of being victims of child abuse and neglect themselves (Carnes, 1983; Earle & Crow, 1989; Murray, 1991). The sex addicts we have treated have recalled a variety of traumas ranging from emotional and/or physical neglect or verbal abuse to sexual humiliation by clergy members, molestation, rape, or incest. Comprehensive treatment of the sex addict cannot regard this history as incidental. Sex addiction, especially among sex offenders, cannot be effectively treated through cognitive or behavioral therapies alone. We do not believe that attempts at cognitive restructuring and behavioral therapy aimed at eliminating the addict's sexual obsessions and compulsive sexual behaviors can succeed unless the pain associated with childhood trauma is considered seriously. In other words, both elements—the immediate behavioral problems and the root causes of those behaviors—must be explored for treatment to be effective.

Treating sex offenders is not for everyone. Some clinicians will find the work too intense, too draining. Others may have difficulty separating the person from his or her behavior: They may regard the crimes as so abhorrent that they cannot stand working so closely with the sex offender. Although we too view our patients' crimes as reprehensible, we do not see the individuals themselves as incorrigible. To exercise a positive influence on these patients, those who choose to work with sex offenders must demonstrate the proper attitude: The therapist must respect and value sex addicts as human beings despite their offenses. Because the issue of sexual abuse outrages all of us, the therapist must first work on his or her own issues associated with childhood trauma or neglect. True compassion for others requires that an individual first be in touch with his or her own pain. This axiom applies equally to both therapists and the victimizing patients they treat.

THE SCINDO SYNDROME MODEL

In helping sex addicts to deal with childhood trauma, to unearth and incorporate childhood trauma, to recognize and acknowledge the connection between past trauma and present behavior, and to understand their own progression from victim to victimizer, we usually introduce them to the concept of the Scindo Syndrome, a treatment model developed by our colleague and associate Marilyn Murray, author of *Prisoner of Another War* (1991). (In addition to seeing referrals from us to her private practice in California, Murray spends nine to 12 weeks a year in our offices doing intensive sessions with some of our patients.) According to the Scindo Syndrome model, childhood trauma and/or deprivation can result in:

- the death of the child;
- crossing over into a nonfunctioning unreality or psychosis; or
- survival through activation of a normal, innate defense mechanism that represses all or part of the memories and affect connected with the trauma or deprivation (Murray, 1985).

This common defense mechanism, which Murray terms a "scindo" (Latin for *split*) allows the child to remain physically alive and to function intellectually within reality. As this model suggests, a child who felt the full impact of the pain at the time might become psychotic or die. By repressing and feeling only a portion of the actual pain involved in a particular incident, however, the child survives the trauma or profound deprivation.

According to this model, the trauma-activated scindo results in the splitting of the personality into three parts:

- *The Sobbing Hurting Child:* This portion of the personality absorbs the pain and carries the affect and the memories connected with the trauma and/or deprivation.
- *The Controlling Child:* This portion of the personality, the innate emotional defense mechanism, takes over, protecting and helping the Sobbing Hurting Child to survive during times of trauma and/or deprivation by taking charge of repressing the memories, pain, and other affect associated with the particular incident.
- *The Original Feeling Child:* This portion of the personality represents the person the child was "born to be," the person the child was prior to the onset of trauma and/or deprivation—a whole, nonfragmented individual with emotions and feelings intact.

Under ideal conditions this partial or total repression, the scindo activated during the course of a traumatic event or profound deprivation, is only a *temporary* response, lasting just long enough to allow the child to survive the incident (just as a person in a car accident often experiences a physiological shock response that inhibits pain until some time after the accident). After the event has ended, the child who has the opportunity to cry and feel the appropriate feelings related to the trauma or deprivation event can own and reintegrate the split-off parts of self. Unfortunately, in many cases this release and reintegration is thwarted. If the child's caregiver(s) is the abuser; the child may have no one to whom (s)he can safely turn to release feelings and receive comfort. Even when the child's parents do not inflict the abuse themselves, they may discourage the expression of any powerful emotion: pain, sadness, anger, hurt. Or the child may be silenced because (s)he has absorbed the concept of stoicism and "strength" (i.e., not expressing emotions) that our culture promotes as the standard by which we should all live.

If the child's environment or family continues to be abusive, the scindo will be activated so often that repression of feelings becomes a conditioned, learned habit, as though the child were in a state of chronic shock. The Controlling Child's primary responsibility always lies in protecting the Sobbing Hurting Child from pain. Yet when the child continues to live in an abusive, dysfunctional environment, the Controlling Child becomes concerned primarily with *survival.* Because the abusive environment inflicts unbearable pain again and again, the Controlling Child can only protect the Sobbing Hurting Child by burying her or him. Sadly, this extreme repression not only buries the Sobbing Hurting Child's negative feelings (pain, anger, loneliness, rejection, etc.), but also the Original Feeling Child's ability to feel positive emotions (joy, love, spontaneity, etc.). The Controlling Child then attempts to stand alone, the sole unburied portion of the victim's personality.

However, the Sobbing Hurting Child, though repressed, has not disappeared altogether. Like a person buried alive, the Sobbing Hurting Child claws, pushes, and scratches, trying to get up and out so that his or her needs might finally be met. To hold down the pain of the Sobbing Hurting Child, the Controlling Child will implement many strategies. These strategies often include attempts to *anesthetize* (through food, alcohol, drugs, sex, etc.) or to *divert* (by directing attention to actions and performance—academics, athletics, work, altruism, perfectionism, and co-dependency). This struggle between the two parts corresponds to the repetitive cycle of numbing and intrusion other clinicians have observed in trauma survivors (Horowitz, 1976). The opposing efforts of the Sobbing Hurting Child to acknowledge the pain of trauma and of the Controlling Child to anesthetize and divert attention away from the pain of these muffled or silent screams may lead to a wide variety of psychological and/or physiological consequences, including compulsive behavior, depression, anxiety disorders, neuroses, affective disorders, multiple personality disorder, and various somatoform disorders.

VICTIM-TO-VICTIMIZER MODEL

In working with both juvenile and adult sex offenders in the Arizona prison system since 1983, Marilyn Murray has developed the following model of the progression from victim to victimizer, which we find useful in treating sex addicts who commit sexual offenses. As a survivor of childhood trauma grows into adulthood and no longer lives in an abusive and/or unresponsive environment, the Controlling Child no longer needs to repress the painful feelings connected with the trauma or deprivation. But by adulthood, repression of feelings has become an entrenched habit. In some cases, the Controlling Child only becomes stronger in adulthood, continuing to employ the outmoded tactics of repressing, anesthetizing, and diverting. Yet, as mentioned earlier, the Sobbing Hurting Child may leak out and begin to beg for attention. Despite being buried, the Sobbing Hurting Child still aches to get her or his needs met and feels as if, "No one is taking care of me." In reaction, the Controlling Child tries various strategies to keep the Sobbing Hurting Child's pain from surfacing. While the young child may choose relatively simple, benign defenses against pain such as immersion in play, withdrawal, eating chocolate chip cookies, escape into reading, as the child grows older, the Controlling Child runs out of options to control the pain. Many traumatized children then begin to turn to less appropriate—and more harmful—resources to divert and anesthetize, including alcohol, drugs, and sex. Turning to one or more of these resources eventually becomes a conditioned response. The addiction becomes an ingrained habit that takes on a life of its own, no longer requiring the surfacing pain of the Sobbing Hurting Child to set it off.

Among sex addicts, the Sobbing Hurting Child leaks out through compulsive sexual behavior. Why should sex addicts, so often victims of sexual abuse themselves, repeat the behavior (either blatantly or in disguised form) that traumatized them? As other clinicians have noted with regard to posttraumatic stress disorders, severe trauma commonly and naturally results in repetitions—consisting of flashbacks, intrusions, and reenactments—which represent the individual's attempt to complete or master his or her emotional response to the original stress (Horowitz, 1976).

Case 9-1

Arnie, an extremely overweight 28-year-old pedophile, was arrested for child molestation. In prison, intensive therapy helped Arnie get in touch with the fears and feelings of his Sobbing Hurting Child, the affect produced by being brutally sodomized at age four. Over the course of the next several months, Arnie's work with his primary therapist focused on dealing with some of the issues raised in intensive therapy. Arnie, who had sexually abused over a dozen preschoolers (children the same age he had been when he was raped), now describes his subsequent molestations as distorted attempts of the Sobbing Hurting Child to show the world: "This is me, this is me, this is what happened to me."

In order to work through the trauma successfully, the survivor must discharge or release the intense emotions that accompanied the trauma, the feelings relegated to the Sobbing Hurting Child. Yet the Controlling Child's attempts to protect the Sobbing Hurting Child by keeping her or him hidden interferes with completion, mastery, and working through the trauma. Whenever the Sobbing Hurting Child intrudes (through flashbacks or behaviors that repeat the trauma in disguised form), the Controlling Child attempts to anesthetize or divert, to block out these agonizing memories and affect. The Controlling Child's attempts to numb prevent grief from surfacing, thereby blocking resolution. Yet the Sobbing Hurting Child's intrusions do not move the survivor toward resolution or mastery either, because these distorted reenactments usually fail to link the associated emotions to their original traumatic source.

Compulsive sexual behavior thus becomes driven by both the Sobbing Hurting Child and the Controlling Child. The Sobbing Hurting Child may scream out to be noticed through sexual behavior: a repetition compulsion that signals the underlying trauma. Yet the Controlling Child may also turn to compulsive sexual behavior: as an anesthetic and diversion that overrides the power and the pain of the Sobbing Hurting Child. Most sex addicts discovered the power of sexuality very early in their lives. Though it may have been introduced in an abusive or inappropriate way, sexual behavior may have aroused the child too. In both childhood and adulthood it provides a release so powerful that it can (temporarily) push aside the traumatic affect. When the bottled-up pain of the Sobbing Hurting Child starts to burst through, the Controlling Child may turn repeatedly to masturbation or other sexual behaviors to deaden the pain of the Sobbing Hurting Child. The dual nature of this turn to sexual behaviors—as both a repetition of trauma and an escape from traumatic affect—launches the addictive cycle. As indicated earlier, however, this addictive cycle, which may begin very early in the addict's childhood, eventually takes on a life of its own, spinning out of the sex addict's control.

The apparent "mutuality of interest" served by sexual acting out causes the Sobbing Hurting Child and the Controlling Child to join forces. The Sobbing Hurting Child in effect issues an ultimatum to the Controlling Child, insisting on the Controlling Child's help: "*I've got to have my needs met and I'll do it any way I can, even if it hurts someone else!*" Chief among these needs for sex addicts are the need to master the trauma, the need to demonstrate the horrors done to the helpless child, and, due to persistent childhood loneliness and neglect, the need for intimacy (or even the illusion of intimacy, however fleeting). The Controlling Child, wanting to quiet the Sobbing Hurting Child's pain (and thereby silence the Sobbing Hurting Child), attempts to meet those needs while at the same time staving off traumatic affect.

When the Sobbing Hurting Child and the Controlling Child connect in this way, they form one or both of the following.

> *The Spoiled Selfish Child*: A sneaky, covert, revengeful, manipulative "game player," the Spoiled Selfish Child can be seductive. Guided by the grandiose beliefs that "I'm special" and "I deserve to have someone take care of me," the Spoiled Selfish Child is committed to doing whatever feels good at the moment.
>
> OR
>
> *The Angry Rebellious Child*: Overtly hostile and aggressive, the Angry Rebellious Child is demanding and blows up quickly. Characteristic statements made by the Angry Rebellious Child include: "Don't tell me what to do!", "I'll do it *my* way!", and "I don't give a ____ what *you* want!"

Both the Spoiled Selfish Child and the Angry Rebellious Child are stubborn and unreasonable. Both will do whatever they want even though they know the action will be *destructive* to themselves and/or other people. Their prevailing attitude toward their destructive behavior(s) could be summarized with the statement, "I know this is bad, but who gives a _____." Both will rationalize their behavior: They become victimizers, but still see themselves as victims. Both demonstrate an unwillingness to look at the consequences of their actions and refuse to take responsibility for their behavior, usually blaming other people or events.

Although a rapist reflects the attitude of a hostile Angry Rebellious Child, most sex addicts who commit sexual offenses typify the Spoiled Selfish Child. They engage in passive-aggressive behaviors, expressing their anger and seeking revenge in sneaky ways, perhaps through incest or other victimizing sexual behaviors. They demonstrate greater distortions in thinking than the Angry Rebellious Child. They will rationalize and justify in an attempt to convince themselves that what they are doing is okay. Yet whether or not sex addicts succeed in self-justification, their actions proclaim, "I want what I want and I want it *now!*"

Since childhood, many sex addicts have thus been torn by powerful, irresistible, and contrary needs. Due to their lingering scindos, they must attempt simultaneously to satisfy denied childhood needs and to squash those needs. This contradiction makes it impossible for either the Controlling Child or the Sobbing Hurting Child to meet his or her needs directly. The Controlling Child cannot completely bury the needs felt by the Sobbing Hurting Child; yet the Sobbing Hurting Child cannot fully satisfy needs that the Controlling Child denies. Unable to satisfy their needs directly, the Sobbing Hurting Child and the Controlling Child team up to satisfy them indirectly: through victimization of self and/or others.

TREATMENT GOALS

As childhood trauma so often plays a significant role in laying the groundwork for sex addiction, treatment of sex addicts must include a thorough examination of childhood issues and possible trauma. *The sex addict and the therapist must deal both with root causes (i.e., childhood trauma) and with immediate behavioral issues (i.e., compulsive sexuality, emotional withdrawal, poor communication) in order to promote full recovery.* If therapy focuses solely on the addictive behaviors without looking at root causes, the patient will merely be sent around the "addiction circle"—that is, the continuing need to anesthetize the Sobbing Hurting Child will result in the replacement of one compulsive behavior by another. Conversely, however, if therapy focuses solely on root causes and ignores the behavior, compulsive acts will continue. Learning the cause of the compulsive behavior does not in itself break the habit. Given that the addictive cycle may be set into motion by childhood trauma, but soon takes on a life of its own, the therapist must address both root causes and behavioral problems in order to arrest it.

The goal of what Marilyn Murray calls "restoration" therapy is the development of what she refers to as The "Feeling Adult" (Murray, 1985). The Feeling Adult functions as a healthy parent or the "chairman of the board": No matter how the various inner children are behaving, the Feeling Adult must take full and total responsibility for what's going on. This goal demands the creation of balance in the individual's life by integrating the three dissociated parts of self: the Original Feeling Child, the Sobbing Hurting Child, and the Controlling Child. The process aimed toward creating this balance and developing the Feeling Adult is threefold:

1. Restructuring the Controlling Child;
2. Releasing the Sobbing Hurting Child; and
3. Restoring the Original Feeling Child.

The primary objective of restoration therapy is not to destroy these three parts of self, but to pull them together—to fit these puzzle pieces together in a healthy way to form a whole, Feeling Adult. The therapist needs to help sex addicts and co-addicts to acknowledge that all three parts of self have value not only to the children, but to the adults they have become and to the adults they are now becoming.

This goal of integration, however, does not involve incorporating the Spoiled Selfish Child and the Angry Rebellious Child. The sex addict (or co-addict) in recovery needs to rid the self of the Spoiled Selfish Child and/or the Angry Rebellious Child, which represent inappropriate and unbalanced constellations of behavior and cognition produced by the Controlling Child and the Sobbing Hurting Child working together (in the absence of the Original Feeling Child). Among sex addicts, the Spoiled Selfish Child and/or the Angry Rebellious Child have become out of control, and have taken control over the person.

The Spoiled Selfish Child and the Angry Rebellious Child do not protect the individual; all of their defense mechanisms are aimed solely toward protecting the addictive behaviors.

In striving toward the goal of reintegrating the Controlling Child, the Sobbing Hurting Child, and the Original Feeling Child while eliminating the Spoiled Selfish Child and the Angry Rebellious Child, the sex addict needs to begin to look at childhood issues in order to see how the sex addiction was formed. The therapist should make sure that the patient understands that this reexamination should strive toward seeing their childhood realistically for the first time, toward seeing with understanding, not with blame. It will help the patient move away from the characteristically rigid thinking of sex addiction to see that childhood was neither "all-good" (the facade) nor "all-bad" (the trauma). We therefore encourage patients to rediscover not only the bad from their childhood, but the good as well.

The objective of such a reexamination is to increase the sex addict's understanding, not to cast blame. While looking at their own pain and the wrongs done to them, sex addicts may also, with the help of their therapist, begin to see their parents with a new sense of empathy and compassion. We may, for example, ask a sex addict to consider what his or her parents were like when (s)he was born. The sex addict needs to recognize that his or her parents were neither saints nor monsters, but rather humans who may have done the best they knew how. (This more realistic perspective also applies of course to the sex addict, who is neither the saint projected through facade nor the monster defined solely by compulsive sexually victimizing behaviors.) At the same time, it should be acknowledged that doing the best they could may not have been healthy for either themselves or their child.

Through reassessing their childhoods, sex addicts can develop a new understanding of both themselves and those close to them. In order to transform unhealthy functioning into healthy functioning, the addict must first grasp the full meaning of unhealthy behaviors: their origins, their often unacknowledged underlying purpose, and their consequences. Recognizing the impact of past experiences on present behavior allows and encourages the addict to break that bond with the past, to refuse to permit the past to continue determining present behaviors. Coming to terms with the past thus frees up and motivates the addict to change the present and the future by developing transformative skills and tools. By first acknowledging and examining, for example, the unhealthy functioning of the Spoiled Selfish Child and the Angry Rebellious Child—and understanding their gestation in reaction to childhood trauma—the addict (or co-addict) can then renounce these constellations of behaviors and attitudes. This lays the groundwork for an exploration of new options, the development of healthier ways of functioning.

The path to healing requires the integration and balancing of all three parts of the person: the Sobbing Hurting Child, the Original Feeling Child, and the Controlling Child. Perhaps the most difficult of the three to access is the Sobbing Hurting Child, the repository of all trauma-related pain. Due to the child's belief that bad things happen only to bad people, the Sobbing Hurting Child takes the blame for all the traumatic events in the individual's life. Sex addicts (and other patients who survived childhood trauma) often hate this part of themselves, which they regard as the bad child, the one who brought the trauma on him- or herself. (Much, if not all, of this process takes place on an unconscious level.) Blamed and reviled by the individual, the Sobbing Hurting Child thus provides the basis for the sex addict's persistent sense of worthlessness.

For this reason, incorporating this part of self is essential to the recovery of sex addicts. Sex addicts must recognize and embrace the Sobbing Hurting Child in order to realize that they are "not the trash, scum, and filth that they all perceived themselves to be..., that buried underneath that mound of trash was a valuable child" (Murray, 1991). Like other trauma survivors, sex addicts often react with amazement to find that there was *ever* anything good in them. And they find it even more amazing to have another person (the therapist) believe this even before they do. This is why therapists who work with compulsive sex offenders, as mentioned earlier in this chapter, must demonstrate the proper attitude. If the therapist cannot love, respect, and value sex addicts as human beings, how can (s)he hope to teach them how to love, respect, and value themselves? If the therapist can help the patient begin to see that Sobbing Hurting Child with the same compassion, empathy, and understanding that the therapist demonstrates, the individual will begin to acknowledge his or her own intrinsic worth.

The Sobbing Hurting Child does have a positive side, one that the recovering sex addict must integrate in order to come to terms with those damaged by his or her victimizing behaviors. The Sobbing Hurting Child provides the basis for empathy and compassion toward both self and others. By helping to increase the addict's empathy for the Sobbing Hurting Child within, the therapist will help build the foundation for increasing the individual's empathy toward the victims of his or her own compulsive sexual behavior. Without understanding their own pain and thus developing an ability to feel empathy and compassion for their victims, sex addicts will never truly understand the consequences of sexually victimizing compulsive behaviors. Owning the pain of childhood trauma, however, will heighten the addict's sensitivity to the defense mechanisms used (by others and by him- or herself) to ward off pain. Getting in touch with one's own personal pain thus makes all people, whether sex addicts or not, better spouses, better friends, better parents–and better therapists.

While helping sex addicts to recognize, accept, and integrate the traumas suffered by the Sobbing Hurting Child, the therapist should take care to balance this work with affirmative, positive therapy that will help bolster the patient during this difficult work. All too often, intensive therapy focuses solely on releasing the Sobbing Hurting Child, on unearthing, processing, and accepting the pain associated with childhood trauma or neglect. Unless properly balanced, this kind of intensive, often illusion-destroying experience can drown the adult with the child. However, if the therapist can take advantage of it, the sustaining force that patients need arises directly and naturally out of the work. In the process of unburying the Sobbing Hurting Child, the Original Feeling Child is also unearthed.

Murray envisions the core of the Original Feeling Child as the individual's spirituality, soul, or quest to know God. As AA and other 12-step groups have long recognized, true spirituality can provide powerful sustenance during the difficult periods of recovery from addiction. Before beginning any intensive therapy designed to overcome a sex addict's (or co-addict's) Scindo Syndrome, the therapist should therefore let the patient know that the process will involve a rediscovery of joy as well as pain. Patients need to know that while uncovering the Sobbing Hurting Child, they will also reconnect with the Original Feeling Child, the child they were created to be. The knowledge that they will retrieve the good inside them, that they will connect with the Original Feeling Child's creativity, talents, spontaneity, and joy–qualities that have been greatly hampered since the onset of trauma—will help sustain the sex addict in the difficult work ahead. And knowing that the only lasting way to get to this Original Feeling Child is to deal first with the Sobbing Hurting Child will help motivate them to undertake this painful work.

The way to get to both the Sobbing Hurting Child and the Original Feeling Child is to convince the Controlling Child that it is safe to let down the defense mechanisms and facades that have protected the individual for so long. The primary function of the Controlling Child has long been to *anesthetize and divert* attention from the trauma and from the Sobbing Hurting Child (as well as the Original Feeling Child). Although intensive therapy aims at getting the Controlling Child to relinquish this function, the goal is not to eliminate or remove the Controlling Child part of the patient, but merely to restructure it and integrate it. Like the Sobbing Hurting Child and the Original Feeling Child, the Controlling Child has an integral role in the psyche of a whole, balanced adult.

The Controlling Child protects the individual from harm. Indeed, without the strength and resiliency demonstrated by the Controlling Child, the sex addict might not have survived childhood trauma at all. To escape what Steven J. Wolin and Sybil Wolin have called the "victim trap"—the posture of endless victimization that plays such an integral part in the addictive cycle—survivors of childhood trauma need to "step back from [themselves] far enough so that [their] injuries diminish within a bigger picture that also includes [their] strengths" (Wolin & Wolin, 1993). Therapists thus need to help sex addicts to appreciate the Controlling Child's efforts, to reframe these survival strategies as signs of resiliency, as attempts to use a child's limited resources to take care of the children they once were. While encouraging patients to appreciate the protective function of the Controlling Child, the therapist also needs to help the addict in recovery to discover and add new strategies to the Controlling Child's repertoire. By encouraging patients to look at the Controlling Child and what (s)he did, both as a child and as an adult, to push down the Sobbing Hurting Child (e.g., maintaining the facade of the perfect child, becoming a workaholic, anesthesizing through alcohol, eating, or sexual behaviors), the therapist can help them see that they need to assign the Controlling Child a new role. Although still protective in nature, the Controlling Child's new function could involve such important elements of recovery as taking re-sponsibility for the addict's actions and setting healthy boundaries that will keep the patient from being victimized or from victimizing others.

Therapy aimed at acknowledging and integrating all three parts pro-duced by trauma-activated or deprivation-induced scindos will help the individual develop balance and integrity both internally and exter-nally. With the three parts of self restored and reintegrated, the sex addict has the opportunity to develop, with the help and training of the therapist, into a Feeling Adult. By bringing together the strength and responsibility of the Controlling Child, the empathy and sensitivity of the Sobbing Hurting Child, and the creativity and spirit of the Original Feeling Child, the sex addict in recovery can begin making the out-ward, behavioral changes that reflect the new internal balance. The dissonance between the projected external image and the internal self-image, the dissonance that helped fuel and was then furthered by the addictive cycle, will thus become less and less pronounced as the work of therapy continues.

THE COURSE OF INTENSIVE THERAPY

In her work with our patients, both sex addicts (about a quarter of our practice) and non-addicts, Marilyn Murray does intensive therapy aimed at resolving childhood trauma. She generally sees only two pa-tients a week: one all morning (i.e., four back-to-back sessions), the other all afternoon (again four straight sessions), for a minimum of five days. Murray has found this bulk of uninterrupted time to be critical for expediting therapy dealing with profound childhood issues. The defense mechanisms associated with a sex addict's (or other patient's) childhood trauma are often too strong to break down in just an hour or even 90 minutes. Indeed, with some patients, it takes a week just to get through these defense mechanisms and allow them the possibility to feel anything related to their childhood traumatization. The length of these sessions also allows patients to withdraw more fully from outside concerns and stressors, thus facilitating therapy by allowing the patient to focus undistracted attention on childhood issues.

We do not incorporate this kind of intensive therapy in the treat-ment of every sex addict. Some do not require it because their defense mechanisms have already begun to crumble through individual and group therapy. Others find such therapy difficult to arrange due to logistical demands, insurance coverage, or other financial considerations. However, even when exploring childhood trauma within the context of individual therapy sessions, we still use the Scindo-Syndrome model and pursue similar treatment goals: restructuring the Controlling Child, connecting with the Sobbing Hurting Child, and reclaiming the Original Feeling Child.

Murray prepares for intensive therapy sessions by becoming completely up-to-date with the primary therapist and familiarizing herself with all test results prior to the first session. She devotes most of this session to taking a detailed case history of the individual. Therapists should keep in mind that it takes very little to traumatize a vulnerable child. A single sentence from a parent spoken at a particularly vulnerable time can traumatize a child. The therapist should, therefore, try to accumulate as much detail about the patient's childhood as possible. For example, a common factor among sex addicts is an extremely lonely, isolated childhood. The family history may reveal that the patient was an only child, or much older or younger than his or her siblings. Left alone at home a great deal, the child often learned to soothe and nurture him- or herself through masturbation.

In addition to information considered standard in taking a family history (e.g., parents, grandparents, siblings, work and education history, religious and ethnic background, medical or mental-health problems, substance abuse), the therapist should also explore the history of interpersonal dynamics in the family. The therapist may ask, for example, how the addict's parents were disciplined and how (s)he would characterize and describe his or her parents' (and grandparents') marriage. Certain pieces of information should be regarded as "red flags." For example, a parent with a full-time military career often indicates a highly regimented and rigid home life. Or learning that a patient's grandparents divorced (since divorce was so much rarer two generations ago) should generally prompt the therapist to dig a little deeper: What was the reason for the divorce? The answer will often point to a larger problem such as alcoholism or multiple affairs.

After compiling a family history, the therapist then needs to take a sexual history. In asking questions about sexuality, the therapist should ask open-ended questions that assume certain sexual experiences. For instance, the therapist will get further by asking, "When did you first masturbate?" rather than "Have you ever masturbated?" Similarly, a question like, "Were you ever sexually abused?" will usually elicit a negative response from a sex addict, in part due to the Controlling Child's defense mechanisms and in part due to the fact that most sex addicts never characterized their early sexual experiences as abuse. Children who are sexually abused, especially boys, are often brainwashed by their abusers, their peers, and the culture in general to believe that they were not being abused, but rather being given an advantage over other children: an early sexual education or a special pleasure denied to most children. For this reason, an open invitation like, "Tell me about your first sexual experiences" will prove much more effective than more pointed questions about abuse. Although they themselves might not characterize their experience as abusive, most sex addicts had the door to sexuality opened early in life. As a result, sexuality became a focus of their lives at a very young age, long before their psyches were equipped to handle it.

After taking the patient's personal, family, case, and sexual histories, Murray introduces patients to the concepts of the scindo syndrome, the trauma-induced split into the Original Feeling Child, the Sobbing Hurting Child, and the Controlling Child, and the goal of developing the Feeling Adult. On the very first day, patients begin receiving homework assignments that will help them to begin thinking in terms of recognizing and integrating the Original Feeling Child, the Sobbing Hurting Child, the Controlling Child, and the Feeling Adult. For example, a patient will usually be asked to keep a journal from each of the four perspectives. The exercise begins with a list of the patient's primary concerns (in the present). Then the patient will write about each of these issues from the perspectives of the Controlling Child, the Sobbing Hurting Child, and the Original Feeling Child. After acknowledging and validating the concerns of the three children, the Feeling Adult is then responsible for resolving the issue. This exercise not only increases patients' awareness of the parts of self, but also introduces a new skill that they will be able to use in real-life situations immediately: It teaches them how to bring every aspect of their being to bear in determining how to handle the issues in their lives. Many of the homework assignments given during such a series of therapy sessions are aimed at developing similar coping and decision-making skills that the patient can use right away.

Most of the remaining half-day sessions are spent exploring and dealing with childhood issues primarily. The therapist's role here involves providing a safe place and time for the patient's memories and feelings to emerge and then to talk about them. These unconscious memories may be mental, emotional, or physical. Although memories can therefore come out at a very cognitive level, they may alternatively involve deeply profound feelings or center on bodily sensations.

CASE 9-1 (*continued*)

Arnie, the child molester described earlier, met with Marilyn Murray in prison. In a single session that lasted several hours, the therapist asked him to tell her everything he could about his family background. Arnie described growing up isolated in a small town, the only child of an alcoholic mother who was seldom at home. Learning that his father had left the family when Arnie was still a toddler, the therapist asked whether there had been any male figures in his childhood. Arnie mentioned that his mother took in a boarder who lived over the garage, a man who sometimes baby-sat for him. Yet despite the initial casualness of his tone, the therapist noticed that while talking about this man, Arnie started to go into a spontaneous regression: a flashback to earlier perceptions, sensations, and feelings. His voice turned childlike as he announced, "I don't like that man." His body began flinching and twisting. In a very small voice, Arnie, who said he was four years old, insisted he had to go to the bathroom. "It hurts really bad, there's blood." Asked why he was bleeding, Arnie went back even further. Suddenly his body started writhing: He said he was lying face down on the bed as his baby-sitter, the boarder, sodomized him. "It hurts so bad," Arnie screamed. "Why are you doing this to me?" As he came back up, slowly returning to the present, he realized that he hadn't told anyone about the rape because the boarder had threatened to kill him. For the first time since that traumatic incident, he had broken through the

Controlling Child's repression and given a voice to that Sobbing Hurting Child.

In recent years, some psychologists (and other interested parties) have begun to question the validity of such recovered memories. False Memory Syndrome (FMS), the belief that a visualization of the past is true even when objective evidence proves it to be false, can so strongly influence an individual's personality that it adversely effects interpersonal relationships. The therapist who explores a sex addict's memories of childhood should take extreme care to remember that not all memories can be trusted. Indeed, as researchers on memory have demonstrated, the faculty can be quite fallible: "Under ordinary circumstances, memory probably represents some combination of judgments, interpretations, and theories about given events and the retrieval of original information" (Lynn & Nash, 1994). Such factors as the cognitive level of development at the time, previous experiences that seem related and may therefore influence the interpretation of that new experience, verbal processing, and states of fear and dissociation may all influence the way people remember an experience. In addition, after the event has become a memory, "new postevent information often becomes incorporated into memory, supplementing and altering a person's recollection" (Loftus, 1993). Memories retrieved through hypnosis may be particularly unreliable. "Recollections obtained during hypnosis can involve confabulations and pseudomemories and not only fail to be more accurate, but actually appear to be less reliable than nonhypnotic recall" (The Council on Scientific Affairs, 1985).

False Memory Syndrome often has its roots in overzealous attempts by the client, the therapist, or both to recover repressed memories. The conviction that repression is a common phenomenon has enormous potential impact in the therapeutic setting. A therapist who, for example, ascribes to the theory that the inability to recall childhood events implies a history of sexual abuse may convey this belief to the client, who in turn may apply the theory and "invent" stories of abuse to fit the formula and thereby please the therapist. Such a belief—whether shared by therapist and client or transmitted from therapist to client—may also promote the transformation of an "innocuous true memory...into an emotionally loaded memory that will be the springboard to a narrative of abuse" (Lynn & Nash, 1994). Patients who demonstrate sex addiction (or any of a host of other current difficulties or disorders) may reap certain psychological rewards from "recovered" memories that confirm their belief in their own victimization. "Creating a fantasy of abuse with its relatively clear-cut distinction between good and evil may provide the needed logical explanation for confusing experiences and feelings" (Loftus, 1993). Finally, "clients may achieve considerable secondary gains from 'abuse memories,' not only in terms of such memories providing a plausible interpretation or explanation of their current plight, but also in terms of their everyday relationships" (Lynn & Nash, 1994).

Although we recognize the fallibility of memory and agree with the cautionary note that patients can reap secondary gains from recovered memories of abuse, we believe that repression of traumatic memories can and does occur. In our own practice, we have seen many patients verify memories recovered in the process of therapy. At the same time, however, we believe that therapists have a responsibility to inform patients that memories more accurately reflect past perceptions than they do objective reality.

To guard against False Memory Syndrome, we employ a number of different strategies. First, to ensure that whatever comes out springs from the patient rather than from the therapist, we avoid using any leading questions. In encouraging the patient to provide experiential details, we use as nonspecific language as possible. For example, we ask such questions as: "Where are you?", "What's happening?", "How old are you?", and "Who is with you?" Second, we try to downplay questions of whether or not what the patient remembers really happened. We do encourage clients, when possible, to verify the veracity of any "recovered" memories. Patients can elicit the memories of other family members as well as friends from that period of their lives. In addition, they can obtain and examine family, school, medical, insurance, psychological, and criminal records. If a memory cannot be verified, the therapist needs to stress the importance of moving on to other information from the patient's personal history, especially information where veracity is not in doubt.

We also adhere to the course laid out by addiction therapist Carol Ross, who has compiled a useful list of recommendations that will help therapists avoid soliciting or eliciting false memories from clients: (1)Therapists should avoid suggesting the possibility of sexual abuse (except in the context of initial assessment, where sexual abuse is just one of many areas explored in taking a personal history) unless patients have already mentioned it themselves; (2) Therapists should "resist the temptation to quickly jump to the conclusion that clients were overtly sexually abused simply because it is plausible" (Ross, 1994). As an example, Ross questions the conclusion that blocked childhood memory invariably indicates a history of abuse; (3) Ross recommends that therapists create a therapeutic milieu in which patients are encouraged to learn "to live with the unknown or the unprovable." As indicated, therapists should also avoid the use of leading questions and not accept as fact memories obtained through hypnosis: "Treat images created in hypnosis as symbolic, not actual facts" (Ross, 1994); (4) "When clients ask your opinion on whether or not their specific memories really happened, a caring response would be, 'I wasn't there when you were five, I don't know. But I am here now and I see/hear that you _____'" (Ross, 1994); (5) Therapists' notes should reflect that these memories represent the patient's perceptions—"X reports that he was sexually abused" rather than "X was sexually abused;" (6) Ross urges therapists to focus not on the *fact* of abuse, but the *perceived effect* of abuse, concentrating on treating "residual traumatic effects" rather than on determining whether or not the memory actually happened (Ross, 1994).

We view this last recommendation as particularly critical. As our patients can rarely offer any substantive proof that what they remember really happened, we try instead to focus the patient on the importance of what the child was *feeling*. This focus on feelings experienced during trauma not only paves the way for integration of dissociated emotions, but also lays the groundwork for the development of genuine victim empathy. What the child *perceives* as happening, rather than what actually happens, does the most profound damage to the psyche. Patients should therefore be cautioned that what they perceive may not necessarily be true. Pinpointing the nature of the trauma itself is not nearly as critical to recovery as releasing and resolving the repressed feelings associated with that trauma. As our colleague has written:

> The actual Trauma itself is damaging, but if the victim is allowed immediate release of the emotions connected with the Trauma; can feel protection and comfort; and, if needed, is provided therapy within a short time...the LONG-term psychological and

physiological pathology will be minimal. *It is the REPRESSION of the emotions connected with the Trauma that causes the greatest LONG-term damage.* (Murray, 1985)

While exploring childhood issues, the therapist should maintain the patient's focus on moving toward integration and adult responsibility. Patients reexperiencing childhood perceptions should always keep one foot firmly planted in the present, adult consciousness. They need to remain aware that they are in the safety of the therapist's office. To maintain this foothold in the present and focus on integration, we often call upon the adult part of a patient to care for the Sobbing Hurting Child. In dealing with the unconscious, we will simultaneously and repeatedly stress the competence and capability of the adult patient. We offer words of support to our patients, for example, saying, "You can do this" (i.e., take care of the Sobbing Hurting Child).

Before ending any session that involves dealing with childhood memories and feelings, it is the therapist's responsibility to make sure the patient is in a good place. This work can be exhausting, shattering, draining, and extremely painful. However, the therapist must see that his or her patients feel relatively secure and stable before telling them that their time is up for the day.

Such intensive therapy often prompts flashbacks—intrusions of childhood perceptions and feelings (not necessarily of childhood events) into present-day consciousness. Flashbacks may occur outside as well as inside the therapist's office. Therefore, the therapist should immediately help the patient plan for "unsupervised" floods of perceptions, sensations, or feelings. With the therapist's help, the patient needs to begin exploring available options to "dump" the Sobbing Hurting Child. This does not mean ridding oneself of the Sobbing Hurting Child, but rather releasing the fears and feelings in safer, more constructive ways that do not victimize self or others. Most sex addicts have never even considered that they may have options other than the escape into compulsive behaviors. But the therapist can help suggest alternatives: writing, drawing, poetry, books, support groups. Indeed, we stress that sex addicts have so many avenues available to them that there is really no excuse to avoid dealing with these issues.

Discovering other ways to deal with the Sobbing Hurting Child will not only better allow recovering sex addicts to take care of themselves, it will help reinforce the often difficult issue of boundaries between patient and therapist. The therapist should avoid becoming the sole member of the sex addict's support system, in other words, the patient's caretaker. This type of therapy does by necessity involve an intense relationship between patient and therapist, but the therapist needs to do all (s)he can to discourage the patient's dependency. This means limiting when the therapist will take phone calls from patients, insisting that patients involved in intensive therapy participate in at least one group, and encouraging patients to contact friends and/or group members between sessions.

Again, some homework assignments developed by Murray help drive home the point that sex addicts undergoing this type of intensive therapy need to explore new ways of expression to deal with the emergence of the Sobbing Hurting Child. (We use the following exercises not only in the context of intensive therapy sessions, but with almost all of our sexually addicted patients.) We may, for example, encourage a sex addict to draw a picture of the Sobbing Hurting Child, then place words or symbols around the picture to indicate what the Sobbing Hurting Child feels. In the subsequent session, when patients talk about the exercise, most start to cry. Because this exercise brings those long-hidden feelings up and out and gives them a form and a face, it can rapidly advance the process of healing.

From the beginning, homework assignments should also encourage the sex addict (or co-addict) to get in touch with the Original Feeling Child. We may ask a patient (with the obvious exception of one whose obsessions or compulsions include child molestation) to go to a park or to the beach, observe a four- or five-year-old child who looks like (s)he did as a child, and notice how the child behaves. This exercise can help the patient to acknowledge and appreciate the child (s)he was created to be–the Original Feeling Child. We may ask the addict to draw the Original Feeling Child as (s)he *would* have looked given a different childhood. Or we may ask the patient to consider the following question: If time and money were no object, what would the Original Feeling Child want to be (i.e., qualities, traits) and do (i.e., activities, deeds)? Always, we encourage our patients–whether sex addicts or not–to put the Original Feeling Child's spontaneity, creativity, and talent to use in the service of healing.

We also use homework assignments and session time to begin looking at the Controlling Child and how (s)he functions. The Controlling

Child has no doubt made use of a wide range of possible anesthetics and diversions, only some of which are victimizing behaviors. While helping patients to examine how they victimize themselves and others, we simultaneously assist them in evaluating which of the Controlling Child's anesthetizing behaviors and diversions are appropriate and which are inappropriate.

CASE 9-2

Bess, who allowed her sex-addicted husband to talk her into joining in on some of his compulsive sexual behaviors (see also Case 7-2), came to us for treatment of her codependency. When asked to portray the ways in which her Controlling Child dealt with the Sobbing Hurting Child, Bess produced the drawing represented in Figure 9-1. Using tears to represent the Sobbing Hurting Child and Band-Aids to demonstrate the strategies of the Controlling Child, Bess was able to see for the first time that the Controlling Child could act in positive as well as negative ways. The exercise helped Bess focus on eliminating her unhealthy coping strategies (at the bottom of the illustration), while turning more to the positive strategies (at the top).

Like most addicts and co-addicts, Bess had a wide repertoire of coping strategies from which the Controlling Child could choose in order to deal with the pain of the Sobbing Hurting Child. Some (talk, pray, journal, laugh) were appropriate, constructive, and healthy; others (isolating, eating, wearing a mask, codependent attachments) were inappropriate and self-destructive. Yet until she did this exercise, she never realized the number of options available to her Controlling Child. By helping to bring to consciousness the extensive repertoire of coping strategies available, the therapist can assist the patient in beginning to make informed, aware *choices* about what to do when in pain. Having it all laid out in front of them allows addicts and co-addicts to identify the behaviors they want to eliminate and those they want simply to modify.

The bulk of intensive therapy is aimed at healing the scindo created as a result of childhood trauma or neglect. After releasing the Sobbing

Figure 9.1. Bess's Drawing.

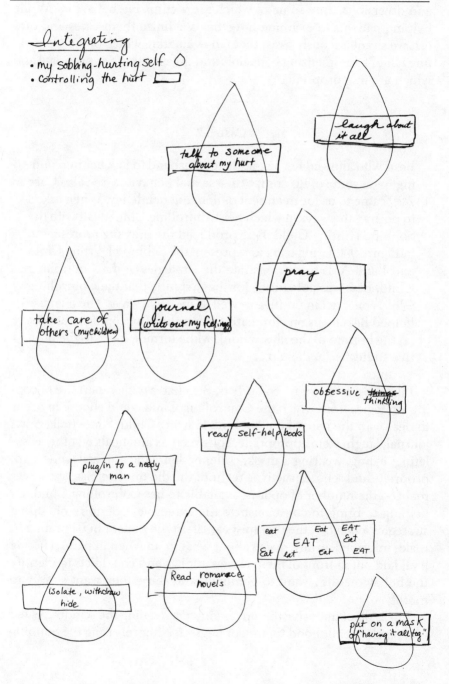

Integrating
- my sobbing-hurting self ○
- controlling the hurt ▭

talk to someone about my hurt

laugh about it all

pray

take care of others (my children)

journal (write out my feelings)

obsessive ~~things~~ thinking

read self-help books

plug in to a needy man

eat Eat EAT EAT EAT Eat eat Eat eat Eat EAT

isolate, withdraw hide

Read romance novels

put on a mask of "having it all tog"

Hurting Child, restoring the Original Feeling Child, and restructuring the Controlling Child, the final day of therapy is devoted to bringing in any significant other(s) whom the patient wants to involve. This may entail meeting with the patient and his or her spouse or partner, parents, siblings, and/or children. During this final session, the patient (with the aid of the therapist) summarizes for the significant other(s) the work done in intensive therapy. The patient also shares with the significant other(s) all homework assignments, a clear and powerful means of communicating experience and furthering the other person's understanding. When a spouse is involved, the therapist helps the patient and spouse recognize the issues that they will need to work on both individually and together.

Case 9-3

After almost three weeks of intensive therapy, William, a sex addict who had engaged in numerous affairs with both men and women throughout his marriage (see Case 7-3), had made enormous strides toward recovery. As the sessions drew to a close, he and his wife Tina faced a major issue: What do we tell the kids? William wanted to come clean and decided to tell all six of his children at the same time. He adopted this strategy for two reasons: He wanted to treat his addiction and recovery as a family issue; and he couldn't bear to go through it more than once. On the last day of the three-week intensive, the entire family—six children, all now adults except the youngest, who was 16, and four spouses—flew into Phoenix for the final session with Marilyn Murray and Ralph Earle as cotherapists. In the previous day's session, William had gone over again and again what he would say to his family. Despite 40 years of compulsive behaviors, he suspected (rightly so, as it turned out) that none of the kids had any clue whatsoever about his sex addiction. Tina, who had fallen apart after William's confession seven years earlier, was seen as the family problem; William was regarded as perfect, the glue that held the family together.

After hearing his shocking confession, each child had the opportunity to say what (s)he felt or thought. Wayne, the oldest, was

furious that his father had remained silent, offering neither support nor compassion, when Wayne had confessed his own compulsive behaviors (alcohol and other drug abuse, sexual affairs)
years earlier. Leslie was angry that she had felt guilty and ashamed
of betraying her family's values when she had had sex with her
fianceé prior to their marriage. Those who had become parents
themselves expressed concern for their own children. (Both therapists at this point reassured the adult children that since William's
sexual behavior had involved only adults, they felt he posed no
danger to his grandchildren.) What seemed to make the children
most angry was not so much their father's behaviors or his hypoc-
risy (although these did shock and enrage them), but rather that
he had let their mother take the rap for his problem for over seven
years, that he had allowed everyone to think she was unstable
and emotionally overwrought while maintaining his own upstand-
ing image. By the end of the day, the children had newfound
respect for their mother and—despite their shock, horror, and
anger—a renewed respect for their father for taking on the monu-
mentally difficult task of finally being honest with them. By role-
modeling positive change and increased intimacy, William and
Tina had set a powerful example for everyone in the family: Less
than three months after this family meeting, four of their children
and one of their in-laws had undergone intensive therapy as well.

The support of significant others can be an important ingredient in
the recovery of sex addicts. With their support and the insights, techniques, and integration acquired through intensive therapy, the patient can then begin the difficult, lifelong journey toward creating balance and developing a Feeling Adult.

The guiding philosophy of this kind of intensive therapy can be
summed up using the metaphor of the body's healing of physical
wounds. We believe that childhood trauma can create a wound not
unlike an infected physical wound: It needs to be lanced in order to
heal properly, but scraping it repeatedly will impede healing. This does
not mean that one or two weeks of intensive therapy will take care of
all childhood (or adult) issues and their intrusion into current affairs.
However, breaking through the sex addict's defenses, accessing traumatic affect, and emphasizing integration of the various parts of the

person will get the ball rolling, allowing much more rapid healing. Intensive therapy offers recovering sex addicts some skills, tools, and vernacular that will allow them to continue the work of recovery with their primary therapist.

Again, finally dealing with childhood issues is *not* the complete cure for sex addicts, especially those who have committed sexual offenses. The therapist needs to help the patient look both at childhood issues (part of *why* I do what I do now) and at current, adult responsibilities (this *is* what I do now, and I cannot continue to do it). Whether this work on childhood issues is done in intensive therapy sessions or in scheduled individual therapy sessions, helping sex addicts who have victimized others to get in touch with their own pain will provide the foundation for the building of victim empathy. And understanding the enormity of the pain they have inflicted on others provides a powerful motivation to stop the cycle of victimization once and for all.

As our colleague has written:

It is my belief that we will finally begin to break the chain of abuse..., when we are able to look within the abuser and find the abused, to find out why a child turns from victim to victimizer, to understand that offenders don't 'just happen,' and to believe that change *is* possible for many offenders–if therapy is provided by qualified, caring professionals, and if the offender is willing to take responsibility for his or her past actions and is willing to face his or her own pain as the process of change takes place. (Murray, 1991)

10

Relapse-Prevention Strategies

Interrupting the Addictive Cycle

For the sex addict in recovery, understanding and prevention are two very different things. No matter how much insight sex addicts have gained into the patterns of their addictive behavior, their cognitive distortions, the childhood origins of their intimacy disorders and sexual obsessions, and other psychological underpinnings of the disease, they cannot be regarded as in recovery until they begin to deal with the immediate behavioral manifestation of their disorder: acting out sexual compulsions. Sex addiction—like other addictions—has no permanent cure, but treatment can cause the disease to go into remission. Keeping sex addiction in remission, however, involves a lifelong challenge that entails continuing attendance at group meetings, efforts to maintain and strengthen interpersonal relationships, and avoidance of triggers—all directed at preventing any kind of lapse or relapse.

Sex addiction involves more than just compulsive *sexual* behaviors; it includes such *non*sexual behaviors as uncommunicativeness, withdrawal, conflict avoidance, repression of feelings and fears, and a lack of self-assertion. Certainly effective treatment for sex addiction must include sex therapy aimed at changing sexual behaviors through: a short-term ban on any touching or masturbation until the addict has "dried out"; teaching basic sex education, cognitively healthy sexuality, appropriate touch, and sexual communication with the addict's partner aimed at heightening sexual intimacy (see Chapter 12). In addition to taking such steps to augment their sex education and enhance their sexual intimacy, however, sex addicts in recovery must also identify other behaviors that need to change. Although a relapse-prevention plan must by definition include strategies to avoid a return to compulsive sexual behaviors, most sex addicts must devote even more attention to changing *non*sexual behaviors: for example, learning to assert themselves appropriately, to develop healthy relationships, to communicate honestly and effectively, to cope with conflict productively, and to express anger, sadness, and other feelings and fears.

Indeed, helping sex addicts to change their self-destructive and other-destructive behavior patterns involves much more than simply eliminating problematic behaviors, whether sexual or nonsexual. Addicts who through therapeutic intervention gradually become aware of the negative consequences of their addictive behavior need more than this awareness in order to effect lasting change. Recovery, though an extremely powerful force in a sex addict's life, cannot be the person's entire life. The high that comes from sexually compulsive behavior provides a strong positive reinforcement for the continuation of the addictive cycle. A monumental challenge for the addict in recovery therefore centers on finding an answer to the critical question: "What am I giving this up *for?*"

Unless (s)he develops an entirely new lifestyle, a new approach to life, the recovering sex addict will probably find it impossible to sustain the process of change, to prevent relapse. Recovery from sex addiction demands serious soul-searching: the development of a sense of what life is all about. It requires the development of a repertoire of positive behaviors that provide lasting rewards and enhance self-esteem in order to overwhelm the dependency on compulsive behaviors that offer merely fleeting rewards. Without involvement in activities that have significant meaning to them, without membership in groups that provide a sense of meaningful connection, sex addicts will have little to offset the painful loss represented by giving up compulsive sexual behaviors. Without connection, sex addicts will not develop the empathy needed to sustain a commitment to recovery. Without a meaning based in reality, sex addicts will lack the determination required to stay on the course of recovery.

What William Glasser has called "reality therapy," brief therapy focusing on the reality of circumstances and the recognition of the effect of one's actions, plays an important part in our relapse-prevention programs. According to Glasser, the therapist can help a patient modify behavior by developing and applying a realistic formula that will make a difference in their lives (Glasser, 1965). This view holds that everyone has the power to make the necessary changes to get from Point A (where they are now, which must be clearly evaluated and understood) to Point B (where they want to be, which also needs to be clearly defined).

In applying reality therapy with sex addicts, we encourage our patients first to audit their own behavior realistically (i.e., to take a "fearless moral inventory"). Once they understand exactly what they are doing and the consequences of their behavior, sex addicts must come to appreciate that they *do* have a choice. Reality therapy—and relapse prevention—depends upon the addicts' determination that they *can* change. Despite any history of failure in trying to control the compulsive behaviors, the sex addict must affirm this power. For this reason, it is essential that in every session therapists offer suggestions of simple, concrete things that can be done by patients before the next session to improve their situation. This helps confirm for them the reality that they can begin making changes right now. Accomplishing even small tasks is empowering and thus augments the course of reality therapy.

The final step in reality therapy involves developing a map of change (the individual's relapse-prevention plan). Somewhere inside them, most sex addicts already know what they need to do. Reality therapy aims to devise and implement the formula that will get them to where they realistically want to be, that is explicitly identifying and actualizing the changes the sex addict needs to make. This strategy is fundamental to the development and execution of an effective relapse-prevention program.

CASE 10-1

When Larry, who had amassed an extensive collection of child pornography, began therapy, he felt helpless and unable to change (see also Cases 4-4 and 5-3). He had choices of which he was not aware. Through therapy, we helped him see that he could take charge of his life, but Larry still faced a critical choice: "Will I or won't I?" With our support and guidance, he mapped out the changes he needed to make. Some of the elements of this map include:

- the knowledge that he must stay away from children in order to stay sober. Larry recognized his belief that "children love me and I'm helpful to them" as a delusion. For whenever he started to befriend and play with children, it would start his mind down the road to sexual fantasy.
- a commitment to devote more time and effort in his relationship with his wife. Larry came to understand that in his marriage, he needed to focus more energy and attention on his wife, rather than just getting stuck in his own stuff.
- the need to expose himself, to make his problem known to his wife, his pastor, and others close to him. In maintaining the secret of his compulsion, he had given it added power over him. By letting others know about it, Larry not only loosened its hold on him, but he simultaneously expanded the circle of people to whom he would be accountable.

Each of these steps in Larry's relapse-prevention program have helped him to become more "real." For the sex addict, becoming real means being in recovery. Addicts must come to the realization that if they are going to have a meaningful life, a life based in reality rather than illusion, if they are going to sustain intimacy, they have no choice but to change. In order to make this choice to change, however, they must first decide that intimacy and a meaningful life is what they want–Point B. Again, they must answer the critical question posed earlier in this chapter: "What am I giving this up *for?*"

The sex addicts we have treated have defined Point B in a number of ways. As the process of self-examination and therapy unfolds, however, these definitions seem to focus on a single theme. As they grow to understand their cognitive distortions, sex addicts want to achieve actual connection with others rather than the mere illusion of connection. As they recognize the facade they have constructed, they want to instill positive self-talk based in reality and recovery to replace the false positive self-talk that serves to conceal the underlying base of lying or negative self-talk. They want to develop genuine self-esteem. They want to establish real control over their behavior rather than the empty promise of overcontrol that in the past almost always preceded loss of control. And they want to achieve true intimacy through communication and relationships instead of the illusion of intimacy offered by compulsive sexual behavior. Sex addicts learn that all of these goals can be achieved. They can move from Point A to Point B, replacing a life based in illusion with a life grounded in reality. And the steps that will take them there make up their unique relapse-prevention program.

ACCOUNTABILITY AND PERSONAL RESPONSIBILITY

One of the most important aspects of relapse prevention calls on the recovering sex addict, often for the first time in his or her life, to assume responsibility for his or her own actions and to remain accountable to self and others. This means that the addict in recovery must accept responsibility for behavior: past, present, and future.

CASE 10-2

As part of a therapeutic exercise, Maria, who had had a string of extramarital affairs over the course of her marriage (see also Cases 2-1 and 4-3), listed actions and areas of her life for which she was personally responsible. Excerpts from this list include:

"I am responsible for having extramarital affairs.
"I am responsible for hurting my husband and my marriage because I had the affairs.
"I am responsible for my life and the lives of my children.
"I am responsible for my marital relationship and for the relationship I have between myself and my children.
"I am responsible for stopping this illness and making myself better for me and my family."

Maria's list not only clearly spells out her responsibility for her actions (the affairs themselves), but also the consequences of those actions (hurting her husband). She also uses this list to strengthen her commitment to recovery, framing it as a responsibility to herself and her family.

To help reinforce this dawning sense of personal responsibility, we encourage addicts to be honest and accountable not only to themselves, but to other people in their lives. This "accountability network" should include, at a minimum, the addict him- or herself, his or her Higher Power, his or her therapist(s), therapy and self-help group(s), and his or her spouse and family (if any). It might also include friends, self-help sponsors, colleagues, officers of the court (if involved), and members of the clergy. In general, the more people involved in a recovering sex addict's accountability network, the better. The therapist can help the individual sex addict to determine an appropriate accountability structure.

CASE 10-3

Calvin, a minister, had involved himself in compulsive sexual affairs before coming to us for treatment. In one of his initial sessions, we asked him, "To whom will you be accountable?" With our help, Calvin developed an accountability network that included his wife, a therapy group we run for clergy members who are sex addicts, another minister in town, the minister of the last church where he worked, and the president of the denomination. To everyone in this network, Calvin detailed his history of sex addiction and made a commitment to keep them regularly informed of his progress and/or his setbacks.

The accountability network serves two functions. It reinforces the therapeutic need and provides an opportunity for the sex addict to come clean, to disclose honestly the history and nature of the problem with all those in his or her network. And it can also serve as an invaluable support network for the sex addict in recovery.

Spouses who are themselves in therapy can become critically important members of the sex addict's accountability network. Because maintaining the secret will only preserve the primary barrier to intimacy between partners, we insist that recovering sex addicts tell the whole story to their spouses (or partners). The day-to-day proximity between spouses makes a co-addict a potentially powerful ally in the sex addict's recovery process. While pursuing his or her own recovery, a spouse may, for example, help identify earlier elements in the addictive cycle (e.g., withdrawal, isolation, victim posturing) and alert the addict when (s)he notices a return to these habits. For this reason, we encourage addicts to try to stay connected with their spouses, to avoid isolation no matter what they may feel or do. As this role of live-in monitor can also heighten tension within the relationship, the couple will need the support and specific guidance of their therapist(s) as they grapple with the demands of the shifting dynamic—and the affect that accompanies it.

CASE 10-4

Ellen and David (see also Cases 1-1, 3-1, 4-1,5-1, 6-1, and 8-1) worked together to identify and confront behaviors that manifest early in his addictive cycle. These behaviors include pouting, putting on a "poor me" attitude, playing victim, jealousy, inappropriate anger, raging, and arranging to be home alone with his stepdaughter Jenny, whom he had molested on numerous occasions. Ellen and David then worked together, as all our couples in recovery do, to develop an "alert list": a relapse-prevention plan based on the specific behaviors they identified. The alert list serves as a contract, spelling out a course of action (e.g., seeing a therapist, family meetings, consulting with a clergy member) that both partners agree to follow whenever the addict reverts to one of the behaviors noted.

As recovery progresses, the therapist can often encourage the sex addict to remain accountable to this network. If a sex addict slips—or if the addict succeeds in avoiding a potentially tempting or troublesome situation—the therapist may ask, "Have you told your spouse yet?" The therapist can help patients see that, rather than waiting for others to call them, it is up to them to contact the people that make up their accountability network, to remain in touch with those to whom they have made a commitment to recovery. In this way, the therapist can bolster recovering sex addicts' responsibility to themselves and to others.

INTERRUPTING THE CYCLE: THE PLAN IN GENERAL

The key to any successful relapse-prevention program lies in interrupting the addictive cycle, as early in the cycle as possible. Toward this end, sex addicts must conduct a thorough self-examination aimed at developing detailed knowledge and full understanding of every individual element of their unique addictive cycle. Interruption of the addictive cycle before it reaches the phase of sexual acting out depends upon the complete and accurate identification of personal triggers: the events, thoughts, and feelings that in recovery serve as yellow lights (be careful) or red lights (STOP!). The therapist must guide the addict to increasing self-awareness in terms of cognition, affect, and behavior. It helps to further this self-awareness if the therapist can help the recovering sex addict begin to see life as a series of choices. For the sex addict, even actions that appear unpremeditated, innocent, and trivial (e.g, taking the "usual" route home, a drive that "just happens" to pass through the city's pornography district) are not inconsequential. Such actions, though they often reflect decisions and choices that may seem unimportant at the time, can nonetheless increase the risk of relapse. To prevent relapse, the sex addict needs to make these apparently trivial choices more conscious. The self-awareness that contributes to relapse prevention is thus twofold. Sex addicts must become aware not only of the past—the addictive cycle, past patterns of behavior, the events, thoughts, and feelings that led up to previous sexual acting out. They also need to heighten awareness of the present—knowing what they are doing right now, where they are heading, how they are behaving, what and how they are thinking, what they are feeling, and what choices they are making.

In identifying triggers, sex addicts should carefully scrutinize all areas of their lives affected by movement into the addictive cycle (Bays, Freeman-Longo & Hildebran, 1990). We encourage sex addicts to consider all of the following areas, any of which can furnish clues that they are slipping back into the addictive cycle:

- social life (e.g., withdrawing)
- work habits (e.g., distraction, absenteeism)
- home life (e.g., sloppiness, anger in marriage)
- attitudes (e.g., self-pity, self-righteousness)
- HALT (i.e., hungry, angry, lonely, tired) or other conditions that add to personal stress
- sleep habits (amount and timing)
- eating patterns (e.g., skipping meals, gorging)

- personal appearance (e.g., lapses in personal hygiene or grooming, or overconcern with looking just right)
- finances (e.g., money problems, misplaced financial priorities)
- alcohol and drugs (usage)
- other behavioral signals (e.g., cruising)

CASE 10-4 (*continued*)

After nearly 17 months of therapy, David prepared the following list of attitudes, behaviors, and emotions that indicated that he had fallen back into the initial phases of his personal addictive cycle. David regarded this list as "red flags," warnings to stop what he was doing and choose another course:

- Isolation
- Not going to groups
- Pouting - quiet
- Lots of *you* statements
- Any use of alcohol
- '*I don't know*' statements
- Pity-potting or whining about things I have no control over
- Competition between myself and wife over work and wages
- Irresponsible financial decisions
- Overeating
- Procrastination of daily responsibilities—e.g., not cleaning apartment, work assignments
- 'Have to' statements rather than choice statements
- Overvalue of material things
- Narcissistic behavior

Once the addict has compiled this kind of early-warning device, (s)he next needs to develop plans to deal with each of these red flags when and if they arise. The sex addict is no stranger to planning. When caught in the grip of the addictive cycle, planning took the form of fantasizing, cruising, and grooming—all of which readied the addict to act out sexually. An active sex addict, for example, about to leave town on business might think, "Oh boy, here's my chance," and plan to carry out his or her compulsive sexual ritual. In recovery, planning serves an entirely different purpose: steeling oneself to avoid relapse. Given the same situation, the addict might instead think, "Uh-oh, this could be trouble," and make plans that will minimize the chances of acting out. The addict in this situation would need to develop answers beforehand to such questions as: How will I fill my time productively? Where can I safely go in the evening? Who will I call for help?

CASE 10-5

Paul, a flight attendant, now gets phone numbers from the SAA. hotline prior to traveling to another city. Paul knows that spending his evenings alone might increase the risk of his acting out. At the same time, he no longer feels comfortable going out with the rest of the flight crew, because too often in the past that had meant stumbling into meaningless sexual affairs. So Paul includes SAA meetings in his itinerary and generally goes out afterward for coffee or a bite to eat with fellow recovering addicts. (SAA, SA, or SLAA meetings can now be found in most U.S. cities.)

CASE 10-6

When Dan, a minister, traveled to other towns, he used to spend much of his time in his hotel room watching X-rated movies and masturbating (see also Case 4-6). Now when he goes on the road, he arranges with the front desk in advance to turn off the cable TV in his room. This prevents the availability of X-rated movies at the touch of a button. When staying in hotels that cannot accommodate this request, Dan asks that the TV be disconnected and taken out of the hotel room entirely.

As these examples show, planning to prevent relapse involves both thorough knowledge of the individual's unique addictive cycle and the development of adequate coping responses *ahead of time.* If addicts do not know beforehand exactly what they will do when they encounter or put themselves into high-risk situations, then they will increase the likelihood that they will fall back into the pattern of compulsive sexual behaviors. *How can I stop?,* one of the finest resources we have found on relapse prevention, calls such relapse prevention plans "escape strategies," and compares them to fire drills (Bays, Freeman-Longo & Hildebran, 1990). If your house begins to burn, you will be much more likely to avoid panic and escape safely if you have already planned what to do when and if you first smell smoke. So too with sex addiction.

In recovery, sex addicts learn that unanticipated high-risk situations can in fact be anticipated—and are best handled when the addict has anticipated and prepared for them. Bays, Freeman-Longo and Hildebran (1990) suggest replacing the time once spent on fantasy rehearsal with relapse rehearsal: addicts imagining high-risk situations and seeing themselves using concrete steps (interventions) from their relapse-prevention plan to get out quickly and safely.

SUCCESSFUL RELAPSE PREVENTION: THE PLAN IN DETAIL

A good relapse-prevention plan never just happens. Every sex addict in recovery faces the challenge of inventing and reinventing his or her own unique relapse-prevention program, one that takes into account every aspect of the addictive cycle, previous patterns of addictive (and contributory) behaviors, and the individual's growing self-knowledge. No relapse-prevention program ever remains constant and unchanged. Rather, a successful program *evolves* based on what the addict has learned about past patterns of behavior—and on what (s)he *continues* to learn from his or her own slips and the slips of others in recovery. The program must also evolve to incorporate changes in work and home life as well as personal changes. For example, a patient may gain new insight through a personal lapse or through therapy that may result in the addition of new behaviors (red flags) to the relapse-prevention program. Or the addict's growth through therapy and recovery programs may affect the amount of therapy needed on a continuing basis; if so, the amount specified in the original relapse-prevention plan would need altering.

A successful relapse-prevention plan incorporates much more than prohibitions against compulsive sexual behaviors. In the past, the addict made time in his or her schedule for acting out. Taking this compulsive sexual behavior out of the schedule will leave a gaping hole in the addict's life. Unless the addict, with the therapist's support and guidance, can find healthier behaviors (e.g., exercise, sleep, elements of a balanced lifestyle) with which to fill this hole, the addict will eventually fill it in by acting out again. For this reason, the addict and his or her therapist should develop a relapse-prevention plan that lists not only *don'ts* that place limits on behavior (e.g., the 3-second rule that restricts sexual fantasies, a part of virtually every sex addict's relapse-prevention program) and highlights behaviors to eliminate (sexual compulsions, withdrawal, etc.), but also *dos* that encourage the development of a healthier lifestyle (e.g., relaxation, eating well, attending self-help meetings, socializing, enjoyable activities).

We detail every relapse-prevention program in a sobriety contract between the recovering sex addict and those in his or her accountability network.

CASE 10-6 (continued)

Dan, a minister who compulsively masturbated, wrote the following sobriety contract:

MY CONTRACT

I. Destructive Behaviors To Abstain From

1. No masturbation without my wife's involvement.
2. No watching pornography or R-rated movies that depict explicit nudity or sexual innuendo.
3. Staying away from adult bookstores.
4. No calling or visiting nude modeling centers inquiring about services, charges, etc.
5. No purchasing pornographic magazines, singles papers, etc.
6. No calling or going to topless bars.
7. No calling escort services inquiring about services, charges, etc.
8. No cruising for prostitutes (particularly on Central Street).

9. No picking up prostitutes.
10. No "sex talking" during a counseling session with a parishioner whereby I initiate the conversation with the attempt to become sexually excited.

II. Positive Behaviors That I Commit To Focus On

1. *To work not more than 60 hours per week* (down from 80–workaholism fuels my sex addiction).
2. *To become emotionally involved with my wife by committing to share my feelings and even my sexual temptations.*
3. *To practice couples communication principles in expressing my wants, needs, expectations, perceptions, thoughts, and feelings.*
4. To begin practicing healthy sexual expression with my wife by beginning to exercise the concept of Sensate Focus.
5. To designate regular time to play golf, swimming, movies, etc., simply for me.
6. To do regular physical exercise.
7. To monitor my feelings and back off from my schedule whenever I overcommit.
8. *To talk out sexual temptation* with my group.
9. If I do act out against my "bottom lines," then I will not hate myself but rather love and be gentle with me.

III. Steps I Commit To Take If I Slip

1. *Force myself to treat me with love and gentleness.*
2. *Confess the slip*:
   (a) to my wife
   (b) to my sponsor
   (c) to my therapist
   (d) to my recovery group

As indicated, the sobriety contract should specifically and concretely spell out not only the negatives the addict promises to change, but also positive, healthy activities that (s)he wants to make part of her or his new life in recovery. In addition, the sobriety contract should spell out as specifically as possible the understood and accepted consequences of any slip or relapse on the part of the addict.

The importance of identifying triggers (particular stressors, anger at spouse, etc.) and venues (on the road, in the red-light district, etc.) of previous acting out cannot be overemphasized. If the addict has not already done so as part of a therapeutic exercise, (s)he should record as complete a list of triggers and venues as possible as part of the process of drawing up a sobriety contract. This will allow and encourage the addict to prepare appropriate plans to avoid these triggers and venues whenever possible and to develop coping strategies for those that are impossible to avoid. (A sex addict preparing for a business trip, for example, may use one of the strategies offered earlier in this chapter or may decide to take the phone numbers of other group members and make a commitment to call them at certain times during the trip—in addition to pledging to make unscheduled calls as needed.)

The sobriety contract should also explicitly state the minimal amount of therapy and self-help in which the sex addict will participate as part of his or her recovery program. To minimize the chance of relapse, a sex addict must continue to do the program, no matter how far (s)he has come in recovery. As we have previously indicated, we design an individualized, customized program for each addict who comes to us for treatment. Every patient we see receives individual therapy and group therapy and attends 12-step groups; where appropriate, a patient might also receive couples therapy, family therapy, expressive therapies, and/or sex therapy. As recovery progresses, the amount of therapy specified in the contract may be adjusted to account for either therapeutic gains or backslides.

A recovering sex addict's sobriety contract and relapse-prevention plan should also address the question of stress reduction or stress management. Efforts to reduce stress depend upon the addict's increased awareness of its physical symptoms—tension in neck and shoulders, rapid breathing, feeling restless or jittery, etc. Sex addicts can then add to their sobriety contracts a promise to use one or more of the many stress-reduction or relaxation techniques available to them. One addict may choose breathing techniques and/or progressive muscle relaxation exercises, whereas another might feel more comfortable with prayer or meditation. Many addicts in recovery find that starting the day with meditation or prayer gets them focused on the program from their first waking moments. Guided imagery—an especially useful technique for sex addicts, who have for years indulged in deviant imagery or sexual fantasy—can help addicts to identify a serene or comfortable place in their minds where they can go to relax and shore up inner resources. Regular exercise (after consultation with a physician) can also contribute to stress reduction. Any one of these stress-reduction techniques should provide the sex addict in recovery with a source of relaxation, revitalization, and renewal. However, given that most people have a tendency to *not* do something when they most need to do it, we encourage addicts to include one or more of these techniques as a scheduled activity mandated by their sobriety contract.

Learning healthy ways to reduce or manage stress is critical to relapse prevention. Sex addicts routinely set up a life of stress, which they then medicate through sexual behaviors. In recovery, most addicts find that a life without high stress is boring. Unfortunately, a life with too much stress can push the addict back into old patterns of coping, perhaps including a relapse to compulsive sexual behaviors. Sex addicts in recovery must therefore carefully examine their lifestyle. Too much of anything—whether it is sex, alcohol, work, exercise, self-help groups, or even therapy—can create excess stress in their lives. Recovering sex addicts need to evaluate and consistently reevaluate what it means to have a balanced life.

The definition of a balanced life differs with each individual addict. The sobriety contract allows every addict the opportunity to spell out the various elements of this personal definition. Recovery challenges the addict to develop a new lifestyle—one that avoids compulsive behaviors, sexual or otherwise, and instead involves exercise, pleasurable activities, relaxation, improved communication, connection and involvement with others, and the realization of intimacy. Creating this lifestyle might necessitate any number of changes, from leaving a partner who refuses to pursue his or her own recovery to finding a new job that involves more supervision and structure and less free, unsupervised time and/or out-of-town travel. For example, David (see Case 10-4) not only stopped molesting his stepdaughter, but during the same period also gave up drinking, quit smoking, and lost weight, too. The goal of a good relapse-prevention program is thus "total package recovery"—not simply the cessation of compulsive behaviors, but the creation of a balanced life.

CASE 10-4 (*continued*)

After 18 months of treatment, David wrote up a revised relapse-prevention program that achieved a balance between positive activities he promised to pursue or continue and negative behaviors to avoid:

- Have learned good communication skills
- Understand I will always be a sex offender but can control it
- Go to three groups per week minimum at this time *with participation*
- Monthly family sessions with therapist
- Monthly individual sessions with therapist
- Daily affirmations
- Strong support group of non-offenders who know my full story
- Continue to develop adult outside interests—e.g., hiking with wife, sports
- Continue to improve self-esteem and image with physical care—e.g., weight reduction, continue cessation of smoking and alcohol
- Be available to others in group to show how my program works
- Continue to work on intimacy with my spouse
- No pornography, no deviant fantasies, do not allow myself to be in situations where I am alone with children under 18
- Continue to become more financially responsible to improve self-esteem
- Deal with conflicts and feelings as they arise using honest communication and problem-solving techniques taught in program"

As mentioned earlier, a successful program of relapse prevention must constantly evolve to take into account new insights, recidivism, new situations in the sex addict's life, and changing conditions.

CASE 10-4 *(continued)*

Nearly one year after David wrote the relapse prevention contract, the court began allowing him to spend single overnights at home, building up over the course of six months to full-time cohabitation. Although this represents an extreme example, given that his compulsive behavior centered on the molestation of his stepdaughter, David's revised sobriety contract included very clear boundaries on permissible behavior. In addition to the 2-second rule regarding sexual fantasies and a therapy regimen that included two aftercare meetings per week, his new sobriety contract placed severe constraints on his conduct inside the home. David could not be in the house unless his wife Ellen was home, and he had to stay in Ellen's sight while inside. He had to remain fully clothed at all times, except when he was alone in the master bathroom (with the door closed) or alone with his spouse in the master bedroom. If he woke up at night to go to bathroom, David agreed to wake Ellen, too. If the kids saw him up in the middle of night, they were to yell out. In addition to these restrictions, David and Ellen also came up with a list of high-risk situations and high-risk activities to be avoided whenever possible.

In addition to helping sex addicts draw up, refine, and revise sobriety contracts, the primary therapist can contribute significantly to relapse prevention. The therapist and addict should, for example, work together to develop appropriate maintenance strategies and emergency responses. In guiding our patients through workbooks such as *How can I stop?* (Bays, Freeman-Longo & Hildebran, 1990), for example, we help them to hone in on the elements of their addictive cycle and come up with a list of alternative behaviors or strategies that will contribute to relapse prevention. Therapists who have extensive experience treating sex addicts can also suggest strategies that they have seen work for others. In addition to helping the addict establish a sobriety contract, the therapist provides a trained eye to help the addict examine his or her lifestyle. The therapist's input can then guide the addict in creating a new lifestyle able to compete with the addiction: a lifestyle that provides a balanced amount of healthy excitement and a supportive connection with at least two other people besides the therapist.

After a sobriety contract and elements of the recovering sex addict's new lifestyle have been established, the therapist can serve as a critical monitor, checking regularly on how (s)he is doing the program. The therapist and patient need consistently to ask such questions as: What's working? What's not working? What's missing? What needs strengthening? Therapists can then encourage patients to review and revise their sobriety contracts in order to reevaluate its adequacy and applicability to current conditions. We often push our patients to strengthen their contracts, that is to say this isn't enough or this isn't strong enough. Such revisions frequently involve adding more people to the accountability network and/or the support structure.

With the help of their therapists, peers in therapy groups or self-help groups, and others, as well as with what they learn from their own mistakes, most recovering sex addicts come to a clear understanding of what they need to do in order to stay in recovery. In time, sex addicts require less and less professional monitoring and can determine for themselves the amount of help they need to maintain their sobriety contracts and stay the course of recovery. We have seen patients who have "graduated" from our program come back, as much as two years later, to participate in group therapy for a week or a month because they knew they needed it at that time. For the ongoing commitment to recovery, made manifest in their sobriety contracts, requires all sex addicts to continue to seek help as needed.

DEALING WITH SLIPS

Like other addictions or compulsive behaviors, sex addiction is not easy to give up. Sex addicts frequently slip back into old patterns of behavior, which sometimes include a return to compulsive sexual behaviors. In discussing recidivism, we distinguish among three types. We define a *slip* as any return to unhealthy behaviors or patterns targeted by therapy. Although slips may involve a return to the primary compulsive sexual behaviors, they may also center on rehearsal (e.g., sexual fantasy accompanied by masturbation), on even earlier stages in the addictive cycle, or on violations of provisions in the addict's sobriety contract. We conceive of a *lapse* as a specific type of slip: one that ends with a return to compulsive sexual behavior. A *relapse* involves repeated slips, including lapses; in other words a full-fledged return to the behavior patterns that define the individual's addictive cycle.

To avoid the negative self-talk and destruction of self-esteem that follows in the wake of "failure," patients should be encouraged by their therapists to form realistic expectations of recovery. In this context, therapists need to take the time to help patients distinguish between what constitutes a slip—and what does not. Approximately three months into sobriety, for example, many sex addicts begin to experience wet dreams (nocturnal emissions). This tends to awaken anxiety in addicts, fear that they have unwittingly broken sobriety. To alleviate this anxiety, we help our patients reframe wet dreams as indications of the progress they have made in recovery. We believe that nocturnal emissions may be a withdrawal symptom, an adjustment made by the body in response to the decrease in sexual activity. After delineating the behaviors that actually would constitute a slip, therapists should help addicts reframe possible slips or even relapses as wake-up calls or warning signals rather than as complete failures. Recidivism indicates that some aspect of the recovery program or the sobriety contract needs adjustment and improvement in order to accommodate the challenges faced by the addict in recovery.

While encouraging realistic expectations, however, the therapist should attempt to demarcate as clearly as possible the thin line between the realistic expectation that slips or lapses *might* occur and giving oneself permission to relapse. All too often, recovering sex addicts negotiate this line poorly, and the realistic appraisal that a lapse "may" happen becomes an excuse to engage in compulsive behavior again. For this reason, we urge the sex addicts we treat *not* to expect that lapses may occur. Rather, we advocate that sex addicts acknowledge that there's a chance it might happen again, but to couple this acknowledgment with the *expectation* that, if they follow their recovery programs and relapse-prevention plans, it *won't* happen again. This approach not only helps foster a sense of urgency and vigilance required for recovery, but also reinforces the understanding that the responsibility for slips or relapses belongs entirely to the individual sex addict.

This understanding becomes critically important with sex addicts whose compulsive behavior has included victimizing behaviors. If the sex addict's compulsive behaviors involve "only" sex with prostitutes, X-rated bookstores, phone-sex services, or masturbation, a lapse or relapse—while leading to sometimes dire consequences in terms of the addict's marriage or other relationships, job, or self-esteem—may be viewed as a possibility (though not a probability, as underscored earlier, if the sex addict truly follows a complete recovery program and appropriate relapse-prevention plan). However, with sex addicts who flash their genitals, commit incest, molest children, or rape, a return to such behaviors cannot be tolerated even as a possibility. (State laws, which differ from state to state, determine whether therapists must report to legal authorities their knowledge of sexual offenses committed, or the risk that further sexual offenses might be committed.) For the patient population of sex offenders, *no lapses are allowed*! We make this a clearly understood provision of our treatment contract with sex offenders.

As indicated in the definitions provided, slips do not necessarily involve a sex addict's primary compulsive behavior. For example, a recovering sex addict who frequented prostitutes may have a slip that does not involve prostitutes, but rather watching an X-rated movie or even going beyond the 3-second limit on sexual fantasies.

CASE 10-4 *(continued)*

After the initial confession to his wife led to his seeking treatment, David never again molested his oldest stepdaughter (or her sisters). Shortly after beginning the gradual process of moving back in with his family, however, David went to the front door of his home in his pajamas, which was an explicit violation of his sobriety contract and the reunification contract prepared by his probation officer, both of which stated that he would be fully clothed except when behind closed doors in the master bedroom or the master bathroom.

A recovering sex addict who slips should always know what to do immediately to avoid a full-blown relapse (just as an addict who does relapse should know in advance what to do to break free of the addictive cycle). As indicated earlier, the sex addict's sobriety contract should clearly spell out the consequences of any slips, lapses, and relapses, thus providing the sex addict with concrete steps to take in order to avoid slipping further into the addictive cycle. Of these steps, the most critical is that sex addicts make a commitment *not* to skip out on group or individual therapy in the wake of a slip. Despite the sex addict's embarrassment or shame at having "failed," (s)he must immediately make her- or himself accountable. Remaining accountable will not only help the addict to avoid a recidivist binge, but will also demonstrate the acceptance of personal responsibility and the willingness to face the consequences of his or her behavior.

CASE 10-7

Henry, who frequented massage parlors and topless bars (see also Case 5-2), had been married to Suzanne less than two months when he began feeling depressed. His wife held and controlled both banking cards and checkbooks, and Henry had to ask her whenever he needed money. As a result, he felt untrusted and demeaned. Rather than let Suzanne (or his therapists or other therapy group members) know how he felt, Henry began to isolate. As his isolation deepened, Henry began "casually" driving through the area of town where most of the strip clubs were located on his way home from work. Eventually, he went directly to the bank, withdrew money from their joint account (after saying he had lost the checkbook), and went to both a topless bar and a massage parlor. To his credit, though he felt extremely depressed about his lapse, Henry came to group therapy the next day. He immediately dealt with the lapse, demonstrating a genuine desire and commitment to change. At the group's urging, Henry immediately confessed to Suzanne and intensified his individual therapy regimen, beginning with a two-hour individual therapy session later that day.

This lapse taught Henry a number of valuable lessons. The group members, his therapists, and his wife helped him with reality testing. Through their combined efforts, Henry realized that his marriage would not last long if he continued to act out. He recognized that he had to stop flirting with triggers; he had to avoid driving through those districts of town. His lapse, its consequences, and the response of his support network forced Henry to become more accountable, to avoid isolating from others, to call people from the group, and to commit to working his program. To date, Henry has not slipped again.

Upon first learning of a slip, a therapist should encourage the patient to report it right away to someone else in the sex addict's accountability network (e.g., the spouse or sponsor). Indeed, the entire story should soon be related to everyone in the addict's network. Since any long-held secret will erode and eventually destroy the efforts to heal the sex addict's primary relationship and restructure it on a new basis of mutual honesty, we strongly emphasize the importance of bringing the spouse into awareness as soon as possible after a slip. In our experience, most recovering co-addicts—despite their anger and disappointment that their partners have slipped and their willingness to carry out agreed-upon consequences—demonstrate respect, and even empathy, for the sex addict who confesses immediately. Often, co-addicts' own experience in recovery and their recognition of their own temptation or tendency to slip back into codependent patterns of behavior augments their understanding that recovery is not easy for the addict either.

The way therapists and sex addicts work together to deal with slips depends upon their nature and frequency. If slips are rare and the sex addict seems to be working his or her recovery program well in general, then the slip should prompt the therapist and patient to reexamine the surrounding circumstances and reevaluate the elements of the addict's relapse-prevention plan. What was going on in the addict's life, in the addict's mind, during the period leading up to the slip? What function might sexual acting out be playing in the system? Had the addict been working the program and following her or his relapse-prevention plan? What—not talking to spouse, not being honest, not going to groups or self-help meetings—had the addict let slide? To what should the addict have been paying more attention? Any slip should cause the addict and his or her therapist to reexamine the program to identify what's *not* working and what *is* working. (A balanced, perspective that acknowledges both the addict's therapeutic gains and progress in recovery in addition to the aspects that still need work is important.) By approaching the occasional slip in the right way, sex addicts (and their therapists) can learn from these mistakes. And what they learn can guide the sex addicts back on track in the pursuit of recovery.

CASE 10-4 *(continued)*

When David went to the front door dressed only in his pajamas, he had clearly violated his sobriety contract. The consequences of such a slip had been clearly written into the contract. David immediately resumed intensive individual therapy (three times a week) to focus on the slip itself, and on the pouting and manipulative behaviors that lay behind it. As the amount of time he was allowed to spend in the home increased, David had become increasingly angry and resentful at having to abide by so many rules and regulations governing his conduct with his own family. When he heard the doorbell ring, David said to himself, "To hell with it," rationalizing his action as "no big deal." After the slip, family therapy, couples therapy, individual therapy, and group therapy all sent David the identical message: Everyone else involved *did* consider it a big deal. David learned that no one in his family, no one in his therapy group, and none of his therapists would condone any attempts to renegotiate his sobriety contract through behavior. Alterations in the agreement could be made only by first talking with the addict's sponsor, therapist, group, and everyone else who would be affected by the change. Most important, David realized that his actions, regardless of how minor *he* considered them, entailed consequences. If he continued these kinds of behavior, the process of reunifying his family would slow and eventually reverse, rather than move forward.

Resenting controls—whether imposed by the addict's own sobriety contract or an outside agency, such as a probation department—is a common problem for sex addicts in recovery. Both David and Henry grew increasingly resentful, angry, and sullen in response to the restrictions placed on their autonomy. Didn't anyone trust them? Could no one treat them like adults? Spouses of sex addicts often resent these rules, too. Like Ellen and Suzanne, many spouses feel they must take on the roles of watchdog and warden. The mutual resentment, more often than not unspoken, intensifies the tension in the couple's relationship—another factor that can contribute to an addict's sense of isolation, and consequently, to the rationalization of slips. To avoid such a progression, therapists can help sex addicts and co-addicts to reframe their understanding of behavioral controls. Addicts need to come to view these controls as limits on behavior that ensure continued recovery, as well as the safety of any potential victims (including themselves). Co-addicts need to understand that although (they are responsible for their own responses—for following through with the agreed-upon consequences of slips, for example—it is the addict who bears primary responsibility for maintaining the sobriety contract.

If a recovering sex addict slips repeatedly, it will lead to more pointed confrontations by his or her therapist(s) and members of therapy groups. Whereas some self-help groups do not necessarily consider slips to be of great consequence, responding by simply urging the recidivist sex addict to get back on the wagon, the therapy groups we lead treat slips as a big deal. Repeated slips invariably lead to serious care-fronting in group meetings, including a reassessment of the patient's commitment to recovery and willingness to change. If the sex addict clearly resists fundamental changes or demonstrates a profound reluctance to recover, we (or long-term group members who have seen this care-frontation technique before) may observe, "You don't seem to want to improve right now." This message clearly indicates that it is not the therapist's or the group's task to *make* the sex addict get better, squarely placing that responsibility instead within the addict's domain.

If, however, the sex addict seems more receptive to therapist and group input, then the therapist should help the patient to regard the series of slips—just as (s)he would a single slip—as an opportunity to learn ways in which (s)he can strengthen the recovery program and relapse-prevention plan. Because a relapse or series of slips can thoroughly demoralize the recovering addict, the therapist—with the support of the group—may find it beneficial to begin with the observation that the sex addict is *not* back to ground zero (as this is rarely the case). One of the goals at this point is to shore up the addict's resources for what will follow by reminding her or him of the gains already achieved through treatment and recovery. Then, the therapist should lead the group in exploring the circumstances surrounding the individual slips. If a pattern emerges, it might signal specific areas of recovery that need to be pinpointed and improved. We find it effective to put such questions directly to the sex addict: "What do you need to do to get back on track?" By treating slips, lapses, and relapses as sources of insight, as teaching tools that can focus sex addicts on what they need to do and how they need to change in order to prevent it from happening again, slips can actually strengthen relapse-prevention plans–and thereby enhance prospects for recovery.

11

What Words Cannot Tell

The Importance of Creative-Art and Sandplay Therapies

Because most sex addicts—and many co-addicts—find it difficult to express their fears and other feelings and have developed a strong, rigid defense system, we often incorporate such expressive modalities as creative-art therapy and sand therapy into our treatment program. Sex addicts and their partners often have suffered severe or repeated trauma during childhood. Yet pain-induced and shame-induced defense mechanisms activated by childhood trauma can block or prevent access to the event and the affect attendant to it. The "alien" and self-negating behavior of sex addiction only reinforces the addict's shame and strengthens these defense mechanisms. Even after sex addicts seek help for their problem—whether voluntarily or under court order—their defense mechanisms may have such a grip on them that they can hardly speak about either their addictive behavior or their childhoods. Because they draw on the right side of the brain, art and sandplay therapies can bypass left-brain-centered defenses. By bringing repressed knowledge and hidden fears and feelings to conscious awareness, art and sandplay therapies can cut through an individual's defenses by taking away the *raison d'etre*: keeping the secret a secret. We have often seen issues unearthed through art or sandplay therapy that other modalities had not yet brought to light, issues that patients can then address further in individual or group therapy. Although we would never rely exclusively on creative-art or sandplay therapies in treating sex addicts and their family members, we have found them useful as adjunctive diagnostic tools, as therapeutic modalities that complement and advance gains made through primary therapy.

Melanie Klein describes her method of treating disturbed children as "play therapy" (Segal, 1989). She concludes that play sometimes offers the only possible means of communication with these children, the only way "to bring out underlying emotional structure for observation and amelioration" (Blau, 1991). The modalities of art and play, essential in the treatment of children, can also well serve many adults. Sex addicts and co-addicts, buffeted again and again by the experience of the addictive cycle, often present as emotionally or psychologically arrested. For this reason, art and play therapies can greatly benefit this population.

Art or play therapies can be used, for example, as an icebreaker for a patient who seems uncomfortable, unwilling, or unable to speak in the therapist's office. When working with children, Dr. Barbara Bagan Prochelo, a registered art therapist on our staff, employs creative-art therapy in early sessions as an indirect means of establishing a rapport and relationship between therapist and patient and as a way for a therapist to get to know the child. Going to a therapist can be scary for anyone, adult or child, but especially for young children victimized—whether directly or indirectly—by their parents' sex addiction and co-addiction. Such children have difficulty trusting any adult. Art therapy can help break down this barrier of distrust.

Case 11-1

At age 13, Michele was referred to us because she had begun to act out sexually with her younger brother. The use of nondirective play and art helped Michele and her therapist to get acquainted. More directed techniques then allowed Michele to begin to tell her story. Asked simply to draw a picture of her little brother, Michele used the medium to begin to express the realities of what had happened and the emotions (her brother's and her own) associated with the abuse. In drawing and discussing the third picture of her brother, Michele began to get in touch with the actual situation and began to feel empathy for her brother. Ultimately, this facilitated a direct and open discussion of everything that had occurred between her and her brother.

The medium of collage often serves as a useful way to connect and communicate, as well as a good way to introduce patients to art therapy. In collage, the patient chooses already formed images and words from magazines and newspapers, needing only to tear them out and paste them onto a piece of paper. One might think that collage, because it depends on an already existing pool of words and images, would be a limited tool for personal expression, but we have seen patients time and again find just the right words and images to express their true feelings. And because collage has clients draw from rather than generate the selection, they often regard it as a less threatening exercise than one requiring that they write something "in their own words" or create something by themselves.

CASE 11-2

Shelley, a sex addict in her 40s, had no concept of healthy sexuality and felt confused about her sexual identity. During her 20 years of marriage, she had had a series of extramarital affairs. She would have short or long periods of sexual sobriety and then act out again. After divorcing her husband, who had also had a number of affairs including one with Shelley's mother, Shelley continued to have a sexual relationship with him. Shelley hit bottom emotionally at the time of the divorce, and sought out professional help.

Early in therapy, Shelley prepared a collage around the issue of her sexuality (see Figure 11.1). The collage revealed to her the sad story of her life: a controlling mother who abused her both psychologically and sexually, an alcoholic father who physically abused her, the innocence of her early childhood shattered by her parents' divorce, and her increasing dependency on food and sex. She had received no sexual education as a child and had equated sex with love. The collage itself, and processing it, helped her begin to get in touch with her sexual self and to realize that she had been living out an unhealthy sexual self. Although processing the collage did not complete her therapy, it helped sharpen her focus on issues of sexuality that she later worked on in individual and group therapy and in Sexaholics Anonymous. Shelley

Figure 11.1. Shelley's Sexuality Collage.

continues to struggle with recovery, but the collage—in highlighting how her own sexuality relates to her experiences with her parents—has helped increase her motivation to break the generational cycle for the sake of her daughters and her grandchildren.

Though patients experience collage as non-threatening, this modality—and other modalities of art therapy—can both mediate and transform consciousness through images or symbolic forms. In processing collages, the therapist should guide patients to the acknowledgment that, though the words and images may have originated from another source, in choosing and arranging them the way they did, they have made these words and images their own.

CASE 11-3

On the surface, Roberta seemed to "have it all": a terrific managerial job in a large corporation, a handsome and successful husband, two beautiful children. However, Roberta's sex addiction threatened to destroy everything she had. For several years, she had been involved in various extramarital affairs and her sex addiction was beginning to get out of control at work. Her obsession with sexual fantasies was eroding her ability to concentrate on her responsibilities, and she had begun propositioning male colleagues. Roberta feared that as a consequence, she might soon lose her job. Despite the damage her addiction was inflicting on both her family and her work, Roberta presented with defensive and defiant denial. She minimized her problem, insisting that she was just an average sensuous woman who liked men.

Roberta prepared a sexuality collage filled with blank white spaces. The piece suggested that she had little understanding of her own sexual identity, of who she was as a sexual being. In processing the collage, Roberta wrote: "I'm desperate for someone, anyone just to love me, and that person just might be desperately wrong for me. *Why don't I deserve love?* What have I done? Why? I'm so sorry. Sorry for anything I have done to cause this pattern. I'm so so sorry. Just take it away. Lift the pain. So badly I want to be loved, just loved. I just wanted love, oh so very badly. I could never express how strong my wish is to feel loved. I want the love that people live for, that people die for. It isn't so much to ask, but it's so unattainable for me. Why can't I be loved? PLEASE!!"

Collages can serve as a vehicle to help sex addicts express and begin to deal with some of their confusion about sex and love, subjects that many people feel uncomfortable talking about. Through this medium, sex addicts can begin to express, as Roberta did, fears of rejection and abandonment that they may never have revealed to anyone before.

In some cases, an adult or child can directly, consciously, and verbally access their fears and feelings, their childhood traumas, or their own victimizing behaviors, then discuss them and the affect associated with them, and integrate them. Yet verbal therapies alone may not adequately access, release, and integrate the denied, repressed, or blocked affect. Words can sometimes get in the way of therapy. Vehicles of conscious control, they can provide a ready means for rationalization and intellectualization, warding off rather than promoting therapeutic insight that might lead to change. In such cases, it sometimes helps to find a vehicle for emotional rather than intellectual expression, a new approach that moves the patient away from words to a more primitive, nonverbal way of relating to self and environment.

When working with either children or adults, the therapist may therefore have greater success in employing symbolic modalities, such as art therapy or play therapy. In *Pictures of a Childhood,* Alice Miller vividly demonstrates the power of art therapy to reveal and heal childhood wounds. Through two analyses, Miller herself had managed to keep the truth and pain of her childhood hidden. Once she began creating small, quickly composed watercolor paintings, as Miller describes it, she gave the once "silent child of long ago the right to her own language and her own story" (Miller, 1986). This modality allowed Miller to release her long-held secrets, to identify the pain of her childhood, to begin her healing journey, and ultimately to contribute to the healing of others. The modalities of art and sandplay therapy can reach deep below the surface, allowing clients to act out or to relate metaphorically the impact of certain situations even when they themselves are not aware of their significance.

Figure 11.2. Laura's Drawing: Isolated from Mother.

CASE 11-4

Laura, the eight-year-old daughter of a single mother in treatment for sex addiction, was asked to draw a picture of herself at home. She portrayed herself (see Figure 11.2) as extremely isolated from her mother, whom she described as being in the bedroom with a man. Although Laura had never verbalized her loneliness, the symbolic modality allowed her to represent what she felt.

As these cases demonstrate, creative-art and sandplay therapies can provide a valuable complement to psychotherapy in the treatment of sex addicts and their families. Administered judiciously by a well-trained therapist, creative-art and sandplay therapies can help accelerate the recovery of both sex addicts and co-addicts. One significant advantage of these therapies stems from their ability to draw on the right hemisphere of the brain (creativity, spirituality, emotions). Centered in right-brain functioning, these therapies are less amenable to conscious controls than traditional psychotherapy. Freed of the conscious controls inherent in verbalization, addicts or co-addicts can produce profound reflections of inner life. Their own creativity can provide unique insight into the spirit and greatly increase their awareness of their own emotional experience, as it did for Laura. Because these therapies tend to bypass conscious controls, they can cut through the rigid defense systems characteristic of both addicts and co-addicts. In analyzing the product of creative-art or sandplay therapy, the addict or co-addict can further overcome defense systems in bringing the emotional or experiential content of the work to conscious, left-brain awareness. This process of creation and analysis can thus help integrate the left brain and the right brain—intellectual and emotional experience.

Sex addicts and co-addicts also benefit from sandplay and creative-art therapies because they are active modalities that demand that the patient participate in the process. The addict or co-addict does virtually all of the work in creative-art and sandplay therapy: Creation, discovery, personal interpretation, and integration all spring directly from the client. The only way to find out with any degree of certainty what an individual image means, for example, is to explore it with the patient, as symbols have not only universal meanings, but uniquely personal ones as well. The demand that they actively participate in every aspect of creative-art and sandplay therapies instead of passively "receiving treatment" helps patients to take personal responsibility and ownership of their experiences.

Finally, sandplay and art therapy can help sex addicts and co-addicts to dissipate and channel emotional energy in a therapeutic way. In the grip of sex addiction or co-addiction, the displaced energy of such repressed emotions as hurt, anger, sadness, and disappointment helps fuel the addictive cycle or co—addictive behaviors. Creative-art and sandplay therapy offer media through which patients can express these emotions and begin to deal with them directly. A skilled creative-art therapist can then use these media to develop a treatment plan designed to achieve such diverse goals as identifying and confronting defense mechanisms, building self esteem, teaching new coping skills, and improving communication.

PERSON, PROCESS, PRODUCT

Creative-art therapists can choose or combine any of three approaches, depending upon the particular needs of individual clients (Ault & Klempner, 1987):

Person-oriented therapy (also called psychoanalytic or dynamically oriented therapy) focuses on the personal symbols included in an individual's work and the associations linked to those symbols. By analyzing and discussing the work's imagery, the patient expresses and thus brings to consciousness hidden or repressed feelings, thoughts, perceptions, attitudes, assumptions, conflicts, or fantasies. Because the symbols (and their associations) chosen are personal in nature, the therapist should guard against the temptation to interpret a patient's symbols for her or him. Insight and understanding develop through the patient's own introspective work, not the therapist's.

Process-oriented therapy "mediates the relationship between a person and the objects and people in the environment" (Ault & Klempner, 1987). Process-oriented therapy concentrates on exploring *how* individuals create rather than *what* they create. The way the individual interacts with the material (clay, sand, etc.) and any others who may be involved in the creative process (including the therapist as overseer and authority figure) often reflects how (s)he relates to the outside world. By concentrating on, for example how they work with the material and how they choose images, etc., addicts or co-addicts can practice new coping skills. All of the creative-arts therapies provide a medium for the creative expression and sublimation of negative emotions. Process-oriented therapy can thus teach patients alternatives to addictive or co-addictive behaviors. We have found process-oriented therapy especially useful in the context of family therapy for sex addicts. In this context, everyone in the family gains the opportunity to observe and identify family dynamics, alliances and antagonisms, while building interpersonal awareness. Family members can in this way become more aware of how they interact with one another and can then begin to develop healthier relationships.

Product-oriented therapy focuses on improving artistic skills and creating better work. This concentration can lead to improved perceptual abilities or coordination as well as the boost in self-esteem that springs from the creation of a beautiful or useful object. When combined with psychotherapy, the encouragement of artistic talent can facilitate the creativity needed to activate other, hidden, healthier functions of the real self (Masterson, 1988). These can include drawing pleasure from beauty, creativity, and skill (a pleasure foreign to many sex addicts and co-addicts) and employing these skills as a means of self-actualization. We do not discount the importance of this aspect of creative-art therapies, however, our primary focus in our work with sex addicts and co-addicts is on person- and process-oriented art therapy.

CASE 11-5

Bob, a health professional in treatment for sexually abusing his children and grandchildren, spoke almost exclusively in medical and psychological terms during his initial session with us. When confronted about this defensive pattern of intellectualizing, Bob explained that he always communicated this way. To get Bob away from the distancing effect of his verbalization, the therapist decided to try person-oriented art therapy. The suggestion that he work with clay caught Bob so off guard that he didn't even think about resisting.

Knowing that Bob had already drawn a picture of his Sobbing Hurting Child and his Controlling Child in therapy with Marilyn Murray, the therapist asked him to do clay pieces representing these parts of himself. Almost as soon as he touched the clay, he became quiet—an unusual condition for him. He focused solely on the clay and his creations. When he had completed the pieces, he was asked to describe the two pieces in the first person. This person-oriented strategy encouraged him to own his work and to begin to identify in a more personal way both with his work and with the feelings associated with the words he used to describe the pieces. Pointing to the figure of the Sobbing, Hurting Child (see Figure 11-3), he said, "This is me with my head held in shame. I was shamed and felt embarrassed as a child. I have wings attached to me, like the wings of an angel. Like the little angel, the perfect child. My mother called me that. I knew I wasn't but I tried to be.... I was really bad. I did try to take care of Mom and protect her from Dad. He was always gone; when he was there, he would scream and throw things at her.

"Afterwards she would take me into her bed and ask me to hold her. I looked good. I was cute. I went to Sunday school. Inside I was so scared of her and of my dad. I was lonely and afraid of everything. With these wings I could also fly away. That's what I did when I was in bed with Mom. I was really not there. I don't have feet but instead fins, like a fish. I couldn't stand up for myself, but I could swim away if I couldn't fly. Maybe I could swim behind a big rock (like the big pillow on Mom's bed that I hid my face in). Or maybe I could find some seaweed and get lost so no one would be able to find me."

Next he talked about the Controlling Child (see Figure 11-4). "This is me, but I have a moat with very deep water and ferocious water creatures around me so that *no one* can get to me. This moat protects and isolates me from others. This taller part of me is composed of all the 'great things' I have done as an adult. Everyone thinks I have so many accomplishments and lots of talents. I do. But that is not who I really am. I have to look good so no one will know what a mess I am. At the top, the tiny knob-like structure that is isolated from the rest, that's me. It is impossible for anyone to get close or to really know me. I am protected, disciplined and controlled. The little knob controls it all."

The tactile, emotional, three-dimensional experience of working with clay allowed Bob to understand more fully and better integrate the parts of himself. He had never before conveyed his true feelings in a therapy session. Yet in talking about the clay figure of the Sobbing Hurting Child, he cried for the first time. He seemed at last to be connecting not only cognitively but emotionally with the extent of his wounding and the ways he learned to control his feelings. Although he admitted to feeling displeasure when initially asked to work with clay, he felt relief afterward. He called it a humbling process for such a highly regarded, arrogant, and ego-centered professional to play with clay.

This person-oriented art therapy not only provided Bob with a catharsis, but also forced him to acknowledge a part of himself that he didn't like—and to begin to integrate this part. The rough and crude yet important images Bob created provided vessels that contained information he previously did not see or did not allow himself to see. When he talked about the product, the process, and himself, he integrated both affect and cognition. This integration was demonstrated symbolically in

Figure 11.3. Bob's Clay Representations: Sobbing Hurting Child.

Figure 11.4. Bob's Clay Representations: Controlling Child.

the way he interacted with the pieces he was describing. When he began talking, he kept the two pieces at a distance from each other. As he continued talking, he moved the pieces closer together. This symbolized the process initiated by this exercise: identifying, expressing, and integrating the various split-off and disowned parts of self.

In a later session, Bob was asked to create a single clay piece that integrated the other two and that would portray his Original Feeling Child. Through this process, Bob was able to see both the negative and positive aspects of both archetypes: the Sobbing Hurting Child and the Controlling Child. With the new awareness uncovered by art therapy, the patient and therapist can then work together to design more productive ways of coping and to establish healthier boundaries.

Given the opportunity and encouragement to express themselves safely, all people can be extremely creative. But sex addicts and co-addicts may at first find themselves constrained in creative-arts or sandplay therapy by the desire to be perfect, even within the confines of the therapist's office. These patients may demonstrate difficulty taking anything but a product-oriented approach to art and play therapy. To combat this perfectionism, when giving directions for an exercise, the therapist should always stress that no one will grade them on the quality of their work. Patients should not worry about doing it the "right" way or the "wrong" way; whatever way they choose is the right way.

SANDPLAY THERAPY

Sandplay therapy has its roots in the medical model of British pediatrician Margaret Lowenfeld and in the Jungian psychoanalytical model of Dora Kalff. This modality can serve as a valuable adjunct in the process of diagnosis, intervention, treatment, and individuation. Originally used only with children and only in the context of individual therapy, some non-Jungian sandplay has more recently been incorporated as an adjunct to couples therapy, family therapy, and even groups.

A mostly nonverbal form of therapy, sandplay enables the patient to express unconscious contents in a tangible, three-dimensional form. A simple, expressive, and direct way to objectify experience through symbols, sandplay can help to expand personal creativity, resolve problems, and facilitate personal growth and development. The process of sandplay therapy involves using sand, water, and a variety of miniature, realistic figures and such natural objects as rocks, shells, and stones to create a picture, scene, or abstract design in a sandtray, telling a story or speaking of associations, and experiencing the symbols used in the process. Sandplay offers a vehicle to the imagination, allowing the individual to become creative. When people put toys in the sand, they seem to tell a story of their heart and spirit. The picture represents in three dimensions some aspect of the patient's psychic situation. Relatively free of ego dominance, this modality can activate deep layers of the unconscious. Representing figures and landscapes of both the inner and the outer worlds, the sand pictures appear to connect and mediate between these worlds.

Sandplay therapy operates under this basic postulate: Deep in the unconscious is an autonomous tendency, given the proper conditions, for the psyche to heal itself. Sandplay seems to "elicit a confrontation and a bringing together of opposite aspects or parts of oneself, which leads to centering and the experience of wholeness" (Bradway, 1985). These qualities make sandplay therapy a valuable adjunctive modality for sex addicts and their families, who often need to reconcile and integrate dissociated parts of themselves (see Chapter 9).

The process of sandplay generally reflects this tendency toward healing. Especially with children but also with some adults, sandplay therapy commonly progresses through three stages: chaos, struggle, and resolution. The first stage, *chaos*, often reflects and objectifies the emotional turmoil and confusion in the child's life. The distressing emotions and/ or repressed feelings brought on by childhood trauma or neglect can overwhelm the young ego. The sandtray offers a safe place for this inner turbulence to surface. This chaotic stage may occur just once in their work with the sandtray, or may last through several sessions.

Case 11-6

Ginny, the daughter of a single mother in treatment for sex addiction, seemed quiet, timid and hesitant in her first sandplay session. The permission to put whatever she wanted in the sand-tray and create any scene she wanted immediately energized her. Moving quickly back and forth from the shelves of minia-tures to the sandtray, Ginny filled the tray with a variety of figures. Working swiftly and silently, Ginny swept sand over some figures, burying and then unburying them, turned other miniatures upside down, and piled figures on top of one another. When she had finished, Ginny wanted to know whether she could leave the scene as it was or if she had to put everything away. Told she could leave her work intact, Ginny seemed pleased. "Now *that's* a mess," Ginny announced, a pronouncement that could equally sum up her home life: an absent father, a mother who brought a parade of men into the home, and a pile of siblings with little or no boundaries.

No matter how chaotic a patient's scene appears, the therapist needs to avoid any urge to "clean it up." Taking the scene apart before the patient leaves would not only deliver a blow to the ego by destroying her or his creative work of art, the product of his or her work, but also effectively short-circuits any chance of the patient processing or analyzing it in depth. After photographing and recording the sandtray and retaining it in the patient's permanent chart (a protocol followed with every sandtray created by any patient), the therapist can then put things back in their place and return the sand to a level and smooth state for the next patient.

In the chaos of a patient's initial sandtray, (s)he usually offers clues to his or her problems—and often to the solutions as well. Laid out in the sandtray, a patient's difficulties and parts of self take on a reality and substance that makes them impossible to deny. After completing the initial sandtray, the patient and therapist need to sift through the chaos to identify important pieces of the puzzle, prioritize elements of recovery into the treatment plan, and begin to address the newly revealed problems.

CASE 11-7

Stan, a sex addict in his mid-30s, created a sandtray scene that clearly exposed many worries, obsessions, and conflicting parts of his personality. His sandtray laid out his realities, his fantasies, and both spiritual and sexual aspects of his self. In one corner, for example, he portrayed going to Disneyland with his wife and children; opposite this scene stood Wonder Woman–a tableau that for him symbolized the opposition of his family life and his compulsive sexual affairs. A Chinese junk about to go under a bridge indicated a recent relapse during a trip to Hong Kong. The chaotic arrangement of the sandtray reflected Stan's own perceptions of himself and his life: out of balance, fragmented, with hardly any connections at all. Although Stan admitted to feeling apprehensive about confronting the contents of his work, he also recognized that he had no hope of recovering unless "I can see it all, everything." In the sandtray he recognized many disowned and repressed parts of himself that he had previously had no awareness of or had refused to accept. Yet in completing the sandtray, Stan recognized that he could no longer repress these "dark" parts of himself, but would have to own them (rather than merely identify them) in order to avoid acting on them.

Stan particularly identified with the figure of a man playing golf, which he saw as a metaphor for his life. "I'm happy when I'm hitting the ball and doing well," he explained. "I get extremely frustrated when I don't do well, actually when I'm not perfect. To do well at golf I need to practice, to play, and to get professional help." Stan smiled, recognizing that he was no longer talking just about golf. "I need to practice healthy patterns of living and appropriate behaviors in my recovery program. The play part means not worrying, obsessing, or living in either the past or the future. Play means to enjoy life, to find meaning and balance in my life, not rigid constraints and perfectionism or black-and-white thinking patterns. The professional help is my ongoing recovery program and therapy."

The second stage of sandplay therapy, *struggle*, reflects the patient's growing empowerment. As children and adults who were victimized during their childhood begin, with the help of sandplay in combination with other therapeutic modalities, to move beyond the trauma and the role of victim, this stage of sandplay therapy enables them to begin identifying with strength. Many patients stage battles involving monsters, cowboys and Indians, knights, and armies. This stage may also involve family miniatures or animal figures. The child (or "adult child") will blow up and destroy people, places and things; indeed, both sides may be annihilated in the beginning of this stage. Often, the struggle becomes more intense and organized over a period of several sessions. In later sessions, the patient may have adversaries imprison one another, rather than killing one another. As a heroic figure often emerges to defeat the "bad guys," it is important to include such powerful images as Superman, Wonder Woman, Batman, or a Fairy Godmother. The patient often identifies with the strength of such victors. The process of struggle laid out in the sandtray can thus prove quite empowering for patients, especially children, who may through this struggle find inner strength, perhaps for the first time feeling powerful despite their small size and physical vulnerability.

The third stage of sandplay therapy, *resolution*, reflects the patient's progression from early chaos to the restoration—or establishment for the first time—of order in his or her life. Sandtrays begin to demonstrate a greater degree of balance and structure. As the child (or adult child) becomes more comfortable and accepting of his or her position in the real world (without necessarily liking that position), the work in the sandtray may make more obvious sense, often becoming more grounded in situations that reflect everyday realities. The patient will have resolved some problems or at least put them in a broader perspective; (s)he may have dissipated some of the energy once poured into those problems. Some patients at this stage demonstrate a sense of completion and wholeness through the ordering and integration of their work (and through the use of such symbols as circles and squares) and often through their words as well: The patient may, for example, brush off her or his hands and announce, "I'm done." Or a child may announce that (s)he only needs to come one or two more times.

CASE 11-8

The 11-year-old son of an abusive, alcoholic father, Justin was a talented actor and performer. The first sandtray he created (see Figure 11.5) offered evidence of how Justin defended himself against his father's abuse: escape into fantasy. Full of fantasy figures, storybook figures, and Walt Disney characters, the sandtray included just one "real" person—representing his father—sitting on the edge of the tray. Five sessions later, Justin produced a dramatically different sandtray (see Figure 11.6), featuring many more naturalistic figures presented in a much more ordered ar-

Figure 11.5. Justin's Sandtray: Alcoholic Father on Edge.

Figure 11.6. Justin's Sandtray: Madonna and Religious Symbols.

rangement. For the first time, Justin also incorporated religious symbols into his work: a mission and a statue of the Virgin Mary. Although his family had no formal religious foundation, Justin had, at age eleven, begun a spiritual journey within himself. This sandtray proved to be a major turning point in Justin's therapy. From the fantasy world that he had so long occupied, Justin began turning to reality and finding sources of healing within himself. Having discovered new ways to comfort himself, he no longer needed to escape into a fantasy world. Although he continued to use his talent as an actor, Justin no longer needed to employ this talent solely for survival or to become identified with his roles.

The initial tray can often reveal the nature of the patient's problem, and even point to the solution. Although none of Justin's subsequent sandtrays included a father figure, the first tray clearly indicated that the absent father was a large part of the boy's problem. Like Justin, many patients—especially children—may not show or tell the therapist a significant factor more than once. The therapist must therefore observe meticulously and carefully all the elements of each individual sandtray, paying particular attention to what the patient shows, doesn't show, or presents in an unusual way (e.g., the father sitting on the edge of the tray). Then the therapist can help the patient thoroughly process these elements, taking care not to overlook something that may prove significant.

Benefits of Sandplay Therapy

Sandplay therapy can allow therapist and patient to achieve a number of therapeutic objectives. First, it provides a safe, non-threatening space for therapy. The sandtray accepts unconditionally whatever the individual chooses to place or play out in it. It also offers a literally and symbolically contained environment, a protected therapeutic space with real physical boundaries in which the process of therapy can unfold. Sandplay thus provides an immediate and safe outlet for the expression of emotions—space for patients to act out and the tools with which to do so. Children benefit from this opportunity to ventilate, in the protected area of the sandtray, feelings that they might otherwise not feel safe in expressing—even through play or art.

CASE 11-9

Jeremy arrived at a session having obviously had an altercation with his father on the drive to the office. Both were visibly upset. In the therapist's office, Jeremy headed straight for the sandtray. For the next 10 minutes, he used soldiers and heavy military equipment to stage a violent, hostile battle, complete with sounds of explosions, machine-gun fire, and violent screams. Then he abruptly stopped, brushed the sand off his hands and announced, "Okay, I'm ready to work now." It was both important and appropriate for Jeremy to express and act out his anger, hostility, and frustration in the sandplay rather than directing it at his father, a younger sibling, or in other inappropriate ways. The rest of the session was devoted to processing his feelings about the argument and about his father. When he returned to the waiting room at the end of the session, he rushed into his father's arms saying, "Let's go, Dad."

With other patients, the therapist can steer sandplay therapy in a direction that produces just the opposite effect. Instead of prompting the release experienced by Jeremy, sandplay can be used to contain and collect out-of-control fears and feelings. Especially in cases involving patients who suffer from anxiety disorders, the act of playing with the sand can have a soothing impact. Slow, rhythmic sandplay can help a patient to slow the heart-rate and calm respiration. In these cases, the sandtray serves as a metaphor for the body.

CASE 11-10

The oldest son of a recovering sex addict, eleven-year-old Kyle suffered from severe anxiety, a not uncommon problem among children of sex addicts. A super achiever, Kyle worried and obsessed about every little thing. Time seemed to control him: During his first sessions, he constantly looked at his watch.

To help Kyle slow his breathing and relax, the technique of simply and slowly moving the sand around in the tray was employed. He would begin the sessions by removing his watch.

Then the therapist would start talking slowly, quietly, and gently while at the same time moving the sand around the sandtray. The therapist then would direct Kyle to attend to his own breathing and to slow it down as he joined in calmly moving the sand around. After several sessions, Kyle was able to relax almost automatically when he arrived in the therapist's office. In time, he learned that he could not be simultaneously anxious and relaxed. Choosing relaxation, he was soon able to use breathing techniques to calm himself whether at home or in school.

Sandplay also allows patients to take an active role in the process of transformation and healing. All individuals in recovery need to take an active and responsible role in their own healing. This is especially true of children, for whom the active modality of sandplay can instill a feeling of empowerment that purely verbal modalities can seldom provide. Sandplay therapy allows patients to take an active role in creating the scene that reflects and amplifies their inner and outer worlds. In addition, the contained environment represented by the sex addict (or other family member) also provides an evolving tableau that allows the patient to take an active role in determining the course of treatment, for example, in setting priorities for recovery.

CASE 11-7 (*continued*)

Stan created a second sandtray, again filled with a chaotic arrangement of incongruent parts. Because he admitted feeling overwhelmed by all these aspects of himself, the suggestion was made to explore and address just one part at a time. The sandtray (see Figure 11.7) thus functioned as a schematic treatment plan, outlining the areas on which Stan needed to concentrate in therapy, but emphasizing that he could attend to just one issue at a time. To ease his sense of being overwhelmed, Stan was encouraged to avoid focusing solely on the negative aspects of self laid out before him, and to begin considering these "dark" parts as repressed potential. This dual perspective allowed Stan to confront reality (a therapeutic imperative) while at the same time drawing hope from this confrontation.

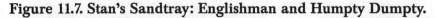

Figure 11.7. Stan's Sandtray: Englishman and Humpty Dumpty.

The first figure analyzed, an English gentleman, represented the image Stan projected to the outside world. As a child, Stan had been the "perfect little boy"; his mother had called him her "little prince." Although he deeply resented his mother for fashioning him in this image—as well as for her lack of appropriate sexual boundaries with her young son—he felt uncomfortable sharing his feelings about his mother. In discussing this figure, he acknowledged that during Focused Action Therapy (psychodrama) at the hospital, he had screamed obscenities at his "mother." Yet he did not want to repeat these words now, wanting to maintain his "good" image even in the therapeutic environment. With repeated encouragement, Stan finally let go of his image and allowed his real feelings to come through.

In exploring a Humpty Dumpty figure he had chosen, Stan explained that he identified with the character: brave, smiling, and flawless on the outside, but fragile, scared, and very angry on the inside. Stan then identified the targets of his anger as women, especially his mother and his former wife. When encouraged to establish congruence between his inner feelings and what he projected to the outside world, Stan began to realize how he displaced and controlled his anger. Although he tried to be "Mr. Nice Guy" all the time, his anger would be acted out either through passive-aggressive behavior or through physical abuse. This incongruence contributed powerfully to his feeling that at any moment he was going to crack apart, just like Humpty Dumpty.

Stan had placed a fantasy fairy-tale figure between the two areas of the sandtray that he described as related to his sexuality and spirituality. When dealing with these parts of himself, Stan explained, he had a tendency to fly off into "Never Neverland." In talking about these areas, he began to appreciate his need to stay grounded in reality.

By tackling each of these sometimes contradictory aspects of himself one at a time, Stan began to appreciate that although recovery would not be easy, neither was it impossible. Instead of leaving the session so overwhelmed, hopeless and depressed that he might never return to therapy, Stan came away from the session with a heightened awareness and understanding of specific things that he wanted to change. In setting his priorities, he had helped determine the direction of his treatment plan—and his recovery.

Sandplay offers a flexible, effective, and creative mode of therapy for patients. The modality taps into the right brain, drawing on creative, holistic, integrative, and spiritual functions. By spiritual, we do not necessarily mean religious, but rather that aspect of a human being's nature through which the individual establishes, nourishes, and maintains a relationship with a Higher Power (e.g., God). In working with children like Justin (see Case 11-8), for example, we are often amazed to see them incorporate a religious or spiritual symbol into their sandplay scenes and use this to begin talking about God. This connection with and facilitation of the patient's spiritual side seems much more apparent with sandplay than with other art therapies. This spiritual element is important in the healing of sex addicts and members of their family, for any child who has suffered victimization (as so many sex addicts have) has been wounded spiritually. And just as a child's mental health is closely connected to his or her religious and spiritual thinking (Coles, 1993), so too is the adult child's.

Sandplay can function as a bridge between the inner and the outer worlds, as well as between the unconscious and the conscious. This modality enables the internal to become externalized, bringing it into conscious awareness for perhaps the first time. Crossing this bridge can help to break through a patient's resistance and denial.

Case 11-11

Margaret, the wife of a sex addict, sobbed deeply as she moved sand through the sandtray and recounted a recent telephone call from her husband's current girlfriend. The young woman on the phone had told Margaret that not only had her husband been having an affair with her for several months, but that he had had numerous affairs throughout their marriage. Margaret was devastated and deeply hurt by her husband's betrayal. As she spoke, Margaret added no miniatures or other figures to the sandtray. Her tears washed down her face, falling into the tray and merging with the water she had poured into the sandtray at the beginning of the session. When she felt able to "come up for air," she noticed that she had unconsciously created a pattern in the sandtray: a large heart, serrated and separated into two parts. This, she said, was her heart, a broken heart.

By serving as an integrative bridge between the unconscious and the conscious, sandplay can make clear what words may be unable to convey—in this case, the depth of Margaret's anguish. Images visualized in the unconscious can be made manifest through the medium of the sandtray. The bridge between the unconscious and the conscious can allow the energy associated with unspoken or repressed emotions or perceptions to be unblocked, released, and dissipated, thereby freeing up energy to be focused in more healthy ways.

Case 11-12

Anna—the 23-year-old daughter of an alcoholic and sexually abusive father, the wife of an active alcoholic, and the mother of a 3-year-old son—presented as a shy, quiet woman, who found it extremely difficult to talk about her dysfunctional home situation. During her first two sessions with us, she related "safe" facts about her family life, denying and minimizing the reality of her current situation and its damaging effect on herself and her son. She reported, for example, that her husband had *only* hit her twice and that *only* when he was drinking did he sleep in the nude with their son. Clearly, Anna was stuck in a rigid defense system of delusion and denial.

Anna worked with a sandtray in her third session. Anna took an unusual approach: Rather than standing the miniatures upright, she chose to lay all the figures down flat in the sand. "I want to see the whole picture," she repeated several times. When she had finished the scene (see Figure 11-8), she explained that her small son was playing with his toy trucks in the far corner with his back turned to his parents, who were engaged in separate activities. Her son was not in his bedroom, she went on, but in the kitchen where he felt safe. The chaos and confusion in the middle of the sandtray represented her family life. The two airplanes and two boats in another corner offered ways she and her son could escape from this crazy place.

Figure 11.8. Anna's Sandtray: Figures Flat.

Anna's creation and her own analysis of the product helped her to begin to acknowledge the unacceptability and inappropriateness of her way of life. In talking about this scene she had created, Anna acknowledged for the first time the mess that was her family life. With a three-dimensional representation in front of her, she could no longer deny her unpleasant reality or the ramifications of the dysfunctional family situation on herself and her son. Her description of the scene helped her to become acutely aware of the fears, isolation, and loneliness of her son—and of herself. And though she recognized her son's helplessness, she also saw that she had the power to plan their "escape." She now had the motivation to change.

Finally, sandplay can also facilitate the transference relationship. Whether referred to as transference, "claiming the therapist" (an especially important task for children), or establishing a witness to the experience, this dynamic is necessary to establish and maintain a therapeutic relationship. Children especially need at least one person to accept and validate them unconditionally. This person might be a family member, a teacher, a friend, a clergy member, or a therapist. Because even a brief encounter with such a significant person can sometimes be helpful, we approach every session with a child as if it might be our only chance to accept and validate them. Sandplay therapy can often make the transference relationship readily apparent. The child (or the adult) may, for example, choose to identify the therapist as either a certain object or an archetypal figure.

Because the objects used in sandplay therapy can serve as transitional objects, the therapist may sometimes find it beneficial to let patients take one home to help anchor the time in therapy (a neurolinguistic programming technique) and to encourage and remind them to continue the therapeutic work beyond the session. The transitional object can thus enhance the therapeutic relationship through the use of evocative memory. Small, colorful rocks have been favorite objects to help ground the therapeutic experience.[1]

---

[1] We often recommend to our patients Byrd Baylor's *Everybody Needs a Rock*, which teaches children—and adults—important lessons about being special, making choices, and appreciating beauty.

CASE 11-13

Luis, a 12-year-old whose father had sexually abused him, chose a colorful rock formation just before he moved out of state with his mother. He explained that he wanted to put it in his aquarium so that every day, when he fed his fish, he would remember some of the things he had done with his therapist.

In this way, objects used in sandplay therapy can help patients recall, incorporate, and further therapeutic insights.

Family Sandplay Therapy

Sandplay can serve as a useful adjunctive therapy not only in an individual context, but in the context of family therapy as well. Because it appeals both to the actual children in the family and to the "inner child" of adult members, sandplay therapy can serve as an equalizer between children and adult family members in a way that traditional talk therapy cannot. It can thus simultaneously offer reparative work to both the actual children and the parents' "inner children."

When combined, sandplay therapy and family therapy can provide the therapist with an opportunity to observe the uniqueness of each family member and the dynamics of the family system. The modality can in this way encourage families to begin exploring family boundaries (or lack of boundaries)—a major issue in the treatment of families of sex addicts. The tangible dimensions of the sandtray impose both physical and symbolic limits on patients, thus providing a container in which to explore boundary issues. The sandtray offers a simple way for family members to create a three-dimensional work that can then be processed to identify and clarify family rules and roles. The reality thus presented in the three-dimensional *product* of a sandtray can help family members work together to confront one another's denial. The *process* of working on a sandtray as a family also provides the therapist access to family dynamics and boundary issues in action. The therapist can clearly see the nature of family alliances in the choices family members make, such as the selection of miniatures and decisions about who will work next, who will work together, and who will work alone.

The therapist then has the opportunity to intervene by offering a more objective view of the family, by restructuring destructive or inappropriate alliances, and by encouraging the formation of healthier ones.

CASE 11-14

Perry, the 12-year-old son of a sex addict, was asked to do a sandtray portraying the family as he saw it. The work showed Perry going off by himself with his dog and his friends. His parents focused all their attention and energy on his 15-year-old sister, who was acting out sexually. Asked to do a second tray showing how he would like his family to be, Perry grouped the figures representing family members in a circle. Through these two sandtrays, his parents (and sister) were able to see something that Perry had never been able to tell them directly. His work with the sandtrays revealed to them his isolation and sense that he was being left out of the family. They saw how the focus on Perry's sister had put him in a position of neglect and how that neglect had begun to affect him. As a result, they resolved to change the family situation, to alter the family dynamics to include Perry.

Working as a group or working individually, family members can learn to particularize their own dilemma, as Perry did, while at the same time learning new ways to communicate and associate with one another. Figures and scenes in a family sandtray may represent actual persons, a feeling or tone, a concept, a fantasy, or an actual situation. Young children may freely show situations in the sandtray using figures—animals, for example, which often seem "safer" than real people— that they may identify with one or more family members. The sandtray may also reveal to both the therapist and others in the family unconscious contents from the psyches of various family members. This revelation can initiate a discussion of emerging family patterns that leads to the exploration and implementation of alternative choices within the family system. The therapist can suggest more conscious choices that family members can begin to implement within the therapy. As part of a comprehensive treatment milieu, family sandplay therapy thus offers families an opportunity to learn new adaptation techniques.

Because the use of sandplay therapy in the context of family therapy is relatively new, the variety of potential applications has not yet been fully explored. Although it can be adapted to whatever orientation a particular practitioner holds, any therapist who elects to combine the two very different orientations of family therapy and sandplay must have a high degree of expertise in both. (Similarly, any therapist who chooses to combine the double orientation of the creative arts and family-systems theory must also be expert in both fields.) Because we have found sandplay a helpful adjunctive modality in the context of family therapy, we believe it offers a variety of possibilities for further study and development.

Cautions Regarding Sandplay and Creative-Art Therapies

Sandplay and creative-art therapies can serve a valuable and valid purpose when employed by a trained clinician within the context of a team approach to treating sex addicts and their families. The creative process and created products involved in these techniques can add new pieces to the puzzle, providing dynamic information that augments the overall picture of the individual and the family and contributes to both individual and family healing. However, we must emphasize that creative-art therapies and sandplay therapy have inherent limitations and should therefore be regarded not as panaceas for this population, but rather, as adjunctive modalities.

Before introducing a patient to creative-art therapies, the therapist should be sure (s)he knows enough about the individual patient and attendant pathology to determine whether these therapies might be of benefit. Intake evaluation, input from the primary therapist and other members of the treatment team, records from previous therapists, and hospitalization records can all assist the creative-art therapist in determining the appropriateness of art or sandplay therapies for a given patient. If the therapist is unfamiliar with the patient, or if (s)he has any doubts at all about the appropriateness of these approaches, then creative-art therapies should *not* be employed. Art therapy and sandplay therapy can reach a deeper, more emotional layer of the psyche, opening up issues and affect that may have been repressed or denied for many, many years. If a client has fragile or weak ego strength or tends toward histrionic behavior or borderline personality (not uncommon diagnoses among sex addicts and their families), this work should not be undertaken unless a qualified clinician can offer close supervision, possibly in a hospital setting.

Therapists should also be cautioned against drawing definite conclusions regarding diagnosis, intervention, or treatment based on a single drawing, sculpture, collage, sandplay experience, or other creative-arts process or product. The therapist must have the opportunity to observe consistency and continuity—or the lack thereof—in every patient's work. Although a single product or process may provide significant clues or powerful insights, a series of work provides much more reliable information.

The creative-art therapist must be first and foremost a competent clinician specially trained in creative-art and/or sand therapy. Not everyone in the treatment team can or will want to do this type of work. On our staff, Barbara Bagan Prochelo is both a registered art therapist (ATR) and a member of the International Society of Sandplay Therapists (ISST). Just as important as receiving professional training, the skilled creative-art and/or sandplay therapist will also have undergone a personal experience of the process. If the therapist does not know, from personal experience, how the process works, (s)he will find it difficult to do and even harder to trust. The patient will sense this hesitancy and find it equally difficult to trust either the therapist or the work.

Although the therapist needs expertise, (s)he must also have the humility to allow the patient, whether child or adult, to lead the process. The therapist's ego and any rigid plans regarding how the process will unfold must remain outside of the therapy room. The therapist must have the intuitive skills to know when to ask questions and when to remain silent. The therapist should take care not to lead, guide, or coerce patients to create, associate, or interpret their work in a particular way. Ethical duty and professional responsibility demand that the client be allowed to produce works that reflect his or her *own* conscious and unconscious issues rather than the therapist's. Although this caution necessarily applies to all therapeutic modalities, it takes on added importance with creative and expressive therapies, which more easily lend themselves to a therapist's projection. If the creative-art therapist keeps all these precautions in mind, the use of these modalities with sex addicts and co-addicts can open up new avenues toward both accessing information and resolving psychological problems.

12

Healthy Sexuality

A New Beginning for Sex Addicts and Co-Addicts

The rebuilding of the relationship between a sex addict and his or her partner necessitates the development, often for the first time, of healthy sexual behavior both individually and as a couple. Some sex therapists have even observed that it is possible, with appropriate interventions, for a couple in which one partner is a sex addict or even a sex offender to attain a higher level of sexual satisfaction within their relationship than those who have no history of sexual deviance (Sedgwick, 1993). Although most married couples in treatment for sex addiction demonstrate heterosexual orientation and behavior, the effectiveness of these interventions has also been studied in married bisexual men who identify themselves as sex addicts (Schneider & Schneider, 1990). Given that many, if not most, sex addicts are involved in primary relationships, recovery programs for sex addiction usually include sex education and sex therapy for couples whatever their sexual preference or gender.

The program of sex education and sex therapy described here, an essential component of what we refer to as edutherapy, applies to couples in recovery together. It addresses issues (explored in more detail below) of sex education, sexual dysfunction, spirituality, and intimacy. The resolution of these issues is so fundamental to the recovery of sex addicts and their partners—often referred to as co-addicts (Earle & Crow, 1990)—that we do not consider this program as a separate entity, but as an essential aspect of the overall therapeutic program. Although we do set aside certain sessions explicitly for sex education and sex therapy, we try to integrate instruction and techniques that promote healthy sexuality throughout the course of therapy.

Certainly, this program can be adjusted to accommodate recovering sex addicts who have no participating partner. Sex addicts who are *not* involved in primary relationships need sex education and sex therapy as much as—if not more than—those who have partners.

SEX EDUCATION

The sex education and therapy part of the treatment regimen embraces the same goal as any quality sex education program: the promotion of accurate, constructive, positive sexual knowledge and attitudes. Unfortunately, many people in our culture have not been exposed to this type of program (Katzman, 1990). When this omission is compounded by the commission of abuse, or other environmental or situational traumas, sexual attitudes become radically distorted and sex addiction may follow.

Earle and Crow (1989) sum up the need for recovering sex addicts to receive a basic sex education as follows:

> With only limited information about how men and women react sexually and because most, if not all, of your own sexual experiences have centered on your compulsive ritual, you may not know what constructive sexual behavior is. What's more, having never allowed emotional involvement or honest communication to be part of your own sexual experience, you may believe that others regard sex the same way you do: as a source of purely physical pleasure. (p. 264)

Case 12-1

John and Mary knew little about healthy sexuality. Neither had received any formal sex education in school or from their families. Sexual curiosity, whether expressed verbally or physically, was suppressed—and even shamed—in both of their childhood homes. A lack of education, however, is an education in itself. The absence of any instruction regarding sexual values or even physiological facts transmitted negative messages about sex: It was literally unspeakable. The informal sex education they received also contributed to their distorted sexual attitudes. John learned from his peers that women existed solely for men's pleasure and that he could always find a girl who would "give in" to his sexual desires. John fantasized constantly about scoring with as many women as possible and then set out to make his fantasies come true. Nonetheless, John was afraid of women and afraid of showing any "feminine" tendencies—e.g., the desire to be stroked or caressed. Mary learned the corollary to this attitude from her peers: that men wanted women for just one thing. If she didn't provide it, others would. Not surprisingly, as adults, neither knew the nature of sexual pleasure or healthy sexuality—or how to achieve them.

John and Mary met each other in a bar. She had just turned 21 and he was also 21. After several hours of drinking together, the couple had had a quick sexual encounter in the back seat of his car. After several more dates, they became engaged. Though they knew little about each other or their families, they married later that same year. John thought marriage would end his sexually compulsive behavior—and it did, for a brief period. Less than a year after his marriage, however, John had returned to his former habits. Three years later, he sought treatment after being arrested for soliciting a prostitute.

SEXUAL DYSFUNCTION

Sex therapy for couples in treatment for sex addiction must also include an exploration of any precipitating or resulting sexual dysfunctions. Butts (1982) indicates that sex addicts often develop "traditional" sexual dysfunctions that may, in turn, contribute to further addiction if left untreated. If the addiction then compounds the dysfunction, the addictive cycle will only gain greater power over the addict. When they started treatment, both John and Mary reported sexual dysfunctions. John had premature ejaculation, and Mary reported hypoactive sexual desire. Other typical dysfunctions experienced by sex addicts and co-addicts include erection difficulties, retarded ejaculation, vaginal or pelvic pain (dyspareunia), and primary or secondary anorgasmia. Vaginismus, a condition in which involuntary spasms or narrowing of the vagina prevent penetration, is less common and it requires specific treatment when it occurs.

As mentioned earlier, many couples (including couples where no sex addiction is present) lack the knowledge, or even a common language for discussion, about sexual issues. As a result, any sexual dysfunctions that do occur frequently remain unrecognized or uncommunicated. Recovering sex addicts and co-addicts receiving appropriate sex therapy thus have a distinct advantage over couples not in treatment in that the therapist, in the course of a thorough sexual history, can quickly assess any dysfunctional or deviant sexual behavior within the relationship and begin to implement appropriate therapeutic modalities. With occasional adaptations along the way, we generally treat sexual dysfunctions in sex-addicted couples according to the traditional regimens prescribed by such clinicians as Barbach (1975), LoPiccolo and LoPiccolo (1978), Masters and Johnson (1970), and Zilbergeld (1992).

SPIRITUALITY

Case 12-1 (continued)

Both John and Mary had been sexually abused during childhood. John recalls that his older brother used to take care of him after school. On more than one occasion, his brother's friends came over to the house, made John undress, and then forced him to parade in front of them naked. They would sometimes make him rub his penis until it became erect. Then the older boys would laugh and tell him he should be ashamed of himself. Mary had been repeatedly molested by an uncle from age 10 to 16.

Many sex addicts (and co-addicts) were victims of childhood sexual abuse. As a result, they suffer from poor sexual self-image. Among survivors of sexual abuse, such issues as power, control, trust, and fear pose additional barriers to a healthy sexual relationship. Judith Herman (1992) points out the similarities in the consequences of prolonged sexual abuse and those of any complex post-traumatic stress disorder. These aftereffects include compulsive or extremely inhibited sexuality, a pervasive sense of shame and guilt, a sense of defilement and ultimately, disruption in intimate relationships. As sexual relations often trigger these psychodynamics, many survivors of sexual abuse suffer from some type of sexual dysfunction (Woititz, 1989). The partner's touch awakens conscious or unconscious memories, with all their accompanying affect. Yet since the partner seldom understands the origins of the triggered behaviors, (s)he may feel at least partially responsible. As a result, the partner may feel rejected or unloved. Whether these codependent attitudes result directly from the relationship dynamics or draw on the partner's own family-of-origin issues, the enabling characteristics of co-addiction usually come into play at this point.

Sex therapy for recovering sex addicts and co-addicts must include the evaluation and treatment of these kinds of deficits in sexual self-image as well as the spiritual aspects of sex (Helminiak, 1989). To create and sustain a positive and healthy sexual relationship, both individuals must see themselves as worthy of giving and receiving sexual pleasure. This is essentially a spiritual issue, profoundly tied to the individual's sense of self-worth, his or her relationship to God and others, and a personal understanding of the place of sex in God's plan.

While recognizing spirituality as a necessary component of sexual "progress," Patrick Carnes (1991) suggests that spiritual sources, particularly organized religions or religious beliefs, may contribute to negative sexual attitudes and eventually to destructive behaviors. Carnes argues that:

Many sex addicts suffered sexual damage from spiritual sources. Religious messages from their childhood equated sex with sin and evil. Lust was to be struggled against for the highest stakes of all: one's soul. The result was wounded, abused children who grew up hating their sexuality and possessing a cynical distrust of religion. (p. 303)

The recognition that shame-based religious messages inflict sexual damage leads Carnes to assert that sex addicts must heal spiritually as well as sexually. Although Sedgwick (1992) makes a distinction between spirituality and religion, she agrees that sex addicts and co-addicts must surrender the addiction to a Higher Power (to quote 12-step programs) or to "God's will." Recognizing that surrendering the addiction can lead to increased feelings of self-worth, a necessary precursor to the development of healthy sexuality, we strongly believe that a healthy sense of spiritual connectedness can promote both individual healing and the healing of the relationship, sexually and emotionally.

INTIMACY

A healthy sexual relationship demands a high level of intimacy between partners. For this reason, while it may not appear so profound at the beginning, the journey from addiction to intimacy to healthy sexuality is a very long and challenging one. In the early stages of treatment, for example, we have heard most sex addicts—and many co-addicts—report that they regard sexual intercourse as a purely physical act. Given this perspective, the notion that spiritual and emotional intimacy are the prelude to healthy sexual relations does not have meaning for many sex addicts.

In addition to knowing little about healthy sexuality, sex addicts and co-addicts tend to have extremely poor social skills. The same self-hatred, guilt, and passive rage that contributed to the development of deviant sexual behavior (Schwartz & Brasted, 1985) hinders the sex addict's ability to achieve spiritual and emotional intimacy. Sex addicts and co-addicts often do not have a clue about how to initiate and maintain a social relationship, either within the marriage or among friends outside of the marriage. Both sex addicts and co-addicts tend to communicate only on a surface level, never sharing deeply felt emotions, fears, or desires. This combination—poor sexual knowledge and inadequate communication skills—inevitably causes the couple's sexual relationship to suffer. In addition to basic sex education, our program therefore teaches healthy social and communication skills—the tools a couple needs to achieve satisfying emotional and spiritual (as well as physical) intercourse.

In defining intimacy, Daniel Araoz (1982) highlights its spiritual and emotional components and their relationship to healthy sexuality:

Intimacy means a commitment to someone else, a commitment to know the other person, to share one's inner life and one's living, including the ups and downs, its backs and forths. Intimacy requires work and perseverence.... Sex has special meaning for humans only because one perceives and welcomes the other as a human being and because of their emotional involvement. (p. 99)

In addition to these spiritual and emotional aspects of intimacy, healthy sexuality also requires certain behavioral aspects. Some of these behaviors need to be present prior to initiating lovemaking. Sherry Sedgwick (1992) refers to this phase as "fore-foreplay." Effective talking and listening skills, for example, need to be an early priority in order to achieve intimacy and healthy sexuality. Considering that every relationship, whether in recovery or not, features conflict, the sex therapy regimen should also include conflict-resolution skills— that is, using improving communication skills to arrive at a consensus— to promote mutual intimacy rather than mutual resentment. A playful outlook can also positively influence intimate communication. Both in and out of bed, healthy sexual partners need to find ways to relax and have fun together—whether taking walks, playing cards or board games, or engaging in sports—in order to further intimacy.

THE SEX EDUCATION AND THERAPY PROGRAM

The long-term objectives of our sex education and therapy program for sex addicts and co-addicts include:

- helping the couple to achieve a meaningful, satisfying sexual and social relationship with each other; and
- helping the addict to eliminate the compulsion to sexually exploit, molest, or abuse any adult or child.

In order to achieve these long-term objectives, we employ the following strategies, each aimed at achieving an immediate objective that builds upon the previous one(s). Although we determine the number and length of therapeutic sessions according to the particular needs and problems of the individual couple, the sex education and therapy program usually consists of three to four 50-minute sessions or their equivalent. Within these sessions and through homework assignments, the recovering sex addict and codependent are encouraged to do the following:

1. Review their sexual history to facilitate diagnostic evaluation and treatment decisions.
2. Discuss their expectations and needs for a healthy, monogamous social and sexual relationship.
3. Learn appropriate facts, attitudes, and behaviors—the basics of formal sex education classes, including relevant anatomy and physiology, the human sexual response cycle, and the development of prerequisites for healthy sexual behavior.
4. Identify any co- or preexisting sexual dysfunctions.
5. Review and implement the steps of "sensate focus," integrating the five senses while working through any concomitant memories of trauma or other negative emotions.
6. Resolve any remaining sexual issues or dysfunctions.

SHORT-TERM GOALS AND STRATEGIES

1. *Review Sexual history.* In the initial session of our sex education and therapy program, a male-female therapy team takes a detailed sexual history from each partner (see Figure 12-1). The history explores family-of-origin relationships, early lessons regarding sex (i.e., what, where, and from whom), first sexual and social relationships, and any history of abuse, in addition to current sexual knowledge, attitudes, and behaviors. Using this data, the therapists evaluate any sexual dysfunctions, sexual incompatibilities, or misconceptions in sexual knowledge and then delineate treatment goals accordingly. In addition, this sexual history-taking often unearths new memories and insights that contribute to the progress of the therapeutic process.

Before taking the couple's sex history, the therapists should know whether the sex addict and co-addict are in an early or later phase of treatment. In the early phase, for example, both partners will likely demonstrate a degree of denial that may affect the genuineness of responses. Taken at a later stage, however, after the couple has acknowl-

Figure 12-1. Sex History Outline.

Client ID

Name	Address	Sex
Age	Height	Weight
Religion	Education	Occupation

Medical Conditions	Use of alcohol or drugs
Medications	Fitness activities

Family History

Parents   Siblings

Any sex addicts or sex offenders in family
Marital status and history, including presence or absence of intimacy
Children

Sex Education and Experience

Age and circumstances when first learned about sex
  Other sex education
  Type of sex play common among teenage peers
  Age and circumstance when first experienced orgasm
  Parents' attitudes toward sex
  Number of sexual partners
  Similarity to present partner's sex education background

Experiences in your life related to physical, emotional, or sexual abuse

What do you think has had the greatest impact on your sexual beliefs?

Feelings about:

  Premarital sex
  Contraception
  Masturbation
  Sexuallty transmitted diseases, including AIDS

Any difficulty discussing sexual matters

Types of Sexual Problems Encountered

  Physical
  Emotional
  Medication effect

Where did you seek answers?

How frequent is your sexual activity?

At this time in your life, how important is sex?

Does your partner express the same feelings?

What, if anything, would you change about your current sexual activities
  or relationship?

edged the addiction and begun their recovery, the history will more accurately reflect the couple's sexuality, allowing the therapists to initiate more direct and effective interventions.

In eliciting responses, the therapist must follow a careful progression from less to more personal questioning. Most people, particularly women, are embarrassed when asked to talk about intimate sexual matters, therefore adhering to this progression will help lay a foundation of trust between therapist and client, so that by the end, most clients feel more comfortable talking about their sexual experiences and feelings. This change in itself often marks the beginning of a new level of communication between couples in recovery.

The sex history can also yield important insight regarding the formation of each person's sexual attitudes. Many women, for example, mistrust men because they recall being told that men only want one thing: sex. Men whose informal sex education emphasized "scoring" and physical sex, on the other hand, have little or no notion of how to fulfill a woman's needs for intimacy and a satisfying sexual relationship. Sexual attitudes based on inaccurate sexual messages can thus provide the fertile soil in which sex addiction grows.

In practicing sex therapy with couples in recovery, we make it clear that partners will share this historical data. In this way, the couple begins to develop critical insights into one another that often cannot be gained in other contexts. We usually spend the first 30–45 minutes of the 90-minute session taking the history: the male therapist questioning the husband; the female therapist, the wife. After a brief exchange of the information gathered, the therapists switch: the male therapist continuing the history with the wife; the female therapist, with the husband. Using the information collected from both partners, the therapists then present the couple with a preliminary diagnosis, set goals for the therapy with the couple, design a treatment plan, and assign homework. We may, for example, ask each partner to compile a list of worries and grievances about sex and their sexual relationship to share and discuss with each other at the next session.

2. *Discuss expectations.* The second phase of our sex education and therapy program follows Maggie Scarf's (1987) talking/listening technique in helping clients clarify their own wants, expectations, hopes, dreams, and eventually goals regarding a satisfying social and sexual relationship. At this stage, the strategy focuses solely on the individual

goals of each person and has no bearing on the partner. This strategy can also prompt each client to identify, perhaps for the first time, any distorted modus operandi concerning sexuality or intimacy, to discover how and where they were learned, and to begin the process of change.

The partners then present their goals to each other. While the first person is sharing expectations and goals, we encourage the partner to listen without interrupting. This gives the partner the opportunity to hear what the other person believes and values regarding social and sexual behaviors and interactions. After the first person has finished, usually after 30 minutes, the other partner takes his or her turn. The therapists should try to ensure that both partners have approximately equal time. The exercise itself generally brings about new understandings of both self and other. In addition, discussing each partner's reactions in the session can highlight each person's exploitative or codependent behavior.

In some cases, one partner, often the man, may demonstrate more reticence than the partner. The therapist can help by offering some prompts in the session, or by asking the more willing partner to start first. Once the couple exhibits greater comfort with the process, the therapist can assign homework, for example, extending the exercise to encompass other aspects of each individual's expectations and hopes. The couple may describe their career aspirations, for instance, or their hopes in relation to establishing a more fulfilling social life, or their desires to master a specific new skill or activity. Each partner must be careful to limit comments to his or her individual experience only. Practicing the exercise in the session can help correct any misinterpretations of instructions or mistaken assumptions of shared meanings.

CASE 12-1 (*continued*)

Although John seemed reluctant the first time we practiced these talking/listening techniques in a session, he later reported that the homework exercise had helped him achieve a new awareness of his wants, expectations, and fears. He had developed new insights into his own fear of women and his desire to be accepted by women as a "whole" man in spite of some "feminine" tendencies. Sharing these revelations with Mary helped build her empathy toward him and eventually paved the way for her forgiveness of John's former compulsive behaviors—as long as they remained in the past.

3. *Learn the basics.* The didactic phase of our sex education and therapy program offers a formal overview of the anatomy and physiology involved in the human sexual response cycle and the necessary stages in the development of a healthy, intimate relationship. We never assume accurate sexual knowledge on the part of sex addicts or co-addicts. Instead, we take clients as far back as "kindergarten" to help them learn correct male and female anatomy and the human sexual response cycle. Even among the general population, some people are not aware of their own genital anatomy and physiology, and many sincerely believe many myths related to sexuality. We have treated women, for instance, who think they have just two orifices instead of three. We have also treated men who were convinced that masturbation would increase the size of the penis. Sex addicts and co-addicts are certainly not better informed than the general public in their knowledge of sexual anatomy. (In fact, most are *less* informed due to the repressive households in which they were reared.)

Fortunately, such organizations as Planned Parenthood and the Sex Information and Education Council of the United States (SIECUS) can supply written information and audiovisual materials that will help the therapist provide accurate facts and promote positive sexual attitudes and behaviors. The many excellent health and sex education textbooks and tradebooks available can also serve as valuable teaching tools. We recommend McCary and McCary (1984), Zilbergeld (1992), and Barbach (1975), among others. To supplement our own educational efforts, we sometimes encourage couples to take a course in human sexuality at a local college or university. Educating the couple about basic sexual anatomy often has a broader impact than the enlightenment of the couple. We encourage them to share the information, *when appropriate,* with children or other family members.

In describing the human sexual response cycle, we use the model developed by Masters and Johnson (1966). Although Masters and Johnson acknowledge its limitations in exploring or evaluating individual psychosexual dynamics, it does provide a helpful baseline for therapists who want to introduce the human sexual response cycle to sex addicts and co-addicts. Therapists can modify or augment this model to provide further information about sexual response. While not denying differences between male and female sexual response, for instance, Masters and Johnson choose to emphasize the similarities. The therapist may want to detail some of the gender differences to enhance understanding of sexual response.

Even children who do receive a formal sex education that provides accurate, positive knowledge and attitudes about sexuality may develop negative attitudes and beliefs through the influence of their family and friends. Children begin in infancy to absorb attitudes and beliefs about love, intimacy, sex, and fidelity from significant others. It is impossible *not* to learn attitudes about sexuality. As mentioned earlier in connection with Case 12-1, the very absence of overt messages can communicate the negative attitude that sex and the human body are dirty, shameful, indeed unspeakable. Verbal messages (e.g., "Masturbation is a sin that will destroy your soul") and experiential messages (e.g., punishment meted out for masturbation or exploring one's own, or another person's, body) of course transmit even more traumatic and enduring messages. Finally, nothing could provide a worse sex education than the experience of being victimized by sexual abuse, as so many sex addicts and co-addicts have been.

During this third stage, we review with both partners a theoretical overview of human development leading to healthy, intimate relationships. We familiarize our clients with the developmental stages that people need to go through in order to arrive at sexual wellness. Benjamin Kogan (1973), drawing on the model of Erik Erikson's (1963) stage theory, posits that sexual development parallels personality development. Applying Erikson's first stage, for example, that of trust versus mistrust during the first year of life, Kogan describes the influence of early infant experiences on the development of such prerequisites of healthy sexual attitudes and behaviors as trust and self-esteem. Using this new knowledge, the therapist can then help both partners see where events or people in their early lives might have detoured them from healthy sexual development. Often, these discussions trigger repressed memories that remained untapped during earlier history taking.

During this stage in the program, we also begin to emphasize the spiritual aspects of development that influence sexual attitudes. As noted earlier, religion can exercise a positive or negative influence on sexual attitudes just as the family of origin can. The therapist carefully assesses the couple's sexual attitudes and beliefs and builds therapy toward the development of inner, or spiritual, qualities that reflect sexual health. These qualities include trust, empathy, patience, understanding, gentleness, relaxation, caring, openness in communication, awareness of one's own and the other person's feelings and boundaries, and optimism. Ideally, the nurturing of these qualities in both partners will result in love, intimacy, and fidelity as the cornerstones of a couple's relationship (see Figure 12-2).

As couples work on developing the spiritual aspects of healthy sexuality, we assign homework in the form of "intimacy requests" (Scarf, 1987). In this exercise, partners take turns asking for special favors as disparate as taking time for a walk together or providing a back rub in a particular way. Unless mutually agreed upon by the couple, these intimacy requests should remain essentially nonsexual. Through this

Figure 12-2. Healthy Sexuality Model.

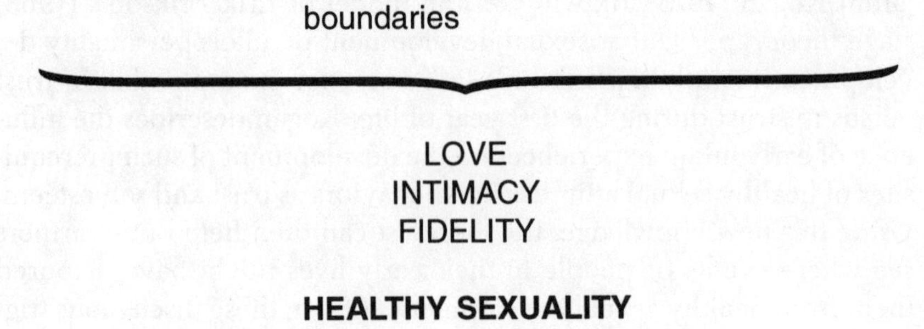

Patience Gentleness Understanding	Openness Awareness of feelings and boundaries	Relaxation Caring	Trust Empathy Optimism

LOVE
INTIMACY
FIDELITY

HEALTHY SEXUALITY

exercise, partners learn to ask for what each wants and begin to place a high priority on making time for each other. A couple who frequently and conscientiously practices this exercise and the talking/listening exercise described earlier will begin to habitualize these behaviors, establishing a degree of intimacy absent in all too many relationships. Then, and only then, can healthy sexual relations ensue.

4. *Identify dysfunctions,* 5. *Implement sensate focus,* 6. *Resolve remaining issues.* The remaining phases of our sex education and therapy program, which focus on any coexisting, "traditional" dysfunctions, are integrated. In practice, the entire process, like the overall addiction treatment regimen to which it contributes, is systemic. The therapist and/or couple may decide to backtrack or move ahead at any time during the course of the program.

Treatment for sex addiction often results in temporary or even long-term hypoactive sexual desire, especially when the addict has observed a period of total abstinence as a necessary part of his or her sobriety contract. In the first stages of recovery from sex addiction, addicts often abstain from both self-pleasuring and sexual relations with their partners until they have begun to deal with such issues as recognizing the cycle of addiction, identifying triggers, developing victim empathy (i.e., connecting with their own Sobbing Hurting Child), and changing arousal patterns. When this phase of the contract expires and the addict learns (s)he can resume sexual activity with his or her partner, the couple seldom feels comfortable at first. Either or both partners may question whether the recovering addict's sexual urges are truly directed toward the recovering co-addict, or are still part of the addiction. Fear of reinitiating the addictive cycle through sexual behavior is common among both recovering addicts and co-addicts. In some cases, hypoactive sexual desire may also predate therapeutic intervention. Before beginning treatment, one or both partners may have passively or actively suppressed their sexual desire toward the partner in an attempt to guard against feeling rejected or hurt by the other.

Sex addicts whose compulsive behavior included extramarital affairs or the use of prostitutes should be tested for all sexually transmitted diseases (STDs), including AIDS, syphilis, gonorrhea, human papilloma virus (HPV), herpes, and chlamydia, prior to ending the period of abstinence. If any of these tests yield a positive result, the sex addict, co-addict, and therapist immediately need to address issues of personal and sexual responsibility. The addict needs to recognize his or her "duty to warn," that is, the necessity of notifying all potential victims of STD transmission so that they too can be tested for the disease(s).

When treating most of the traditional dysfunctions—including hypoactive sexual desire, erection difficulty, premature ejaculation, retarded ejaculation, vaginismus, dyspareunia, or anorgasmia—we introduce "sensate focus" exercises to the couple. Because the texts cited earlier offer a complete description of these exercises, we will describe them only briefly here.

Sensate focus consists of a series of sequential steps that the couple performs at home. In the first step, the couple performs grooming and other preparations for the exercise; this may include the sensual experience of showering together. Next, one partner selects a position that feels most comfortable on the couple's bed. The other partner then begins sensually touching the other person. The "touchee," preferably through verbal communication, determines the quality and location of the touch. In this early stage, touching should exclude the breasts and genitals. The couple should focus on the sensations involved in touching and in being touched, and on the emotions experienced as the giver or recipient of the partner's touch. The couple then exchanges roles and repeats the process. After the exercise, the couple details their responses in their journals and shares them in the next therapy session.

In the next phase of the exercise, the couple may include the breasts and genitals in the touching. The therapist should remind the couple that the goals of the exercise are heightened awareness of physical and emotional sensations and the building of intimacy. While both partners should remain focused on the sensations of touch and emotional response rather than on sexual intercourse, the lovemaking can include intercourse if *both* partners consent. Again, both partners are asked to record their responses in their journals and share them in the next therapy session. In addition to enjoying the physical aspects of sensation, couples often discover many interpersonal and intrapersonal dynamics, both positive and negative, which can help advance the recovery process.

Finally, when the couple has completed all phases of the edutherapy program, we assess their progress together and address any remaining sexual issues or questions. Respecting the systemic nature of the larger treatment regimen, the sex therapist consults with the primary therapist and presents the couple's case to the entire therapy team. To reiterate, the hope and expectation for the couple is the establishment or reestablishment of healthy intimacy and sexual relations and the elimination of any distracting, disruptive, or destructive behaviors that have undermined all previous efforts to create a positive, loving relationship.

13

Forgiveness
Choosing a Path Toward
Spiritual Recovery

As we have consistently suggested in previous chapters, we do not believe that treatment of the sex addict can be considered complete unless it addresses the question of spirituality. Developing spirituality does not necessarily mean that sex addicts need to undergo a religious conversion to a specific church. (Indeed with some sex addicts, spiritual recovery may require leaving their church for a while or switching to a less shame-based church.) Spiritual recovery can occur independent of organized religion or a 12-step program. But it does require sex addicts to discover and nurture that aspect of their nature through which they establish, nourish, and maintain a relationship with a higher power (e.g., God) and with other people.

In the context of recovery, spirituality involves acknowledging and dealing with the addict's deepest levels of pain and suffering as well as the pain (s)he has inflicted upon others. Anyone who has suffered childhood victimization (as so many sex addicts have) has been wounded spiritually. And as Marilyn Murray has suggested, the only lasting way for a sex addict (or other survivor of childhood abuse) to reconnect with the Original Feeling Child—which Murray envisions as the core of the individual's spirituality, soul, or quest to know God—involves first uncovering and confronting the Sobbing Hurting Child, the pained victim of childhood trauma (Murray, 1991). Discovering a foundation for personal spirituality through the confrontation of pain both suffered and inflicted not only provides the basis for authentic victim empathy, an indispensable element of recovery from sex addiction, but also for a rediscovery of the good inside the addict: a reconnection with the Original Feeling Child's creativity, talents, spontaneity, and joy.

In the grip of their addiction, most sex addicts live joyless lives, regarding life in general—and their lives in particular—as essentially meaningless. Feeling unconnected to a Higher Power or others, they suffer through a series of injuries, humiliations, abasements, and abuses inflicted by the dog-eat-dog world in which they live. If sex addicts believe in God, they tend to put rigid and absolutist faith in either a harsh, punitive, unforgiving, and vindictive God or a "sugar daddy" who dispenses grace and forgiveness freely without demanding any responsibility or accountability.

The issue of forgiveness, central to both of these conceptions of God, plays a critical role in the spiritual integration of the sex addicts (and other sexual abuse victims) we see in therapy. For sex addicts, forgiveness must encompass not only forgiving themselves for behavior that has hurt themselves and others, but also, because so many sex addicts were themselves abused as children, forgiveness of *their* abusers—and equally important in many cases, forgiveness of and by God. When we emphasize forgiveness in attending to spiritual recovery, we stress that we neither mean a forgiveness that minimizes the abuses suffered nor a forgiveness that says it doesn't matter. Nor do we advocate a forgiveness that prohibits or preempts anger at the one(s) who victimized the addict as a child, at the enormous legacy of pain created by the childhood abuse, or at the addict's later offenses to him- or herself and others. Rather, we envision forgiveness as an invaluable strategy that will help anyone deal with the inevitable injuries derived from human contact in an imperfect world. Among sex addicts, the strategy of forgiveness applies not only to the insidious injuries experienced during an abusive childhood, but also to the abuses heaped upon themselves and others through compulsive sexual behaviors.

STEPS TOWARD FORGIVENESS

When we introduce the concept of forgiveness to our sexually addicted patients, we envision it as a five-step process. The first step involves defining the offenses, identifying with as much detail as possible the injurious behaviors that often seem unforgivable. The next two steps require the identification of the range of emotions associated with these offenses and finding an appropriate outlet for expression of this affect. Next, the addict—with the therapist's instrumental guidance and support—needs to set appropriate boundaries that will guard against further abuses and injuries. Last comes forgiving: the decision to cancel the debt and take charge of life.

A therapist working through the issue of forgiveness with a sexually addicted patient—or any other patient—could first encourage the addict to describe with as much specificity as possible the severity and extent of the injury caused by the abuse they suffered during childhood—and of the injuries inflicted on others through their compulsive sexual behavior. Unless the patient can adequately delineate what has happened, revealing the truth insofar as (s)he understands it, (s)he cannot truly know what (s)he needs to forgive.

CASE 13-1

Nate, a compulsive masturbator and voyeur in his mid-40s, voluntarily hospitalized himself due to increasing irritability and potential explosiveness toward his wife of 25 years and their two daughters. Accused by two female coworkers of voyeurism, Nate also had a history of visiting massage parlors for sexual gratification—a compulsion he admitted to his wife just prior to his hospitalization.

At first, Nate strongly denied that his childhood had been abusive. "I was just a bad kid," he rationalized, "and gave my mother a very hard time. She had to do what she had to do to take care of me." As therapy progressed, however, Nate slowly began to appraise his childhood more realistically. Abandoned by his father, Nate felt equally shunned by his mother, who consistently abused him physically and verbally. Nate was repeatedly told by his mother that he would "never amount to anything." Until his adolescence, Nate's childhood involved a repetitive cycle of his acting rebellious (in his mother's words), then getting whipped by his mother and sent to his room.

By the time he became a teenager, Nate thoroughly identified with his abusive mother. In a pattern typical among child abuse victims, the only way Nate could make sense of the abuse was to agree on a profound emotional level with his mother's assessment. He believed that he was a bad person, that there was something wrong with him, that his mother's abuse was his own fault—a belief that, as the words quoted demonstrate, he clearly continued to hold when he began therapy more than 30 years later. In a futile attempt to overcome this assessment and to escape further abuse, Nate conformed ever more closely throughout his adolescence to what he believed his mother wanted, doing his best to do all she expected, to become the model child he believed she wanted.

Since the age of 12, Nate had thus labored under the misconception that he could forgive his mother without acknowledging the truth about his experiences with her and how he felt about her. Nate's gallant attempts to cover up what he truly thought and felt had in some measure served to normalize his relationship with his mother during his adult years. But the toll it took upon Nate emotionally and spiritually was incalculable. Not only did he suffer from a variety of physical symptoms, but he experienced deep depression and increasingly displaced himself as well as his anger upon those closest to him.

After delineating the offenses committed by others against themselves and by themselves against others, the offenses that addicts have never forgiven, the second step in the process involves the identification of the emotions associated with the abuse. This invariably involves the addict's recognition of anger toward him- or herself and the abuser. A natural response to abuse, anger is often suppressed in its original traumatic context and eventually may be repressed altogether. Most victims of childhood abuse experience anger as an unsafe emotion, a feeling too dangerous to access directly and release symbolically, that is through confession and confrontation. Because the helpless victims of abuse often fear reprisals should they express their anger directly, they can express it only indirectly, principally through behaviors that prove destructive to themselves and/or others. Typically any anger expressed outwardly is done obliquely—through passive-aggressive behavior, being hypercritical of others, carrying a chip on one's shoulder, displacement to safer persons, or withdrawing from others—in short, adopting anger as a way of defending oneself from potential additional harm from others.

In addition, the shutdown of anger among child-abuse victims often results in profound emotional and psychological depression. In the long run, the various emotions cannot be suppressed differentially. For this reason, victims of child abuse find it impossible to repress their anger without simultaneously suppressing their positive emotional responsiveness. Repression of anger may also contribute to a wide variety of physiological complaints—the symptomatic expression of anger through the body.

CASE 13-1 (continued)

Nate was very angry in a polite sort of way. His core being, the reality behind the facade of conformity he had first adopted in his adolescence, lay in anger and resentment. Inwardly, he loathed both his mother and himself. Yet the intensity of his own hidden rage frightened Nate so profoundly that he became unwilling to express any emotion at all—at least not directly. Nate suffered from a wide range of physiological symptoms, including high blood pressure, frequent headaches, and an abnormal pattern of sleep and wakefulness that he had tolerated for years.

Initially, Nate demonstrated extreme reluctance to unearth the affect associated with his mother's emotional abuse—just as he had at first resisted seeing his mother as an abuser at all, and then had tried to avoid specificity regarding the extent of his abuse. Over the course of several weeks, we dealt with his fear, with the frustration of his personal needs for support and encouragement, and with the anger that ossified into hatred as a means of protecting himself. During this stage of the forgiveness process, we did not attempt to deal with this affect in any final or complete way. Rather, we encouraged him to identify and explore, authentically and truthfully, the strong feelings that had been blocked for so long.

After identifying the associated affect, the next step involves a search for suitable ways by which sex addicts can express these feelings and fears. The therapist can make use of a variety of techniques in the early stages of treatment that suitably avoid the patient having a premature confrontation with an abuser. Some of the techniques include writing a letter that the patient does not plan to mail, role playing in group therapy, taking a variety of parts in psychodrama (Focused Action Therapy), talking to an empty chair, and using a soft bat to beat upon pillows and a punching bag. At this stage of therapy, the patient needs only to confirm the reality and authenticity of the feelings rather than directly express them to his or her abuser. As the sex addict gains psychological strength and becomes less emotionally vulnerable, an appropriate time and occasion may present itself for a direct confrontation, if necessary.

CASE 13-1 (*continued*)

Nate's gains in therapy had made it possible for him to confront his mother appropriately, something he had never believed possible or thought necessary before. He not only confronted his mother's abusiveness, but also shared with her how he had managed his own anger and hatred toward her when he was a child. While Nate's mother initially seemed to receive this communication rather well, within a week or two she had changed her tune. She accused Nate of wronging her in talking with her the way he did; she expressed the desire to meet with him alone in order to convince him that his grievance centered not on her, but on unresolved problems with his wife. Though Nate readily admits the continuing need to work on issues with his wife, he now has the clarity of vision to see that his current difficulties in no way exonerate his mother from her own abusive behavior.

As Nate's encounter with his mother demonstrates, the sex addict and therapist must begin to discuss appropriate boundaries to put in place in order to protect the addict responsibly from the past victimizer. Such boundary issues—like the other steps in the process of forgiveness—demand tireless working and reworking on the part of the addict and his or her therapist. For appropriate boundaries must be established not only in those relationships that have proved harmful in the past, but also to protect the sex addict from any potential victimizers in her or his present life.

CASE 13-1 (continued)

Nate also needed to set boundaries regarding his interaction with his wife, Elena. Elena had taken on much the same role that his mother had played long ago. When, for example, Nate learned of an affair that Elena had been carrying on for years, she told him that she preferred the other man to him, adding "I have never really cared much for you ... in all the years we've been married." These words reiterated the dynamic of Nate's relationship with his mother. In therapy, we began devoting considerable time and energy toward the goal of setting appropriate boundaries regarding his responsibility in the failure of their marriage, and regarding how much stock he would put in Elena's judgment of his personal worth.

The final step in the process of forgiveness involves the sex addict's decision to cancel the debt, to forgive the one(s) who created the void in his or her life. Again, this decision should result neither in the minimization of the damage nor in the immediate weakening of the inevitably strong emotion associated with the experience of abuse (though in the long run the process *does* help dissipate powerful, unexpressed feelings). To the contrary, genuine forgiveness often enables a victim to feel and express more appropriately anger about the injustices of life.

CASE 13-1 (continued)

When Nate began his treatment, the possibility of taking a stand against his mother's abuse was entirely foreign to his thinking. Only painstaking patience and the commitment to recover allowed him finally to confront his mother about her abusive behavior and to admit the anger that he had nurtured in order to protect himself and cope with the abuse. Supported by some family, a few friends, and his therapist, Nate's eventual confrontation with his mother, while traumatic in prospect and extremely difficult in practice, has finally begun to be a freeing experience. The new freedom has arisen not from his mother's response, but rather from Nate's own willingness to take a stand in his own behalf and from his determination to continue his honest expression of what he has felt, what he has thought, and what he has done to cope with his abusive experience.

WHY FORGIVE THE "UNFORGIVABLE"?

The healing force of forgiveness allows the addict to turn away from a codependent focus upon actions that *some other person* needs to do in some particular way in order for the addict to recover. This dependency upon another to "fix" the addict, whether this fixing relates to the abuse suffered during childhood or to the craving, expressed through addiction, for the illusive and unattainable "enough" (a substitute for what the addict did not get as a child), locks up the addict emotionally and spiritually—and locks up the offender with the addict in a negative emotional bond. In insisting that a perpetrator or even the addict him- or herself pay the debt incurred through past abuse, the sex addict is thus bound in dependency to another in his or her attempt to heal. The sex addict becomes an eternal victim, locked in the victim stance that plays such an integral part in the addictive cycle (see Chapter 4). In investing another person with such power over his or her own well-being, the sex addict essentially turns over the responsibility for his or her life to the very one(s) who perpetrated, and perhaps still perpetrates, the abuse.

Sex addicts who continue to try to collect the debts that others have caused in their lives meet with little success, and sometimes incur even more damage. First, the "debtor" may not even acknowledge the debt or damage (s)he has created. Second, the debtor may actually increase the debt through further abuse or neglect. Perhaps the debtor has died or is ill and is not even available for repayment. Even on those rare occasions when an available debtor seems willing to try to repair the damage, (s)he may simply not have the resources to do so. How, for instance, does one restore the innocence of childhood? Although a genuine mutuality of concern and acknowledgment of the debt can make it possible for victims to receive what they truly need from the one(s) who wronged them, an adequate strategy for healing must not depend upon what someone else may or may not do. The individual must come to rely on her- or himself to begin to experience more wholeness in life.

Those who reject forgiveness lose sight of the fact that they may choose from any number of different pathways toward healing, regardless of the nature and the extent of injuries caused by themselves and others. The number of possible roads to recovery are as abundant as the kinds of trees that live along side them. However, if sex addicts focus exclusively on those who have inflicted abuse or injury on them, no matter how dastardly the offense(s) may have been, they bind themselves to a single-minded and often unattainable solution to their needs.

Rather than focusing upon the apparent necessity for *one particular person to do some particular thing in order for the sex addict to be okay again,* learning to forgive enables sex addicts to free themselves to embrace new provisions for their needs, to be responsive to the myriad creative pathways healing can take. The release of forgiveness enables sex addicts, not just intellectually but emotionally, to look to new alternatives for healing—new people, new relationships, new circumstances, new behavioral initiatives. The strategy of forgiveness thus makes possible a fresh beginning, a focus on remedying the sex addict's flaws and "defects of character" in a creative manner, instead of concentrating upon the people who have wronged him or her.

CASE 13-1 *(continued)*

Without minimizing the trauma of his childhood (and adulthood), Nate recognized that he had to release his mother from his own expectation of what she should be (but was not able to be) for him. The process of genuine forgiveness has enabled Nate to let go of illusions. And this "letting go" has begun to provide Nate with the basis for an increased ability to care for himself, believe in himself, and affirm his personal worth in a new way. He still needs the nurturing of others, of course, as well as their support and encouragement, but whereas once it was only his mother or his wife who could do what he needed, his well-being no longer depends upon any particular person.

If sex addicts learn to make forgiveness a habitual practice, it can help them to avoid the hook of codependency in the present and the future, and free them from the codependency of the past. Despite the growing strength of sobriety, others will continue, whether intentionally or unintentionally, to hurt the recovering addict. And though addicts who embrace forgiveness may not be able to take away the power of others to hurt them, they will no longer need to depend on others to heal the hurts.

When working on the issue of forgiveness with sex addicts, therapists need to attend not only to the matter of forgiving the patients' original abusers (if any), but to the equally imperative necessity for these patients to learn to forgive themselves. The steps to self-forgiveness follow the same progression as do the steps to the forgiveness of others. However, many sex addicts demonstrate an even more profound resistance to the need to let go of the abusive manner in which they treat themselves and others. Indeed most sex addicts find it impossible to reach such a conclusion emotionally without first taking a stand against the abuse suffered at the hands of the original abuser.

CASE 13-1 (*continued*)

Nate had so identified with his abuser that when he began therapy, he routinely berated, demeaned, and abused himself (and others), not only with his addictive behaviors, but verbally and emotionally as well. Without the intervention of the kind of intensive therapy undertaken first in the hospital and then as an outpatient, we suspect he would very likely have escalated the abuse until, deploring his life ever more profoundly, he found a way to take his life. For his life, lived as it was as a stand-in for his former abuser, had clearly become intolerable.

In one of our therapy groups, Nate recently recalled a "vision" he had always had of how his life would end up. "I saw myself old before my time, taking space in a shabby hotel within a run-down part of the city. I want to have a prostitute come to dull my pain, but I'm too despicable a man. I can't even pay a woman to be with me. That's the way I've always seen it ending.

"But not anymore. I'm beginning to really believe I'm worth more than that. I'm beginning to see that God doesn't think I'm no good, and I'm inclined much more to agree with God. Not just about my need to forgive and be forgiven, but just about me."

The process of forgiveness stimulates and later supports an increasingly truthful admission, confession, and taking a stand on the side of a continuing commitment to truthful living. This ongoing expression of a more honest, transparent, and open life seems to us the essential hallmark of spiritual integrity. Trust in relationships is enhanced, while manipulation and control diminish. For through forgiveness, recovering sex addicts (and codependents) begin to recognize in a more personal and comprehensive way the nature of their dependence upon a Higher Power, and their healthy interdependence with others.

The strategy of forgiveness enables sex addicts in recovery not to deny their past injuries and current difficulties, not to minimize them, not to squelch the appropriate expression of their feelings about them, but rather to make the turn to begin to consider the abundant ways and surprising sources from which healing and well-being may come. In forgiving themselves and others, sex addicts thus open themselves up to the real possibility of relational and personal wholeness in a world of diverse persons, all dependent upon the care of a benevolent Higher Power.

References

Abel, G., Blanchard, E., Becker, J., & Djenderedjian, A. Differentiative sexual aggressives with penile measures. *Criminal Justice & Behav* 1978;5:315–332

Adams-Tucker, C. Proximate effects of sexual abuse in childhood: a report on 28 children. *Am J Psychiatry* 1982;139:1252–1256

Araoz, D. *Hypnosis and Sex Therapy.* New York: Brunner/Mazel, 1982

Augsburger, D. *Caring Enough to Confront.* Ventura, Calif: Regal, 1983

Ault, R., & Klempner, Y. *Art Therapy: The Healing Vision.* Topeka, Kan: Menninger Foundation, 1987

Barbach, L. *For Yourself: The Fulfillment of Female Sexuality.* New York: Doubleday, 1975

Bateson, G. The cybernetics of self: a theory of alcoholism. *Psychiatry* 1971;34(1):1–18

Bays, L., Freeman-Longo, R. *Why Did I Do It Again?* Orwell, VT: Safer Society Press, 1989

Bays, L., Freeman-Longo, R., Hildebran, D. *How Can I Stop?* Orwell, VT: Safer Society Press, 1990

Black, C. *It Will Never Happen to Me!* Denver: MAC Publishing, 1981

Blau, T.H. *The Psychological Examination of the Child.* New York: Wiley, 1991

Bowen, M. *Family Therapy in Clinical Practice.* New York: Aronson, 1978

Bradshaw, J. *Homecoming: Reclaiming and Championing Your Inner Child.* New York: Bantam Books, 1990

Bradway, K. *Sandplay Bridges and the Transcendent Function.* San Francisco: C.G. Jung Institute; 1985

Brooks, B. Preoedipal issues in a postincest daughter. *Am J Psychotherapy* 1983;37(1):129–136

Butts, J. The relationship between sexual addiction and sexual dysfunction. *J Health Care for the Poor and Underserved* 1982;3:128–135

Carnes, P. *Out of the Shadows: Understanding Sexual Addiction.* Minneapolis: CompCare, 1983

Carnes, P. *Don't Call It Love: Recovery from Sexual Addiction.* New York: Bantam Books, 1991

Carnes, P. *Out of the Shadows: Understanding Sexual Addiction* (2nd edition). Center City, MN: Hazelden, 1992

Coles, R. *The Spiritual Life of Children.* Boston: Houghton Mifflin, 1993

The Council on Scientific Affairs. Scientific status of refreshing recollection by the use of hypnosis. *JAMA* 1985;253:1918–1923

Courtois, C. *Healing the Incest Wound.* New York: Norton, 1988

Earle, R. *Come Here/Go Away.* New York: Pocket Books, 1991

Earle, R., Crow, G., (with Osborn, K.) *Lonely All the Time: Recognizing, Understanding and Overcoming Sex Addiction, for Addicts and Co-Dependents.* New York: Pocket Books, 1989

Earle, R., & Crow, G. Sexual addiction: understanding and treating the phenomenon. *Contemp Fam Ther IntlJ* 1990;12:89–104

Elbow, M., & Mayfield, J. Mothers of incest victims: villains, victims, or protectors? Families in Society. *J Contemp Human Svces* 1991;72(2):78–86

Erikson, E. *Childhood and Society.* New York: Norton, 1963

Ferguson, A. On conceiving motherhood and sexuality: a feminist materialist approach. In: *Mothering: Essays in Feminist Theory.* Totowa, NJ: Rowan & Allenheld, 1984

Fossum, M., Mason, M. *Facing Shame.* New York: Norton, 1986

Funderburk, W. Electroencephalographic studies in chronic alcoholics. *Electroenceph Clin Neurophys* 1949;1:360–370

Giarretto, H. Humanistic treatment of father-daughter incest. *J Humanistic Psych* 1978;18:59–76

Gil, E. *Treatment of Adult Survivors of Childhood Abuse.* Walnut Creek, Calif: Launch Press, 1988

Glasser, W. *Reality Therapy: A New Approach to Psychiatry.* New York: Harper & Row, 1965

Greenleaf, J. Co-alcoholic–Para-alcoholic: Who's who and what's the difference? Presented at the National Council on Alcoholism Annual Alcoholism Forum, New Orleans; April 12, 1981

Hagood, M. Group art therapy with mothers of sexually abused children. *Arts in Psychother* 1991;18(1):17–27

Helminiak, D. Self-esteem, sexual self-acceptance, and spirituality. *J Sex Educ Ther* 1989;15:200–210

Herman, J. *Trauma and Recovery.* New York: Basic Books, 1992

Hewitt, L., Barnard M. Group work with mothers of incestuously abused children. *Australian Soc Work* 1986;39(2):35–40

Horowitz, A. Guidelines for treating father-daughter incest. *Social Casework* 1983;64(9):515–524

Horowitz, M. *Stress Response Syndromes.* New York: Aronson, 1976

Jacobs, J. Reassessing mother blame in incest. *Signs* 1990;15(3):500–514

James, B. *Treating Traumatized Children: New Insights and Creative Interventions.* Lexington, Mass: Lexington Books, 1989

Jung, C. *Aion.* Princeton, NJ: Princeton Univ Press, 1951

Jung, C. *The Archetypes and the Collective Unconscious.* Princeton, NJ: Princeton Univ Press, 1968

Katzman, E. Education for sexual health care. *J Nursing Educ* 1990;19:141–142

Katzman, E. Healthy sexuality: a new beginning for sex addicts and co-addicts. (Unpublished paper)

Koch, K., Jarvis, C. Symbiotic mother-daughter relationships in incest families. *Social Casework* 1987;68(2):94–101

Kogan, B. *Human Sexual Expression.* New York: Harcourt Brace Jovanovich, 1973

Lalumiere, M., Quinsey, V. Polygraph testing of child molestors: are we ready? *Violence Update* 1991;1(11):3–11

Laws, D.R. *Relapse Prevention with Sex Offenders.* New York: Guilford, 1989

Lewis, Michael. *Shame: The Exposed Self.* New York: The Free Press (1992)

Loftus, E.F. The reality of repressed memories. *Am Psychologist* 1993;48(5):518–537

LoPiccolo, J., & LoPiccolo, L., eds. *Handbook of Sex Therapy.* New York: Plenum, 1978

Lynn, S.J., & Nash, M.R. Truth in memory: ramifications for psychotherapy and hypnotherapy. *Am J Clin Hypnosis* 1994;36(3):194–208

Marlin, E. *Hope: New Choices and Recovery Strategies for Adult Children of Alcoholics.* New York: Harper & Row, 1987

Masters, W., & Johnson, V. *Human Sexual Response.* Boston: Little, Brown, 1966

Masters, W., Johnson, V. *Human Sexual Inadequacy.* Boston: Little, Brown, 1970

Masterson, J.F. *The Search for the Real Self: Unmasking the Personality Disorder of Our Age.* New York: Macmillan, 1988

McCary. S., & McCary, J. *Human Sexuality.* Belmont, Calif: Wadsworth, 1984

McConaghy, N. Sexual dysfunction and deviation. In: Bellack A., Hersen M., eds. *Behavioral Assessment.* Needham Heights, Mass: Allyn & Bacon, 1988

Miller, A. (Hannum H. trans). *Pictures of a Childhood.* New York: Farrar, Straus & Giroux; 1986

Miller, S., Miller, P., Nunnally, E.W, & Wackman, D.B. *Couple Communication I: Talking and Listening Together.* Littleton, Colo: Interpersonal Communication Programs, 1991

Minuchin, S. *Familes and Family Therapy.* Cambridge, Mass: Harvard Univ Press, 1974

Murray, M. *The scindo syndrome.* Unpublished masters thesis, 1985

Murray, M. *Prisoner of Another War.* Berkeley, Calif: PageMill Press, 1991

Nichols, H., & Molinder, I. *Multiphasic Sex Inventory.* Tacoma, Wash: Nichols & Molinder, 1984

Overton, D. State-dependent learning produced by addicting drugs. In: Fisher, S., & Freedman, A., eds. *Opiate Addiction: Origins and Treatment.* Washington, DC: Winston, 1973

Paitich, D., Langevin, R., Freeman, R., Mann, K., Handy, L. The Clarke shq: a clinical sex history questionnaire for males. *Arch Sexual Behav* 1977;6:421–436

Peniston, E., & Kulkosky, P. Alpha-theta brainwave training and beta-endorphin levels in alcoholics. *Alcoholism: Clin Exper Res* 1989;13(2):271–279

Peniston, E., & Kulkosky, P. Alcoholic personality and alpha-theta brainwave training. *Med Psychother* 1990;3:37–55

Prochelo, B. Sandplay as a way to the psyche: an approach to treatment and recovery. *Arizona Psychologist* 1991;10–13

Prochelo, B. Creative art therapies. (Unpublished paper)

Ross, C. Memories: from the obscure to the obvious. (Unpublished paper)

Scarf, M. *Intimate Partners: Patterns in Love and Marriage.* New York: Ballantine, 1987

Schneider, J.P. *Back from Betrayal.* San Francisco: Harper & Row, 1988

Schneider, P., & Schneider, B. Marital satisfaction during recovery from self-identified sexual addiction among bisexual men and their wives. *J Sex Marital Ther* 1990;16:230–250

Schwartz, M. Compulsivity as post-traumatic stress disorder: treatment perspectives. *Psychiatric Annals* 1992;22(6):333–338

Schwartz, M., & Brasted, W. Sexual addiction: self-hatred, guilt, and rage contribute to this deviant behavior. *Marital Aspects of Human Sexuality* 1985;19:103–107

Scott, R., & Flowers, J. Betrayal by mother as a factor contributing to psychological disturbances in victims of father-daughter incest: an MMPI analysis. *J Soc Clin Psych* 1988;6(1):147–154

Sedgwick, S. *The Good Sex Book: Recovering and Discovering Your Sexual Self.* Minneapolis: CompCare, 1992

Sedgwick, S. The good sex program: Recovering and discovering sexuality. Presented at Building Bridges: Sexual Recovery and Restoration Conference, Scottsdale, Ariz, June 10, 1993

Segal, H. *Klein.* London: Karnac Books and the Institute of Psycho-analysis, 1989

Stein, D., Hollander, E., Anthony, D., Schneier, F., Fallon, B., Liebowitz, M., & Klein, D. Serotonergic medications for sexual obsessions, sexual addictions, and paraphilias. *J Clin Psychiatry* 1992;53(8):267–271

Stern, M.J., & Meyer, L. Family and couple interactional patterns in cases of father/daughter incest. In: *Sexual Abuse of Children: Selected Readings.* Washington, DC: Govt Printing Office; 1980

Strand, V. Treatment of the mother in the incest family: the beginning phase. *Clin Soc Work* 1990;18(4):353–366

Tachiki, K. Personal communication; 1993

Wegscheider-Cruse, S. *Another Chance: Hope and Health for the Alcoholic Family.* Palo Alto, Calif: Science and Behavior Books, 1981

Whitfield, C.L. *Healing the Child Within: Discovery and Recovery for Adult Children of Dysfunctional Families.* Deerfield Beach, Fla: Health Communications, 1987

Wickes, F.G. *The Inner World of Childhood: A Study in Analytical Psychology.* Boston: Sigo Press, 1988

Woititz, J. *Adult Children of Alcoholics.* Pompano Beach, Fla: Health Communications, 1983

Woititz, J. *Struggle for Intimacy.* Pompano Beach, Fla: Health Communications, 1985

Woititz, J. *Healing Your Sexual Self.* Deerfield Beach, Fla: Health Communications, 1989

Wolin, S., & Wolin S. *The Resilient Self: How Survivors of Troubled Families Rise Above Adversity.* New York: Villard, 1993

Zilbergeld, B. *The New Male Sexuality.* New York: Bantam Books, 1992

Recommended Reading

Adult Children of Alcoholics. Woititz, J. (Health Communications, 1985)

Another Chance. Wegscheider, S. (Science and Behavior Books, 1981)

Back From Betrayal. Schneider, J. P. (Harper & Row, 1988)

Choicemaking. Wegscheider-Cruse, S. (Health Communications, 1985)

Co-dependence: Misunderstood—Mistreated. Schaeff, A. W. (Harper & Row, 1986)

Co-dependent No More. Beattie, M. (Hazelden, 1987)

Come Here/Go Away. Earle, R. (Pocket Books, 1991)

Don't Call It Love: Recovery From Sexual Addiction. Carnes, P. (Bantam, 1991)

Everybody Needs a Rock, Baylor, B.

A Gentle Path Through the 12 Steps. Carnes, P. (CompCare Publishers, 1993)

Grandchildren of Alcoholics. Smith, A. W. (Health Communications, 1988)

Healing for Damaged Emotions. Seamands, D. (Walker & Company, 1987)

How Can I Stop? Bays, L., Freeman-Longo, R., & Hildebran, D. (The Safer Society Press, 1990)

How to Survive the Loss of a Love. Cosgrove, M., Bloomfield, H. H., & McWilliams, P. (Prelude Press, 1991)

Is It Love or Is It Addiction? Schaeffer, B. (Harper Collins, 1987)

Lonely All the Time. Earle, R., & Crow, G. with Osborn, K. (Pocket Books, 1989)

Men Who Hate Women and the Women Who Love Them. Forward, S., & Torres, J. (Bantam, 1987)

Out of the Shadows. Carnes, P. (CompCare Publications, 1983)

Please Understand Me. Keirsey, D., & Bates, M. (Prometheus Nemesis Book Co., 1984)

Premenstrual Syndrome Self-Help Book: A Women's Guide to Feeling Good All Month. Lark, S. (PMS Self-Help Center, 1984)

Prisoner of Another War. Murray, M. (PageMill Press, 1991)

Recovery: A Guide for Adult Children of Alcoholics. Gravitz, H. L., & Bowden, J. D. (Simon & Schuster, 1985)

The Road Less Traveled. Peck, M. S. (Touchstone Books, 1978)

Self-Parenting. Pollard III, J. K. (Generic Human Studies Publishing, 1987)

Stage II Relationships: Love Beyond Addiction. Larsen, E. (Harper & Row, 1987)

The 12 Steps: A Spiritual Journey. (Recovery Publications, 1994)

The 12 Steps: A Way Out. (Recovery Publications, 1987)

Under the Influence. Milan, J., & Ketcham, K. (Bantam, 1981)

Who Am I And Why Am I In Treatment. Freeman-Longo, R. & Bays, L. (The Safer Society Press, 1988)

Why Am I Afraid to Tell You Who I Am? Powell, J. (Tabar Publishing, 1969)

Why Did I Do It Again? Bays, L. & Freeman-Longo, R. (The Safer Society Press, 1989)

Women Who Love Too Much. Norwood, R. (Pocket Books, 1986)

Name Index

Subject Index